OSAGE COUNTY
OKLAHOMA

〃〃〃〃

| 0 Miles | 5 | 10 | 15 |

| 0 Kilometers | 10 | 15 |

Sand Creek

●Bartlesville

●Okesa

●T. LOUIS SCHOOL ■ Pawhuska

Bird Creek

H O M A

O M A

●Bigheart

WASHINGTON
COUNTY

Hominy Creek

Hominy
●

TULSA
COUNTY

Arkansas River

● Tulsa

© 2016 Jeffrey L. Ward

KILLERS *of* *the* FLOWER MOON

ADAPTED FOR YOUNG READERS

KILLERS *of* the FLOWER MOON

The Osage Murders and the Birth of the FBI

ADAPTED FOR YOUNG READERS

DAVID GRANN

Crown Books for Young Readers
New York

A NOTE ABOUT LANGUAGE USE

This book follows the *AP Stylebook,* which recommends using the term *American Indians* or *Native Americans* when referring to two or more people of different tribal affiliations, and stating the specific affiliation when referring to a singular person or nation. For historical accuracy, direct quotations and the official names of organizations have not been changed.

Library of Congress Cataloging-in-Publication Data
Names: Grann, David, author.
Title: Killers of the flower moon: the Osage murders and the birth of the FBI / David Grann.
Other titles: Osage murders and the birth of the FBI
Description: First edition. | New York: Crown Books for Young Readers, [2021] | "Adapted for young readers." | Includes bibliographical references and index. | Audience: Ages 10 & up | Audience: Grades 7–9 |
Summary: "This essential book introduces young readers to the Reign of Terror against the Osage people—one of history's most ruthless and shocking crimes"—Provided by publisher.
Identifiers: LCCN 2021022997 (print) | LCCN 2021022998 (ebook) | ISBN 978-0-593-37734-5 (hardcover) | ISBN 978-0-593-37735-2 (library binding) | ISBN 978-0-593-37736-9 (ebook)
Subjects: LCSH: Osage Indians—Crimes against—Case studies—Juvenile literature. | Murder—Oklahoma—Osage County—Case studies—Juvenile literature. | Homicide investigation—Oklahoma—Osage County—Case studies—Juvenile literature. | United States. Federal Bureau of Investigation—Case studies—Juvenile literature. | Osage County (Okla.)—History—20th century—Juvenile literature.
Classification: LCC E99.O8 G675 2021 (print) | LCC E99.O8 (ebook) | DDC 976.6004/975254—dc23

The text of this book is set in 11.2-point Charlotte Std. Book.
Interior design by Cathy Bobak

Printed in the United States of America
10 9 8 7 6 5 4 3 2 1
First Edition

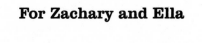

For Zachary and Ella

Contents

Foreword by Dennis McAuliffe Jr.   ix

Chronicle One: The Marked Woman

1. The Vanishing   3
2. An Act of God or Man?   15
3. King of the Osage Hills   21
4. Underground Reservation   33
5. The Devil's Disciples   53
6. The Million Dollar Elm   65
7. This Thing of Darkness   75

Chronicle Two: The Evidence Man

8. Department of Easy Virtue   95
9. The Undercover Cowboys   102
10. Eliminating the Impossible   107
11. The Third Man   113
12. A Wilderness of Mirrors   118
13. A Hangman's Son   122
14. Dying Words   130
15. The Hidden Face   136
16. The Quick-Draw Artist, the Yegg, and the Soup Man   143

17. The State of the Game   153

18. A Traitor to His Blood   172

19. The Double Agent   183

20. So Help You God!   191

21. The Hot House   204

Chronicle Three: The Reporter

22. Ghostlands   217

23. A Case Not Closed   233

24. Standing in Two Worlds   242

25. The Lost Manuscript   252

26. Blood Cries Out   257

Acknowledgments   271

Who's Who   277

Glossary   282

A Note on the Sources   286

Archival and Unpublished Sources   288

Notes and Selected Bibliography   289

Illustration Credits   308

Index   311

Foreword

IN JANUARY 1926, NEWSPAPERS ACROSS THE COUNTRY reported that the U.S. government had investigated a murderous "Reign of Terror" against oil-rich Osage Indians "that will astound the Nation when the details are known." Almost 100 years later, those details are still astounding the nation, thanks to David Grann's monumental *Killers of the Flower Moon*.

If all books were written like this one, well, you'd read more books without prodding from parents and teachers. How many history books have you read that are written like a murder mystery, a detective story, a whodunit? This book is all that and more. You won't want to put it down. The book tells the story impartially and impersonally—just the facts, please—allowing you to see for yourself and form your own judgments. Those conclusions, because they're yours, will have a powerful and profound impact on you.

From the opening pages you may wonder how people can be so cruel and evil to one another! But this is what racism, individual and systemic, looks like. And once you see it and recognize it on your own, you'll always be able to spot it and—our future hope rests with you—counter it.

So read this book with your eyes wide open—the way they are when you watch a scary show. This is a scary story. And you'll see history, perhaps for the first time, stripped of the sugarcoating that books and documentaries (and, yes, your parents and teachers) have put on difficult details of our history to make them easier for young people.

There's no sugarcoating in this book. The events recorded in it are difficult to take in at times.

To understand our history—and our country today—you must include Native Americans (too many books leave us missing in action). And no account is complete without the Osages. If you understand Osage history, *this history,* you'll better understand our country's past in all of its complexities—those difficult, troubling, and recurring events that will challenge, even haunt, you all your life.

Close your eyes and examine your mental picture of Native Americans. Are one of their tribes the richest people per capita in the world, driven around by chauffeurs in Pierce-Arrow luxury cars? I didn't think so. Are they the most murdered people per capita in the world?

Ask yourself again after you read *Killers of the Flower Moon.*

It's important for you to know that one of the most sinister crimes in U.S. history was committed against Native Americans—Osages—not in the cavalry carnage of the late 1800s but just last century. This time the killers did not ride in and wipe out a village in one swift burst of violence. Instead, they tried to wipe out its people slowly, by pretending to care about them and then killing them off one by one, over time. It still sends chills up my spine to think about it.

Evil things happened, yes, but that's not all that happened. Not all whites on the Osage reservation were bad. Osage people survived. We're still very much alive. The Osage Nation thrives. The killers failed in their ultimate purpose.

There was some justice—though not a lot of it. Remember, the killers in the book were only those who got caught, and their murders were only the few the authorities investigated. Sadly, there were many more still unnamed—victims and killers. Naming some of the killers and putting faces on some of their victims, telling their stories with dignity, restores something their murders stole from them and gives justice a second chance. *Killers of the Flower Moon* brought the story of the Reign of Terror out of the shadows where it lay buried on the Osage reservation for much of the past century. People are talking about the murders now, not just in Osage County, Oklahoma, but across the country. They didn't much before. They're asking questions about their grandparents and great-grandparents—white and Osage. What did they do? What was done to them? These questions and discussions will lead to more research and storytelling—on pages and screens. The list of names on a future Reign of Terror victims' memorial will grow. The same with the Reign of Terror's shameful list of perpetrators.

Every time this history is learned, justice is served, and the victims—all of them, not just those named in this book—are honored.

Do your part.

I asked an Osage, who was visiting my house on the reservation, what she thought of young people reading *Killers of the Flower Moon*.

"Kids reading *Killers*?" she said. "Wow! That's great!"

"Why should they read it?" I asked her.

"Because it's history!" she said. "It's our history! Osage history! Oklahoma history! American history!"

She glanced out a window at a street just blocks away from

where many people in this book lived and died and killed, and she said:

"If they don't learn it, that history could repeat itself."

Dennis McAuliffe Jr., an Osage tribal member and an editor at the *Washington Post*, is the author of *The Deaths of Sybil Bolton: Oil, Greed, and Murder on the Osage Reservation.*

The Marked Woman

1

The Vanishing

IN APRIL, MILLIONS OF TINY FLOWERS SPREAD OVER THE blackjack hills and vast prairies in the Osage territory of Oklahoma. There are Johnny-jump-ups and spring beauties and little bluets. The Osage writer John Joseph Mathews said that the galaxy of petals makes it look as if the "gods had left confetti." In May, when coyotes howl beneath an unnervingly large moon, taller plants, such as spiderworts and black-eyed Susans, begin to creep over the tinier blooms, stealing their light and water. The necks of the smaller flowers break and their petals flutter away, and before long they are buried underground. This is why the Osage Indians refer to May as the time of the flower-killing moon.

On May 24, 1921, Mollie Burkhart, a resident of the Osage settlement town of Gray Horse, Oklahoma, began to fear that something had happened to one of her three sisters, Anna Brown. Thirty-four, and less than a year older than Mollie, Anna had disappeared three days earlier. She had often gone on "sprees," as her family called them: dancing and drinking with friends until dawn. But this time, one night had passed and then another, and

Anna had not shown up on Mollie's front stoop as she usually did. When Anna came inside, she liked to slip off her shoes, and Mollie missed the comforting sound of her moving, unhurried, through the house. Instead, there was a silence as still as the plains.

Mollie had already lost her sister Minnie nearly three years earlier. Minnie's death had come with shocking speed, and though doctors had named it a "peculiar wasting illness," Mollie had her doubts. Minnie had been only twenty-seven and had always been in perfect health.

Like their parents, Mollie and her sisters had their names inscribed on the Osage Roll, which meant that they were among the registered members of the tribe. It also meant that they were worth a fortune. In the early 1870s, the Osage had been driven from their lands in Kansas onto a rocky, presumably worthless reservation in northeastern Oklahoma. Decades later, they discovered that this land was sitting above some of the largest oil deposits in the United States. And to get that oil, prospectors had to pay the Osage.

In the early twentieth century, each person on the tribal roll began receiving a quarterly check. The amount was initially for only a few dollars, but over time, as more oil was tapped, the payments grew into the hundreds, then the thousands. And virtually every year, they received more and more, until the tribe members had collectively accumulated millions and millions of dollars. (In 1923 alone, the tribe took in more than $30 million, which would be worth more than $400 million today.) The Osage were considered the wealthiest people per capita in the world. "Lo and behold!" the New York magazine *Outlook* exclaimed. "The Indian, instead of starving to death . . . enjoys a steady income that turns bankers green with envy."

The public had become transfixed by the tribe's prosperity, which contradicted many of the images of American Indians that could be traced back to the brutal first contact with whites—the original sin from which the country was born. Readers were fascinated by stories about the Osage's brick mansions and chandeliers, their diamond rings and fur coats and chauffeured cars. One writer marveled at Osage girls who attended the best boarding schools and wore sumptuous French clothing.

At the same time, reporters seized upon any signs of the traditional Osage way of life, which seemed to stir in the public's mind visions of "wild" Indians. One article noted a "circle of expensive automobiles surrounding an open campfire, where the bronzed and brightly blanketed owners are cooking meat in the primitive style." Another documented a party of Osage arriving at a ceremony for their dances in a private airplane.

Gray Horse was one of the reservation's oldest settlements. These outposts—including Fairfax, a larger town of nearly fifteen hundred people, and Pawhuska, the Osage capital, with a population of more than six thousand—seemed like fevered visions. The streets clamored with cowboys, fortune seekers, bootleggers, soothsayers, medicine men, outlaws, U.S. marshals, New York financiers, and oil magnates. Automobiles sped along paved horse trails, the smell of fuel overwhelming the scent of the prairies. There were restaurants, advertised as cafés, and opera houses and polo grounds.

Although Mollie didn't spend as lavishly as some of her neighbors did, she had built a beautiful, rambling wooden house in Gray Horse near her family's old lodge of lashed poles, woven mats, and bark. She owned several cars and had a staff of servants. The servants on the reservation were often Black or Mexican, and in the early 1920s a visitor to the reservation expressed contempt at the sight of "even whites" performing "all the menial tasks about the house to which no Osage will stoop."

Mollie was one of the last people to see Anna before she vanished. That day, May 21, Mollie had risen close to dawn, a habit ingrained from when her father used to pray every morning to the sun. She was accustomed to the chorus of meadowlarks and sandpipers and prairie chickens, now overlaid with the *pock-pock*ing of drills pounding the earth. Unlike many of her friends, who shunned Osage clothing, Mollie wrapped a traditional blanket around her shoulders. She also didn't cut her hair in a flapper bob, but let her long black hair flow over her back, revealing her striking face, with its high cheekbones and big brown eyes.

Her husband, Ernest Burkhart, rose with her. A twenty-eight-year-old white man, he looked like an extra in a Western picture show: short brown hair, slate-blue eyes, square chin. Only his nose disturbed the portrait; it looked as if it had taken a barroom punch or two. Growing up in Texas, the son of a poor cotton farmer, he'd been enchanted by tales of the Osage Hills—that last American frontier where "cowboys and Indians" were said to still roam. In 1912, at nineteen, he'd packed a bag, like Huck Finn lighting out for the Territory, and gone to live with his uncle, a domineering cattleman named William K. Hale, in Fairfax.

"He was not the kind of a man to ask you to do something—he told you," Ernest once said of Hale, who became his surrogate

Mollie Burkhart

Ernest Burkhart

father. Though Ernest mostly ran errands for Hale, he sometimes worked as a taxi driver, which is how he met Mollie, chauffeuring her around town.

Ernest had a tendency to drink liquor and play stud poker with shady men. Beneath his roughness, though, there seemed to be a tenderness and a trace of insecurity about him, and Mollie fell in love with him. Born a speaker of Osage, she had studied English in school. But Ernest still made the effort to learn her native language until he could talk with her in it. Mollie suffered from diabetes, and he cared for her when her joints ached and her stomach burned with hunger. After he heard that another man had affections for her, he muttered that he couldn't live without her.

It wasn't easy for them to marry. Ernest's roughneck friends ridiculed him for wanting to marry an Osage woman. And though Mollie's three sisters had wed white men, she felt a responsibility to have an arranged Osage marriage, the way her parents had. Still, Mollie, whose family practiced a mixture of Osage and Catholic beliefs, couldn't understand why God would let her find love only to then take it away from her. So in 1917, she and Ernest exchanged rings, vowing to love each other till eternity.

By May 1921, they had a daughter, Elizabeth, who was two years old, and a son, James, who was eight months old and nicknamed Cowboy. Mollie also tended to her aging mother, Lizzie, who had moved into the house after Mollie's father passed away. Lizzie once feared that Mollie would die young, because of her diabetes, and she begged her other children to take care of her. In truth, Mollie was the one who looked after all of them.

May 21 was supposed to be a delightful day for Mollie. She liked to entertain guests and was hosting a small luncheon. After getting dressed, she fed the children. Cowboy often had bad earaches and she'd comfort him till he felt better. Then she issued instructions to her servants as everyone in the house bustled about—except her mother, who'd fallen ill and stayed in bed. Mollie asked Ernest to call Anna and see if she'd come over to help tend to Lizzie for a change. Anna, as the oldest child in the family, held a special status in their mother's eyes and was the one her mother spoiled.

When Ernest told Anna that her mama needed her, she promised to take a taxi straight there. She arrived shortly afterward, dressed in bright red shoes, a skirt, and a matching blanket. In her hand was an alligator purse. Before entering, she'd quickly combed her windblown hair and powdered her face. Mollie noticed, however, that Anna was drunk.

Mollie couldn't hide her displeasure. Some of the guests had already arrived. Among them were two of Ernest's brothers, Bryan and Horace Burkhart, who had been lured to Osage County by oil and often assisted Hale on his ranch. One of Ernest's aunts, who spewed racist notions about American Indians, was also visiting, and the last thing Mollie needed was for Anna to cause a commotion.

Anna slipped off her shoes and began drinking whiskey. Mollie

Mollie (right) with her sisters Anna (center) and Minnie

knew that Anna had been very troubled of late. She'd recently divorced her husband, a settler named Oda Brown, and since then had spent more and more time in the reservation's boomtowns that had sprung up to house and entertain oil workers.

At Mollie's house, Anna began to flirt with Ernest's younger brother, Bryan, whom she'd sometimes dated. He was more brooding than Ernest and had yellow-flecked eyes and thinning hair, which he wore slicked back. A lawman who knew him described him as a troublemaker. When Bryan asked one of the servants at the luncheon if she'd go to a dance with him that night, Anna said that if he fooled around with another woman, she'd kill him.

Meanwhile, Ernest's aunt was muttering, loud enough for all to hear, about how mortified she was that her nephew had married an American Indian. It was easy for Mollie to subtly strike back, because one of the servants attending to the aunt was white—a blunt reminder of the town's social order.

Anna continued causing a ruckus. She fought with the guests, fought with her mother, fought with Mollie. "She was drinking and quarreling," a servant later told authorities. "I couldn't understand her language, but they were quarreling." The servant added, "They had an awful time with Anna, and I was afraid."

That evening, Mollie planned to look after her mother while Ernest took the guests into Fairfax, five miles to the northwest, to meet his uncle Hale and see a play. Bryan, who'd put on a cowboy hat, his catlike eyes peering out from under the brim, offered to drop Anna off at her house.

Before they left, Mollie washed Anna's clothes, gave her some food to eat, and made sure that she'd sobered up enough that Mollie could glimpse Anna's usual bright and charming self. They lingered together, making up and sharing a moment of calm. Then Anna said good-bye, a gold filling flashing through her smile.

With every night that passed without her sister's return, Mollie grew more anxious. Bryan insisted that he'd taken Anna straight home and dropped her off before heading to the play. After the third night, Mollie, in her quiet but forceful way, pressed everyone into action. She sent Ernest to check on Anna's house. He jiggled the knob to her front door—it was locked. From the window, the rooms inside appeared dark and deserted.

Ernest stood there alone in the heat. A few days earlier, a cool rain shower had dusted the earth, but afterward the sun's rays beat down mercilessly through the blackjack trees. This time of year, heat blurred the prairies and made the tall grass creak underfoot. In the distance, through the shimmering light, he could see the skeletal frames of oil derricks.

Anna's head servant, who lived next door, came outside, and Ernest asked her, "Do you know where Anna is?"

The servant said she'd stopped by Anna's house before the shower to close any open windows. "I thought the rain would blow in," she explained. But she said the door was locked and there was no sign of Anna.

News of her absence spread through the boomtowns, traveling from porch to porch, from store to store. Fueling the unease were reports that a thirty-year-old Osage man, Charles Whitehorn, had vanished a week before Anna did. Friendly and funny, Whitehorn was married to a woman who was part white, part Cheyenne. A local newspaper noted that he was "popular among both the whites and the members of his own tribe." On May 14, he'd left his home, in the southwestern part of the reservation, for Pawhuska. He never returned.

Still, there was reason for Mollie not to panic. It was possible that Anna had slipped out after Bryan had dropped her off and headed to Oklahoma City or across the border to Kansas City. Perhaps she was dancing in one of those jazz clubs she liked to visit, unaware of the chaos she'd left trailing in her wake. And even if Anna had run into trouble, she knew how to protect herself. She often carried a small pistol in her alligator purse. She'll be back home soon, Ernest reassured Mollie.

A week after Anna disappeared, an oil worker was on a hill a mile north of downtown Pawhuska when he noticed something poking out of the brush near the base of a derrick. The worker came closer. It was a body. The victim had been shot twice in the head.

It was hot and wet and loud on the hillside. Drills shook the earth, and derricks swung their large clawing arms back and forth. Other people gathered around the body, which was impossible to identify in its current condition. One of the pockets held a letter. Someone pulled it out, straightened the paper, and read it. The letter was addressed to Charles Whitehorn, and that's how they first knew it was him.

Around the same time, a father and his teenage son as well as another man were squirrel hunting by Three Mile Creek, near Fairfax. While the men were getting a drink of water from a creek, the boy spotted a squirrel and pulled the trigger. The boy watched the squirrel tumble over the edge of a ravine. He chased after it, making his way down a steep wooded slope and into a gulch, where the air was thicker and where he could hear the murmuring of the creek. He found the squirrel and picked it up. Then he screamed, "Oh Papa!" By the time his father reached him, the boy had crawled onto a rock. He gestured toward the mossy edge of the creek and said, "A dead person."

It was the body of what appeared to be an American Indian woman. She was on her back, with her hair twisted in the mud.

The men and the boy hurried out of the ravine and raced on their horse-drawn wagon through the prairie, dust swirling around them. When they reached Fairfax's main street, they couldn't find any lawmen, so they stopped at the Big Hill Trading Company, a large general store that had an undertaking business as well. They told the owner, Scott Mathis, what had happened. He alerted his undertaker, who went with several men to the creek. There they recovered the body, then laid it inside a wooden box, in the shade of a blackjack tree. The undertaker tried to determine if the woman was Anna Brown, whom he'd known. But he and the other men couldn't make an identification.

Mathis, who had managed Anna's finances, contacted Mollie, and she led a grim procession toward the creek, which included Ernest, Bryan, Mollie's sister Rita, and Rita's husband, Bill Smith. Many who knew Anna followed them, along with the curious.

Vultures circled in the sky as Mollie and Rita stepped close to the body. The sisters recognized Anna's blanket and the clothes that Mollie had washed for her.

Rita began to weep, and her husband led her away. Mollie, trying to stay composed, mouthed the word "yes." It was Anna. Mollie eventually retreated from the creek with Ernest, leaving behind the first hint of the darkness that threatened to destroy not only her family but her tribe.

2

An Act of God or Man?

A CORONER'S INQUEST, AN INVESTIGATION MADE UP OF jurors and led by a justice of the peace, was quickly held at the ravine. Inquests were left over from a time when ordinary citizens had to investigate crimes and maintain order. For years after the American Revolution, the public opposed the creation of police departments, fearing that they would become forces of repression. Instead, citizens themselves chased after suspects.

In the mid-nineteenth century, after the growth of cities, police departments began to emerge in the United States. But even by the time of Anna's death, elements of citizen policing remained in some more remote and rural places.

The justice of the peace chose the jurors from among the white men at the ravine, including Scott Mathis. They were charged with determining whether Anna had died by an act of God or man. If it was determined to be a felony, then they would be tasked with trying to identify who committed the crime. Two doctors, the brothers James and David Shoun, who cared for Mollie's family, had been called to perform an autopsy. Leaning over Anna's body in the

The ravine where Anna Brown's body was found

wooden box, with members of the inquest huddled around them, they began to diagnose the dead.

After an examination, the Shoun brothers determined that Anna had lost her life between five and seven days earlier. The doctors shifted her head slightly and discovered a perfectly round hole in the back of her skull. "She's been shot!" one of the Shouns exclaimed.

There was a stirring among the men. Mathis then took a look and thought that a .32-caliber bullet had caused the wound. There was no longer any doubt: Anna's death had been cold-blooded murder.

Lawmen were then still largely amateurs. They rarely attended training academies or learned the new scientific methods of detection, such as the analysis of fingerprints and blood patterns. Frontier lawmen, in particular, were primarily gunfighters and trackers. They were expected to stop crimes and to catch a known gunman alive if possible, dead if necessary. "An officer was then literally the law and nothing but his judgment and his trigger finger stood between him and extermination," the *Tulsa Daily World* said in 1928, after the death of a veteran lawman who'd worked in the Osage territory. Because these enforcers received pitiful salaries and were prized primarily for being quick draws, it's not surprising that there wasn't always a clear line between good lawmen and bad lawmen. The leader of the Dalton Gang, an infamous nineteenth-century band of outlaws, once served as the main lawman on the Osage reservation.

At the time of Anna's murder, the Osage County sheriff was a fifty-eight-year-old, three-hundred-pound frontiersman named Harve M. Freas. A 1916 book about the history of Oklahoma described Freas as a "terror to evil doers." But there were also murmurings that he was cozy with criminals and that he gave free rein to gamblers and bootleggers like Kelsie Morrison and Henry Grammer. A rodeo champion, Grammer had once served jail time for murder, and he controlled the local distribution of illegal liquor known as moonshine. One of his workers later admitted to authorities, "I had the assurance that if I was ever arrested . . . I would be turned out in five minutes."

When Sheriff Freas was told about Anna's murder, he was already busy with Whitehorn's slaying, and he initially sent one of his deputies to collect evidence. Fairfax had a town marshal, the equivalent of a police chief, who joined the deputy and the Shoun brothers at the ravine. To identify the murder weapon, the lawmen needed the bullet, but it was nowhere to be seen.

They went down to the creek where Anna had been found.

Though there was still no sign of the bullet, one of the lawmen noticed a bottle on the ground, which was partially filled with a clear liquid. It smelled like moonshine. The lawmen believed that Anna had been sitting on the rock, drinking, when someone came up behind her and shot her.

The marshal spotted two distinct sets of car tracks running between the road and the gulch. It looked as though both cars had come into the gulch from the southeast, then circled back.

No other evidence was collected. The lawmen, untrained in forensic methods, didn't make a cast impression of the tire marks, or dust the bottle for fingerprints, or check Anna's body for gunpowder residue. They didn't even photograph the crime scene, which, in any case, had already been contaminated by the many observers.

Someone, though, found one of Anna's earrings and brought it to Mollie's mother, who was too ill to travel to the creek. Lizzie instantly recognized it. *Anna was dead.* As with all Osage, Lizzie considered the birth of her children to be the greatest blessing of Wah'Kon-Tah, the mysterious life force that pervades the sun and the moon and the Earth and the stars. This was the force around which the Osage had structured their lives for centuries, hoping to bring some order out of the chaos and confusion in the world. The force was invisible, remote, giving, awesome, and unanswering. Many Osage had given up their traditional beliefs, but Lizzie had held on to them. Now someone, *something,* had taken her oldest and most favored daughter before her allotted time—a sign, perhaps, that Wah'Kon-Tah had withdrawn his blessings and that the world was slipping into greater chaos. Lizzie's health grew even worse, as if grief were its own disease.

Mollie (right) with her sister Anna and their mother, Lizzie

Mollie relied on Ernest for support. A lawyer who knew them both noted that Ernest's "devotion to his Indian wife and his children is unusual . . . and striking." He comforted Mollie as she threw herself into organizing Anna's funeral. There were flowers to be purchased, along with a white metal coffin and a marble tombstone. Undertakers charged the Osage sky-high rates for a funeral, taking advantage of them. By the time the undertaker hired by Mollie was done tallying the accessories, including gloves for the gravedigger, the total cost was astronomical. As a lawyer in town said, "It was getting so that you could not bury an Osage Indian at a cost of under

$6,000"—a sum that, adjusted for inflation, is the equivalent of nearly $80,000 today.

The funeral was arranged to reflect the family's Osage and Catholic traditions. Mollie, who had gone to a missionary school in Pawhuska, regularly attended Mass. She liked to sit in the pews as the Sunday morning light came through the windows and listen to the sermon of the priest. She also liked socializing among friends, and there was plenty of that on Sundays.

After the funeral service for Anna, Mollie guided her family and the other mourners to a cemetery in Gray Horse, a quiet, isolated spot overlooking the endless prairie. Mollie's father and her sister Minnie were buried there, side by side, and next to them was a freshly dug grave for Anna, with a tombstone bearing the inscription "Meet Me in Heaven." Mollie and her family placed enough food in the casket for Anna's three-day journey to what the Osage refer to as the Happy Hunting Ground.

The older mourners, like Mollie's mother, began to recite Osage prayer-songs, hoping that Wah'Kon-Tah would hear them.

Standing at the grave site with Ernest, Mollie could hear the old people's song of death, their chants mixed with weeping. Oda Brown, Anna's ex-husband, stepped away, looking grief-stricken. Precisely at noon—as the sun, the greatest manifestation of the Great Mystery, reached its zenith—Mollie watched the glistening white coffin sink into the ground.

3

King of the Osage Hills

THE KILLINGS OF ANNA BROWN AND CHARLES WHITE-
horn caused a sensation. A banner headline in the *Pawhuska Daily
Capital* read, TWO SEPARATE MURDER CASES ARE UNEARTHED ALMOST
AT SAME TIME. Was it just a coincidence that both victims had been
wealthy Osage Indians in their thirties? Or was this, perhaps, the
work of a repeat killer?

Lizzie relied on Mollie to deal with the authorities. During
Lizzie's lifetime, many of the Osage had been separated from their
traditions. Louis F. Burns, an Osage historian, wrote that after oil
was discovered, the tribe had been "set adrift in a strange world,"
adding that "there was nothing familiar to clutch and stay afloat
in the world of white man's wealth." In the old days, an Osage clan,
which included a group known as the Travelers in the Mist, would
take the lead whenever the tribe was undergoing sudden changes.
Though Mollie often felt bewildered by the upheaval around her,
she took the lead for her family—a modern traveler in the mist.
She spoke English and was married to a white man, and she had
resisted the temptations that had hurt many young members of the
tribe, including Anna.

To some Osage, especially elders like Lizzie, oil was a cursed blessing. "Someday this oil will go and there will be no more fat checks every few months from the Great White Father," an Osage chief said in 1928. "There'll be no fine motorcars and new clothes. Then I know my people will be happier."

Mollie pressed the authorities to investigate Anna's murder, but most white officials seemed to have little interest. So Mollie turned to Ernest's uncle. William Hale was one of the most successful businessmen in the county, and he had campaigned for law and order—for the protection of what he called "God-fearing souls."

Hale, who had an owlish face, stiff black hair, and small, alert eyes set in shaded hollows, had settled on the reservation nearly two decades earlier. He seemed to have come out of nowhere— a man with no known past. Arriving in the territory with little more than the clothes on his back and a worn Old Testament, he began what a person who knew him well called a "fight for life and fortune" in a "raw state of civilization."

Hale found work as a cowboy on a ranch. Before trains crisscrossed the West, cowboys drove cattle from Texas to Osage territory, where the herds grazed on the lush bluestem grass, and then on to Kansas, for shipment to Chicago and other cities. These cattle drives fueled the American fascination with cowboys, but the work was hardly romantic. Hale toiled day and night for very little money. He rode through storms—hail, lightning, sand—and survived stampedes, when he had to guide the cattle into smaller and smaller circles so they wouldn't trample him. His clothes carried the stench of sweat and manure, and his bones were frequently battered, if not broken. Eventually, he hoarded and borrowed enough money to buy his own herd in Osage territory. "He is the most energetic man I ever knew," a man who invested in his business recalled. "Even when he crossed the street he walked as if he were going after something big."

But Hale soon went bankrupt—a bitter failure that only stoked the furnace of his ambition. After he started over in the cattle business, he often slept in a tent on the windy plains, alone in his fury. Years later, a reporter described how he'd pace before a fire "like a leashed animal. He nervously rubbed his hands into the flames. His rather ruddy face was aglow with cold and excitement."

He became an expert cattleman. And as his profits rose, he bought up more territory from the Osage and neighboring settlers until he owned some forty-five thousand acres of the finest grazing land in the county, as well as a small fortune. Then he went to work on himself. He replaced his ragged trousers and cowboy hat with a suit, a bow tie, and a felt hat, his eyes looking out through distinguished round-rimmed glasses. He married a schoolteacher and had a daughter who adored him. He recited poetry. Pawnee Bill, the legendary Wild West showman and the onetime partner of Buffalo Bill, described Hale as a "high-class gentleman."

He was named a reserve deputy sheriff in Fairfax. The position enabled him to carry a badge and to lead posses, and he sometimes kept one pistol in his side pocket and another strapped to his hip. They represented, he liked to say, his authority as an officer of the law.

As Hale's wealth and power grew, politicians courted his support, knowing that they couldn't win without his blessing. He outworked and outwitted his rivals, making plenty of enemies who wanted him dead. "Some did hate him," a friend admitted. Still, Mollie Burkhart and many others considered him Osage County's greatest benefactor. He had aided the Osage before they were flush with oil money, donating to charities and schools and a hospital. He even assumed the label of preacher, signing his letters "Rev. W. K. Hale." A local doctor said, "I couldn't begin to remember how many sick people have received medical attention at his expense, nor how many hungry mouths have tasted of his bounty." Later, Hale wrote a letter to an assistant chief of the tribe, saying, "I never had better friends in my life than the Osages. . . . I will always be the Osages true Friend." In this last remnant of the American frontier, Hale was revered as the "King of the Osage Hills."

Hale frequently came by Mollie's house to pick up Ernest. Not long after Anna's burial, he showed up to pay his respects to Mollie and her mother. He vowed to get justice for Anna.

He had always expressed affection for Anna—"We were mighty good friends," he said—and had served as a pallbearer at her funeral. Mollie remembered seeing Hale huddled with Ernest during one visit, apparently talking about hunting down whoever had murdered her sister.

A short time later, Mollie went to testify at a hearing in Fairfax. The U.S. Department of the Interior's Office of Indian Affairs—which oversaw government relations with tribes and was later renamed the Bureau of Indian Affairs—had a field agent assigned to the Osage territory who knew Mollie. He said that she was "willing to do everything she can in order to . . . bring the guilty parties to justice." The authorities had provided a translator for Mollie, but she waved him off and spoke in succinct English, the way the nuns had taught her as a child.

William Hale competing in a roping contest when he was a cowboy

A transformed Hale standing with his daughter and wife

Mollie described for the jurors the final time that Anna visited her house. She said that her sister had left around sundown. In a later proceeding, a government official asked her, "How did she go?"

"She goes in a car."

"Who was with her?"

"Bryan Burkhart."

"Did you notice which direction they went?"

"Towards Fairfax."

"Was anyone else in the car with Bryan and Anna?"

"No, just Bryan and Anna . . ."

"Did you see her anymore alive after that?"

Mollie stayed composed. "No," she said.

"You saw her body after it was found?"

"Yes."

"How long was it about after this time you saw her leave your mother's place with Bryan Burkhart, you saw her body?"

"About five or six days."

"Where did you see the body?"

"At the pasture . . . just right there."

While Mollie seemed eager to answer every question, to make sure that nothing was missed, the justice of the peace and the jurors asked her barely anything. Perhaps they discounted her because of their prejudice—because she was an Osage and a woman. The panel spent more time questioning Bryan Burkhart. Many locals had begun to whisper about him. After all, he was the last person seen with Anna before she went missing.

Bryan lacked the good looks of his brother Ernest, Mollie's husband, and there was something cold about his appearance. He had uncomfortably steady eyes. Hale had once caught him steal-ing his cattle and, to teach his nephew a lesson, he filed charges against him.

The county prosecutor asked Bryan about the day that he said he'd given Anna a ride to her house. "When you brought her back, where did you go?"

"Come to town."

"When was this?"

"About five, or four-thirty."

"You haven't seen her since then?"

"No, sir."

At one point, the county prosecutor paused and asked, *"Positive?"*

"Yes, sir."

At a later hearing, Ernest was also questioned. A law-enforcement official pressed him about his brother: "You understand he is the last person seen with this woman, Anna Brown?"

"I understand," Ernest replied, adding that Bryan told him "he left her at her house. That is his story."

"Do you believe it?"

"Yes, sir."

Bryan was jailed by the authorities after the first hearing. To Mollie's distress, they even held Ernest, too, in case he was cover-ing for his younger brother. But both men were soon turned loose. There was no evidence tying Bryan to the crime, other than the fact that he'd been with Anna before she disappeared. When Er-nest was asked if he had any information as to how Anna met her death, he said no, adding, "I don't know of enemies she had or anyone that disliked her."

Lawmen seize a moonshine still in Osage County in 1923.

The main theory was that her killer was someone from outside the reservation. Once, the tribe's enemies had battled them on the plains. Now they came in the form of train robbers and stickup men and other desperadoes. The passage of Prohibition, outlawing alcohol, had only added to the territory's feeling of lawlessness by creating, in the words of one historian, "the greatest criminal bonanza in American history."

Few places in the country were as chaotic as Osage County, where the amount of oil money—by one account, more than the value of all the Old West gold rushes combined—had drawn every kind of villain from across the country. An official with the U.S.

Al Spencer Gang members jokingly hold up others in their crew.

Department of Justice warned that there were more fugitives hiding out in the Osage Hills than "perhaps any other county in the state or any state in the Union." Among them was the hard-boiled stickup man Irvin Thompson, who was known as Blackie. A lawman described him as "the meanest man I ever handled." Even more notorious was Al Spencer, the so-called Phantom Terror, who had made the transition from galloping horses to speeding getaway cars and had inherited from Jesse James the title of the region's most infamous outlaw. Members of Spencer's gang, including Dick Gregg and Frank "Jelly" Nash, were themselves ranked among the most dreaded outlaws of the day.

A more unnerving theory about Anna's death was that her killer was living among them, hiding in sheep's clothing. Mollie and others began to suspect Anna's ex-husband, Oda Brown, who called himself a businessman but spent most of his time partying. In retrospect, his grief had seemed almost too intense. After Anna divorced him, she had denied him any inheritance, leaving virtually all of her fortune to her mother. Since the burial, Brown had hired a lawyer and tried unsuccessfully to fight the will. The investigator concluded that Brown was "absolutely no good and capable of doing almost anything for money."

Several weeks after the funeral, a man who'd been arrested in Kansas for check forgery sent a letter to Sheriff Freas claiming that he had information about Anna's murder. Upon receiving the message, the sheriff set out for the Kansas jail in what the press described as a "fast automobile." Hale, who had been tipped off about the potential breakthrough, rushed to the jail as well. Under interrogation, the forger, a fidgety twenty-eight-year-old man, claimed that Brown had paid him $8,000 to murder Anna. The forger also described how he'd killed her.

Soon after his confession, a posse of lawmen swept in and seized Brown when he was in Pawhuska on business. The *Pawhuska Daily Capital* heralded the news: ANNA BROWN SLAYER CONFESSES CRIME. It added, ODA BROWN, HUSBAND OF WOMAN, ALSO ARRESTED.

Mollie and her family were devastated by the report that Anna's ex-husband was responsible for her murder, but they took comfort in the thought of his facing justice. Within days, however, authorities said that there was no evidence to support the forger's claims—no evidence that he had been in Osage County at the time of the murder or that Brown had ever contacted him. The authorities had no choice but to release Brown. "There's a lot of talk," the sheriff was quoted as saying. "But you have to have proof, not talk."

❁

Like many officials, the county prosecutor owed his election at least in part to William Hale, who had helped turn out the vote for him.

Hale met with him about Anna's murder. Eventually, the county prosecutor decided to look again for the bullet that investigators had missed during Anna's autopsy. He even got a court order to unbury Anna. But, once again, the Shoun brothers found nothing. The bullet appeared to have vanished.

By July 1921, the justice of the peace had completed his investigation, stating that Anna Brown's death had come at "the hands of parties unknown"—the same finding as delivered in the Whitehorn inquest. The justice locked away in his office the little evidence that he'd gathered, in case more information came to light.

Meanwhile, Lizzie—who'd once had the same energy and determination as Mollie—had grown sicker. Each day, she seemed to drift further away. It was as if she had the same peculiar wasting illness that had consumed her daughter Minnie.

Desperate for help, Mollie turned to the Osage medicine men, who chanted when the eastern sky was red like blood. She also looked to the new breed of medicine men, the Shoun brothers, who carried their potions in black bags. Nothing seemed to work. Mollie kept vigil over her mother, one of the last tethers to the tribe's ancient way of life. Mollie could not cure her, but she could feed her, and she could brush her long, beautiful silvery hair from her face—a face that was lined and expressive, that maintained its aura.

One day that July, less than two months after Anna's murder,

Lizzie stopped breathing. Mollie couldn't revive her. Lizzie's spirit had been claimed by Jesus Christ, the Lord and Savior, and by Wah'Kon-Tah, the Great Mystery. Mollie was overwhelmed with grief. As an Osage mourning prayer went:

Have pity on me, O Great Spirit!
You see I cry forever,
Dry my eyes and give me comfort.

Bill Smith, the husband of Mollie's sister Rita, was one of the first to wonder if there was something curious about Lizzie's death, coming so soon after the murders of Anna and Whitehorn. Bill had also expressed deep frustration over the authorities' investigation, and he had begun looking into the matter himself. Like Mollie, he was struck by the peculiar vagueness of Lizzie's sickness. No doctor had ever pinpointed what was causing it. Indeed, no one had uncovered any natural cause for her death. The more Bill searched, the more he was certain that Lizzie had died of something dreadfully unnatural: poison. And Bill was sure that all three deaths were connected—somehow—to the Osage's underground reservoir of black gold.

4

Underground Reservation

THE MONEY HAD COME SUDDENLY, SWIFTLY, MADLY. Mollie had been ten years old when the oil was first discovered, and she had witnessed firsthand the ensuing frenzy. But, as the elders in the tribe had told her, the tangled history of how their people had gotten hold of this oil-rich land went back to the seventeenth century, when the Osage territory stretched west from what is now Missouri, Kansas, and Oklahoma, all the way to the Rockies.

In 1803, President Thomas Jefferson purchased from the French the Territory of Louisiana, which contained lands dominated by the Osage. Jefferson told his secretary of the navy that the Osage were a great nation and that "we must stand well, because in their quarter we are miserably weak." In 1804, a delegation of Osage leaders met with Jefferson at the White House. He told the navy secretary that the Osage, whose warriors typically stood well over six feet tall, were the "finest men we have ever seen."

At the meeting, Jefferson addressed the Osage as "my children" and said, "It is so long since our forefathers came from beyond the great water, that we have lost the memory of it, and seem to have grown out of this land, as you have done. . . . We are all now of one family." He went on to say, "On your return tell your people that I take them all by the hand; that I become their father hereafter, that they shall know our nation only as friends and benefactors."

But within four years, Jefferson had forced the Osage to give up their territory between the Arkansas River and the Missouri River. An Osage chief stated that his people "had no choice, they must either sign the treaty or be declared enemies of the United States." Over the next two decades, the Osage were forced to hand over nearly a hundred million acres of their ancestral land, ultimately finding refuge in a 50-by-125-mile area in southeastern Kansas. And it was in this place where Mollie's mother and father had come of age.

Mollie's father, who was born around 1844, went by his Osage name, Ne-kah-e-se-y. A young Osage man then typically wore fringed buckskin leggings and moccasins and a breechcloth. A finger-woven belt held his tobacco pouch and tomahawk. His chest was often bare, and his head was shaved, except for a strip of hair that ran from the crown to his neck and that stood straight up, like the crest of a Spartan's helmet.

Along with other warriors, Ne-kah-e-se-y defended the tribe from attacks, and before heading into battle he would have painted his face black with charcoal and prayed to Wah'Kon-Tah, confirming that it was time, as the Osage put it, "to make the enemy lie reddened on the earth." As Ne-kah-e-se-y grew older, he became an important figure in the tribe. Deliberate and thoughtful, he had an ability to study each situation before choosing a course of action. Years later, when the tribe created its first court system, which decided mostly minor crimes, he was elected one of the three judges.

Lizzie also grew up on the reservation in Kansas, where she helped to provide for her family, harvesting corn and hauling wood over distances. She wore moccasins, leggings, a cloth skirt, and a blanket around her shoulders, and she painted the part in the middle of her hair red, to symbolize the path of the sun. An Indian Affairs agent would later describe her as "industrious" and a "person of good character."

Twice a year, when Lizzie and Ne-kah-e-se-y were young, their families and the rest of the tribe would pack their few earthly possessions: clothing, bedding, blankets, utensils, dried meat, and weapons. Then they would lash their belongings to horses and set out on a sacred two-month buffalo hunt. When a scouting party spotted a herd, Ne-kah-e-se-y and the other hunters raced on their horses across the plains, the hooves pounding the earth like drums, the manes whipping the riders' sweating, gleaming faces. A French medical student who joined the tribe on a hunt in 1840 said, "The race is a merciless one. . . . Once the bison is reached, the animal tries to escape in another direction, he doubles to deceive his enemy; then seeing himself overtaken, he becomes enraged and turns against his aggressor."

Ne-kah-e-se-y would coolly draw his bow and arrow, which the Osage considered more effective than a bullet. When a bison was fatally wounded, the tail was cut off—as a trophy for the conqueror. Nothing was left to waste: the meat was dried, the heart was smoked, and the intestines were made into sausages. Oils from the bison's brain were rubbed over the hide, which was then transformed into leather for robes and lodge coverings. And still there was more to reap: horns were turned into spoons, sinews into bowstrings, and tallow into fuel for torches. When an Osage chief was asked why he didn't adopt the white man's ways, he replied, "I am perfectly content with my condition. The forests and rivers supply all the calls of nature in plenty."

The Osage had been assured by the U.S. government that their Kansas territory would remain their home forever, but before long they were under siege from settlers. Among them was the family of Laura Ingalls Wilder, who later wrote *Little House on the Prairie* based on her experiences. "Why don't you like Indians, Ma?" Laura asks her mother in one scene.

"I just don't like them; and don't lick your fingers, Laura."

"This is Indian country, isn't it?" Laura said. "What did we come to their country for, if you don't like them?"

One evening, Laura's father explains to her that the government will soon make the Osage move away: "That's why we're here, Laura. White people are going to settle all this country, and we get the best land because we get here first and take our pick."

Though, in the book, the Ingallses leave the reservation under threat of being removed by soldiers, many squatters began to take the land by force. In 1870, the Osage—driven from their lodges, their graves plundered—agreed to sell their Kansas lands to settlers for $1.25 an acre. Nevertheless, impatient settlers massacred several of the Osage. An Indian Affairs agent said, "The question will suggest itself, which of these people are the savages?"

The Osage searched for a new homeland. They debated buying nearly 1.5 million acres from the Cherokee in what was then called Indian Territory—a region south of Kansas that had become an end point on the Trail of Tears for many tribes ousted from their lands. The unoccupied area that the Osage were eyeing was bigger than Delaware, but most whites regarded the land as "broken, rocky, sterile, and utterly unfit for cultivation," as one Indian Affairs agent put it.

That is why Wah-Ti-An-Kah, an Osage chief, stood at a council meeting and said, "My people will be happy in this land. White man cannot put iron thing in ground here. White man will not come to this land. There are many hills here . . . white man does not like country where there are hills, and he will not come." He continued, "If my people go west where land is like floor of lodge, white man will come to our lodges and say, 'We want your land.' . . . Soon land will end and Osages will have no home."

So the Osage bought the territory for seventy cents per acre and, in the early 1870s, began their exodus. "The air was filled with cries of the old people, especially the women, who lamented over the graves of their children, which they were about to leave forever," a witness said. After completing their

The Osage chief Wah-Ti-An-Kah

An Osage camp on the new reservation

trek to the new reservation, members of the tribe built several camps. The biggest one was in Pawhuska, where the Office of Indian Affairs erected an imposing sandstone building for its field office. Gray Horse, in the western part of the territory, consisted of little more than a cluster of newly built lodges, and it was here that Lizzie and Ne-kah-e-se-y, who married in 1874, settled.

The series of forced migrations, along with such "white man's diseases" as smallpox, had taken a terrible toll on the tribe. By one estimate, its population had dwindled to about three thousand— a third of what it had been seventy years earlier. An Indian Affairs agent reported, "This little remnant is all that remains of a heroic race that once held undisputed ownership over all this region."

Although the Osage still went on buffalo hunts, they were chasing not only food but the past. "It was like life in the old days," a white trader who accompanied them recalled. "The old men of the band were wont to gather about the campfires in a reminiscent mood and there recount the tales of prowess on the war-path and in the chase."

By 1877, there were almost no more American buffalo to hunt. Their extinction was hastened by the authorities, who encouraged settlers to wipe out the animals, knowing that, in the words of an army officer, "every buffalo dead is an Indian gone." U.S. officials increasingly forced tribes to abandon their traditions, and they tried to turn the Osage into churchgoing, English-speaking tillers of the soil. The government owed the tribe yearly payments for the sale of its Kansas land, but it refused to distribute them until able-bodied men like Ne-kah-e-se-y took up farming. Even then, the government insisted on making the payments in the form of clothing and food rations. An Osage chief complained, "We are not dogs that we should be fed like dogs."

Unaccustomed to the white man's farming methods and deprived of buffalo, the Osage began to go hungry. Their bones soon looked as if they might break through their skin. Many members of the tribe died. An Osage delegation, including the chief Wah-Ti-An-Kah, was urgently sent to Washington, D.C., to ask the commissioner of Indian Affairs to abolish the ration system. According to an account by John Joseph Mathews, members of the delegation wore their best blankets and leggings, while Wah-Ti-An-Kah wrapped himself in a red blanket so that you could see little more than his eyes, dark wells that burned with an entire history.

The delegation went to the commissioner's office and waited for him. When the commissioner arrived, he informed an interpreter, "Tell these gentlemen that I am sorry that I have another appointment at this time—I am sorry I had forgotten about it until just now."

As the commissioner tried to leave, Wah-Ti-An-Kah blocked his path to the door and let go of his blanket. To the shock of even his fellow Osage, he was naked except for his breechcloth and his moccasins, and his face was painted as if he were leading a war party.

Wah-Ti-An-Kah told the interpreter, "Tell this man to sit down." When the commissioner complied, the chief said, "We have come [a] long way to talk about this."

The commissioner said, "Surely this man who doesn't know how to act—who comes to my office almost naked, with war paint on his face, is not civilized enough to know how to use money."

Wah-Ti-An-Kah replied that he was not ashamed of his body. After he and the delegation pressed their case, the commissioner agreed to end the ration policy. The chief then picked up his blanket and said, "Tell this man it is all right now—he can go."

Like many others in the tribe, Mollie's parents tried to hold on to their customs. Bestowing a name was one of the most important Osage rituals; only then was someone considered a person by the tribe. Mollie, who was born on December 1, 1886, was given the Osage name Wah-kon-tah-he-um-pah. Her sisters were also known by Osage names: Anna was Wah-hrah-lum-pah; Minnie, Wah-sha-she; and Rita, Me-se-moie.

But as settlers began to move onto the reservation, they threatened the Osage's culture and traditions. They didn't look like the Osage, or even like the Cheyenne or the Pawnee. The settlers seemed unwashed and desperate, like William Hale, who would eventually appear on his horse, in his ragged clothes—a man from nowhere. Even newcomers like Hale who formed close ties to the tribe argued that the white man's road was inevitable and that the only way for the Osage to survive was to follow it. Hale was determined to transform not only himself but the wilderness from which he came—to fence off the open prairie and to create a network of trading posts and towns.

In the 1880s, John Florer, a Kansas frontiersman who referred to Osage territory as "God's country," established the first trading post in Gray Horse. Mollie's father, Ne-kah-e-se-y, liked to linger outside it, in the shade, and sell animal pelts. Mollie got to know the son of a trader, who was one of the first white people she'd ever seen. His skin was as pale as the belly of a fish.

The trader's son kept a journal, and in it he noted a profound life change experienced by Mollie and her family. One day, he said, a trader began to refer to Ne-kah-e-se-y as Jimmy. Soon, other traders began to call Mollie's father Jimmy, and before long it had replaced his Osage name. "Likewise his daughters who often visited the store, received their names there of," the trader's son wrote. And that's how Wah-kon-tah-he-um-pah became Mollie.

Mollie—who, like her mother, then wore leggings, moccasins, a skirt, a blouse, and a blanket—slept on the floor in a corner of her family's lodge and had to do many grueling chores. But there was a relative peacefulness and happiness to that time. Mollie could enjoy the ceremonial dances and the feasts, and playing water tag in the creek, and watching the men race their ponies in the emerald fields.

In 1894, when Mollie was seven, her parents were told that they

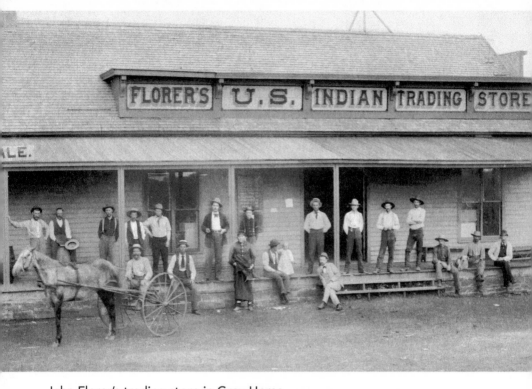

John Florer's trading store in Gray Horse

Mollie's father (right)
in front of Florer's
trading store

had to enroll her in the St. Louis School, a Catholic boarding institution for girls that had been opened in Pawhuska. An Indian Affairs commissioner had said, "The Indian must conform to the white man's ways, peacefully if they will, forcibly if they must."

Mollie's parents were warned that if they didn't follow these rules, the government would withhold its yearly payments, leaving the family starving. And so, one morning in March, Mollie was taken from her family and bundled into a horse-drawn wagon. As she and a driver set out for the two-day journey to Pawhuska, Mollie could see Gray Horse, the seeming limit of her universe, gradually disappear until all that was visible was the smoke rising from the tops of the lodges. In front of her, the prairie stretched to the horizon like an ancient seabed. There were no settlements, no souls, as if she'd slipped over the edge of the world.

Hour after hour, mile after mile, Mollie crossed the wild, empty landscape, not yet carved into a country. Eventually, the light began to fail, and the driver and Mollie had to stop and set up camp. When the sun sank below the prairie floor, the sky would turn blood-red and then black, the darkness diluted only by the moon and the stars, from where the Osage believed that many of their clans descended. Mollie had become a traveler in the mist. She was surrounded by the forces of night, heard but not seen: the gibbering of coyotes and the howling of wolves and the screaming of owls, which were said to carry an evil spirit.

The next day, the prairies gave way to timber-covered hills. Mollie and her driver rode until they came upon a dilapidated red-painted wooden structure. It was an Osage trading store, and nearby was a grubby rooming house and a blacksmith shop. The muddy trail turned into a wider, even muddier trail, with a scattering of trading stores on either side.

Mollie had reached Pawhuska. Although the reservation's capital then seemed a small, grimy place—a "muddy little trading post," as one visitor described it—it was likely the biggest settlement Mollie had ever seen. She was taken about a mile away, to a forbidding stone building that stood four stories high: the St. Louis Catholic missionary school, where she was left in the care of women in black-and-white nuns' habits. Mollie went through the front door—Mathews once described the entrance to another Osage boarding school as a "big, black mouth, bigger and darker than a wildcat's."

Mollie had to remove the traditional Osage blanket from her shoulders and put on a plain dress. She wasn't allowed to speak Osage—she had to catch the white man's tongue—and was given a Bible.

Each hour of the day was scheduled, and students were lined up and marched from point to point. They were taught piano, penmanship, geography, and arithmetic. Mollie was supposed to fit into white society and be transformed into what the authorities thought of as the ideal woman. So while Osage boys at other institutions learned farming and carpentry, Mollie was trained in the "domestic arts": sewing, baking, laundering, and housekeeping. "It is impossible to overestimate the importance of careful training for Indian girls," a U.S. government official had written, adding, "Of what avail is it that the man be hard-working and industrious, providing by his labor food and clothing for his household, if the wife, unskilled in cookery, unused to the needle, with no habits of order or neatness, makes what might be a cheerful, happy home only a wretched abode of filth and squalor? . . . It is the women who cling most tenaciously to heathen rites and superstitions."

Many Osage students at Mollie's school tried to flee, but lawmen chased after them on horseback and bound them with ropes,
hauling them back. Mollie attended class eight months each year.
And when she did return to Gray Horse, she noticed that more and
more girls had stopped wearing their blankets and moccasins and
that the young men had exchanged their breechcloths for trousers and their scalp locks for broad-brimmed hats. Many students
began to feel embarrassed by their parents, who didn't understand
English and still lived by the old ways. An Osage mother said of her
son, "His ears are closed to our talk."

Mollie was forced to attend the St. Louis School.

Mollie's family was straddling not only two centuries but two civilizations. Her family's distress increased in the late 1890s as the U.S. government pressured the Osage to submit to a new policy called allotment, which would end the Osage's communal ownership of their land. The reservation would be divvied up into 160-acre parcels, with each tribal member receiving one allotment. The rest of the territory would then be opened to settlers. The allotment system, which had already been forced on many tribes, was designed to end the old way of life and turn American Indians into private-property owners. This system would also make it easier for outsiders to buy up their land.

The Osage had seen what had happened to the Cherokee Out-

The land run of 1893

let, a vast prairie that was part of the Cherokee territory and was near the western border of the Osage reservation. After the U.S. government purchased the land from the Cherokee, it announced that at noon on September 16, 1893, any settler would be able to claim one of the forty-two thousand parcels of land—if he or she got to the spot first! For days leading up to that moment, tens of thousands of men, women, and children, from as far away as California and New York, gathered along the boundary. The ragged, dirty, desperate mass of humanity stretched across the horizon, like an army pitted against itself.

Finally, after several settlers who'd tried to sneak across the line early had been shot, the starting gun sounded—A RACE FOR LAND

SUCH AS WAS NEVER BEFORE WITNESSED ON EARTH, as one newspaper put it.

A reporter wrote, "Men knocked each other down as they rushed onward. Women shrieked and fell, fainting, only to be trampled and perhaps killed." The reporter continued, "Men, women and horses were laying all over the prairie. Here and there men were fighting to the death over claims which each maintained he was first to reach. Knives and guns were drawn—it was a terrible and exciting scene; no pen can do it justice. . . . It was a struggle where the game was empathically every man for himself and devil take the hindmost." By nightfall, the Cherokee Outlet had been carved into pieces.

Because the Osage had purchased their territory, it was harder for the government to force them to give up their communal land and divide it into individual allotments. The tribe, led by one of its greatest chiefs, James Bigheart—who spoke seven languages, among them Sioux, French, English, and Latin, and who had taken to wearing a suit—was able to hold off the process. But pressure was mounting. Theodore Roosevelt had already warned what would happen to an American Indian who refused his allotment: "Let him, like these whites, who will not work, perish from the face of the earth. . . ."

By the early twentieth century, Bigheart and other Osage knew that they could no longer avoid what a government official called the "great storm" gathering. The U.S. government planned to break up Indian Territory and make it a part of what would be a new state called Oklahoma. (In the Choctaw language, "Oklahoma" means "red people.") Bigheart had succeeded in delaying the allotment process for several years—the Osage were the last tribe in Indian Territory to have their land divided up. This gave the Osage more power to make a better deal, since government officials were eager to avoid any final roadblocks to statehood. In 1904, Bigheart sent a talented young lawyer named John Palmer across the country "to keep his finger on the Washington pulse." The orphaned son of a white trader and a Sioux woman, Palmer had been adopted as a child by an Osage family and had since married an Osage woman. A U.S. senator from Oklahoma called Palmer "the most eloquent Indian alive."

James Bigheart, one of the Osage's greatest chiefs

For months, Bigheart and Palmer and other members of the tribe negotiated with government officials over the terms of allotment. The Osage succeeded in getting the government to divide the land only among members of the tribe, increasing each individual's allotment from 160 acres to 657 acres. The Osage also managed to slip into the agreement what seemed, at the time, like a curious provision: "That the oil, gas, coal, or other minerals covered by the lands . . . are hereby reserved to the Osage Tribe."

The tribe knew that there were some oil deposits under the reservation. More than a decade earlier, an Osage Indian had shown John Florer, the owner of the first trading post in Gray Horse, a rainbow sheen floating on the surface of a creek. The Osage Indian dabbed his blanket at the spot and squeezed the liquid into a container. Florer thought that the liquid smelled like the axle grease sold in his store, and he rushed back and showed the sample to others, who confirmed his suspicions: it was oil. With the tribe's approval, Florer and a wealthy banking partner obtained a contract known as a lease, which allowed them for a price to drill for oil under the reservation. Few imagined that the tribe was sitting on a fortune, but by the time of the allotment negotiations several small wells had begun operating. And the Osage shrewdly managed to hold on to this last realm of their land—a realm that they could not even see.

The Osage created a system in which any wealth obtained from oil resources would be communally controlled by the tribe. Like other Osage, Mollie and her family members each received what was called a headright—an equal share of any oil profits. When Oklahoma became the forty-sixth state the following year, members of the tribe were able to sell their individually owned plots of land in what was now Osage County. But to keep the oil under tribal control, no one could buy or sell headrights. These could only be inherited. And so while much of the land on the surface was eventually divided and sold off to people outside the tribe, the oil beneath it could not be. Mollie and her family had become part of the first underground reservation.

The tribe soon began leasing areas to more and more white prospectors to drill underground in search of oil. Mollie saw workers—tool dressers, rope chokers, mule peelers, gang pushers—toiling furiously. These men built wooden structures that rose into the sky, like temples, and they chanted their own private language: "Bounce, you cats, bounce. Load up on them hooks, you snappers. That's high. Ring her off, collar-pecker. Up on the mops. Out, growler-board." Many wildcatters dug dry wells, or "dusters," and scurried away in despair. One Osage remarked that such white men "ack like tomorrow they ain't gonna be no more worl."

George Getty, a lawyer from Minneapolis, began his family's quest for oil in the eastern part of Osage territory, on a parcel of land, Lot 50, that he'd leased for $500. When his son, Jean Paul Getty, was a boy, he visited the area with him. "It was pioneer days," Jean Paul, who founded the Getty Oil Company, later recalled. "No motorcars, very few telephones, not many electric lights. Even though it was the beginning of the twentieth century, you still very much felt the influence of the nineteenth century." He went on to say, "It seemed a great adventure. My parents never saw the charm of it all that I did."

One damp spring day in 1917, Frank Phillips—a wildcatter who'd previously sold a tonic to prevent baldness—was out with his workers on Lot 185, less than half a mile from Lot 50. They were on a platform drilling when the derrick began to tremble, as if a locomotive were rushing by. From the hole in the ground came a rumbling, gurgling sound, and the workers began to run, their screams smothered by what had become a roar. A driller grabbed Phillips and pulled him off the platform just as the earth burst open and a black column of oil spewed into the air.

Each new find seemed more breathtaking than the last. In 1920, E. W. Marland, who was once so poor that he couldn't afford train fare, discovered Burbank, one of the highest-producing oil fields in the United States.

Many of the Osage would rush to see a gusher when it erupted, scrambling for the best view, while making sure not to cause a spark. Their eyes would follow the oil as it shot fifty, sixty, sometimes a hundred feet in the air. With its great black wings of spray, arcing above the rigging, it rose before them like an angel of death. The spray coated the fields and the flowers and smeared the faces

Workers strike oil in Osage territory.

of the workers and the spectators. Still, people hugged and tossed their hats in celebration. Bigheart, who had died not long after the allotment deal was done, was hailed as the "Osage Moses." And the dark, slimy, smelly mineral substance seemed like the most beautiful thing in the world.

5

The Devil's Disciples

MOLLIE'S HEADRIGHT GAVE HER MORE THAN MONEY. IT gave her the clout to at least try to pressure white authorities to pursue a killer of American Indians. After Lizzie died in July 1921, Mollie's brother-in-law Bill Smith presented his suspicions to police that Lizzie had been slowly poisoned. But by August, they had still not looked into the case. Nor had any progress been made in solving Anna's murder. To prod investigators, Mollie's family issued a statement saying that because of "the foulness of the crime" and "the dangers that exist to other people," they were offering a $2,000 cash reward for any information leading to the capture of those responsible. The Whitehorn family offered a $2,500 reward to catch Charles's slayers. And William Hale promised his own reward to anyone who caught the killers, dead or alive. "We've got to stop this bloody business," he said.

But the situation with law enforcement continued to worsen. The Oklahoma attorney general soon charged Sheriff Freas, who was investigating the murders, with permitting bootlegging and gambling. Freas denied the charges, but while the case awaited trial, the sheriff's attention was distracted. Given this turmoil, Hale announced that it was time to hire a private eye.

During much of the nineteenth and early twentieth centuries, private detective agencies often did the work that was ignored by incompetent and corrupt sheriff and police departments. In books and in the popular imagination, the all-seeing private eye displaced the crusading sheriff as the symbol of rough justice. Like Sherlock Holmes, he relied upon the startling powers of reason and deduction, the ability to *observe* what the Watsons of the world merely saw. He found order in a scramble of clues and, as one author put it, "turned brutal crimes into intellectual puzzles."

Yet the reality was that many private detectives were untrained and unregulated and often had criminal records themselves. Because they were widely seen as burglarizing other people's secrets, they were known as "the devil's disciples." In 1850, Allan Pinkerton founded the first American private detective agency. In advertisements, the company's motto, "We Never Sleep," was written under a large, unblinking eye, which gave rise to the term "private eye." Pinkerton admitted that his detectives must at times "depart from the strict line of truth" and "resort to deception." Yet even many people who despised the profession deemed it a necessary evil.

Hale recruited a brooding private detective from Kansas City, who went by the name of Pike. To keep his cover, Pike met Hale at a hidden spot near Whizbang, a boomtown in Osage County. As smoke from the oil fields melted into the sky, Hale gave Pike details of the case. Then Pike slipped away to start his investigation.

At the direction of Mollie and her family, Anna's estate also hired private detectives. The estate was being overseen by Scott Mathis, the Big Hill Trading Company owner, who had long man-

The Big Hill Trading Company was run by Scott Mathis, who was a guardian of Anna and Lizzie.

aged the financial affairs of Anna and Lizzie as a guardian. The U.S. government, believing that many Osage were unfit to handle their own money, had required the Office of Indian Affairs to determine which members of the tribe it considered capable of managing their own trust funds. Over the tribe's strong objections, many Osage, including Mollie, Lizzie, and Anna, were deemed "incompetent," and were forced to have a local white guardian overseeing and authorizing all of their spending, down to the toothpaste they purchased at the corner store. One Osage who had served in World War I complained, "I fought in France for this country, and yet I am not allowed even to sign my own checks." The guardians were usually drawn from the ranks of the most prominent white citizens in Osage County.

Mathis put together a team of private eyes, as did the estate for Whitehorn. That summer, the team hired by Mathis began to infiltrate the county. Each agent identified himself, in his daily reports, only by a coded number to protect his identity. At the outset, operative Number 10 asked Mathis, who'd been a juror for the inquest, to show him the crime scene. "Mathis and myself drove out to the place where the body was found," Number 10 wrote.

One of the investigators spoke to Anna's main servant. She revealed that after the inquest, she'd obtained a set of Anna's keys and had gone, with Anna's sister Rita Smith, to Anna's house. Incredibly, no one from the sheriff's office had searched the place yet. The women eased open the door and stepped through the silence. They could see Anna's jewelry and blankets and pictures, the accumulated treasures of her life, now resembling the ruins of a lost city. The servant, who had helped dress Anna the day she disappeared, recalled, "Everything was just as we left it"—except for one thing. Anna's alligator purse, which she had taken to Mollie's luncheon, was now lying on the floor, the servant said, with "everything torn out of it."

Nothing else in the house appeared to have been stolen, and the presence of the bag meant that Anna had likely returned to her house at some point after the luncheon. Mollie's brother-in-law Bryan seemed to be telling the truth about having brought her home. But had he taken her back out? Or had she gone away with someone else?

Number 10 turned to another potentially rich vein of clues: the records of Anna's incoming and outgoing telephone calls. In those days, phone calls were patched through by operators at switchboards, who frequently kept written records of the calls. According to the log of a Fairfax operator, at about 8:30 on the night Anna disappeared, someone had rung her house from a phone belonging to a business in Ralston, a town six miles southwest of Gray Horse. The records showed that someone had picked up. That meant that Anna was likely still in her house at 8:30—further evidence that Bryan had been truthful about taking her home.

The private detective, sensing that he was on the verge of a breakthrough, hurried to the Ralston business where the call was made. The owner insisted that he hadn't called Anna's house and that nobody else would have been allowed to make such an expensive call from his phone. Backing up his claims, no Ralston telephone operator had a record of the call being patched through to the Fairfax operator.

"This call seems a mystery," Number 10 wrote. He suspected that an operator had been paid to destroy the original log ticket, which revealed the true source of the call. Someone, it seemed, was covering his or her tracks.

Number 10 wanted to look closely at Oda Brown. "General suspicion points towards the divorced husband," he wrote. But it was getting late and he finished his report, writing, "Discontinued on case 11 P.M."

A week later, another operative from the team—Number 46—was sent to find Brown in Ponca City, twenty-five miles northwest of Gray Horse. A savage storm blew across the prairie and turned the streets into rivers of mud, so the private detective didn't arrive in Ponca City until dark, only to discover that Brown wasn't there. He was said to be visiting Perry, Oklahoma, where his father lived. The next day, Number 46 took a train south to Perry, but Brown wasn't there, either. He was now said to be in Pawnee County. This is what Sherlock Holmes stories leave out—the tedium of real detective work, the false leads and the dead ends.

From place to place Number 46 went until, in Pawnee County, he spied a slender, cigarette-smoking, shifty-looking man with rust-colored hair and flat gray eyes: Oda Brown. He was with a Pawnee woman whom he'd reportedly married after Anna's death. Number 46 stayed close, shadowing them. One day, Number 46 approached Brown, trying to befriend him. Eventually, Number 46 wormed his way deeper into Brown's confidence. When Brown mentioned that his ex-wife had been murdered, Number 46 tried to get Brown to reveal where he'd been at the time of her death. Brown, perhaps suspecting his new friend was a professional snoop, said that he'd been away with another woman, though he wouldn't name the location. Number 46 studied Brown closely. According to the Pinkerton manual, a criminal's secret becomes an "enemy" within him and "weakens the whole fortress of his strength." But Brown didn't appear at all nervous.

While Number 46 was working on Brown, another operative, Number 28, learned a seemingly vital secret from a young Kaw Indian woman who lived near the western border of Osage County. In a signed statement, the woman claimed that Rose Osage from Fairfax had admitted that she'd killed Anna after Anna had tried to steal her boyfriend, Joe Allen. Rose said that while the three were riding in a car, she'd shot Anna, then with Joe's help, left her body by Three Mile Creek. Rose's clothes were covered with Anna's blood, the story went, so she took them off and discarded them in the creek.

It was a grim tale, but operative Number 28 was excited by the discovery. In his daily report, he said that he'd spent hours pursuing this "clue that seems to be a lead on the case."

The private detectives, though, struggled to confirm the informant's story. No one had spotted Anna with Rose or Joe. Nor were any clothes found in the stream by the body. Was it possible that the informant was simply lying to get the reward?

Sheriff Freas urged the private detectives to remain skeptical about Rose and her boyfriend as suspects. Then he offered a counter-rumor: two hard-boiled characters from the oil camps had supposedly been seen with Anna shortly before her death and had then skipped town. The private detectives agreed to look into the sheriff's story. But they refused to drop the case against Rose. Number 28 vowed, "We are going to follow out this theory."

The private detectives shared what they knew with Bill Smith, who was still leading his own investigation. The twenty-nine-year-old had been a horse thief before attaching himself to an Osage fortune: first by marrying Mollie's sister Minnie, and then by marrying Mollie's sister Rita only months after Minnie's death from the mysterious "wasting illness" in 1918. When Bill drank, he was known to hit Rita. A servant later recalled that after one fight between Bill and Rita, "she came out kind of bruised up." Rita often threatened to leave him, but she never did.

Rita had a sharp mind, yet those close to her thought that her judgment was impaired by what one person described as "a love that was truly blind." Mollie had her doubts about Bill. Had he,

Mollie's sister Rita

in some way, been responsible for Minnie's death? Hale made it clear that he didn't trust Bill, either, and at least one local lawyer thought that Bill was abusing "the sacred bond of marriage for sordid gain."

But since Anna's murder, Bill had, by all appearances, tried hard to find the culprit. When Bill learned that a tailor in town might have information, he went with a private detective to ask him questions, only to find that he was spreading the now-familiar rumor that Rose Osage had killed Anna in a fury of jealousy.

Desperate for a break, the private detectives decided to eavesdrop on Rose and her boyfriend. At the time, laws governing electronic surveillance were not well defined and the detectives installed a Dictograph—a primitive listening device that could be tucked in anything from a clock to a chandelier. The detectives, hiding in another room, began listening to the staticky voices of Rose and her boyfriend through earphones. But, as is so often the case with surveillance, the rush of excitement gave way to the boring details of other people's daily lives. The private eyes eventually stopped bothering to jot down the meaningless information that they overheard.

Using more conventional means, however, the detectives made a startling discovery. The cabdriver who'd taken Anna to Mollie's house on the day she vanished told them that Anna had asked him to stop first at the cemetery in Gray Horse. She had climbed out and stumbled to her father's tomb. For a moment, she stood near the spot where she, too, would soon be buried, as if offering a mourning prayer to herself. Then she returned to the car and asked the driver to send someone to bring flowers to her father's tomb. She wanted his grave to always be pretty.

While they continued to Mollie's house, Anna leaned toward the driver. He could smell alcohol on her breath as she divulged a secret: she was going to have "a little baby."

"My goodness, no," he replied.

"I am," she said.

"Is that so?"

"Yes."

Detectives later confirmed the story with two people close to Anna. She had also confided to them the news of her pregnancy. Yet no one knew who the father was.

One day that summer, a stranger showed up in Gray Horse to offer his help to the private eyes. The man, who was armed with a .44-caliber snub-nosed English Bulldog revolver, was named A. W. Comstock, and he was a local attorney and the guardian of several Osage Indians. Some locals thought that Comstock, with his broadly curving nose and tan complexion, might be part American Indian—an impression that he did little to discourage. "The fact he represented himself to be an Indian would make him get along pretty well with the Indians, wouldn't it?" another lawyer skeptically remarked.

Given Comstock's many contacts among the Osage, the private eyes now took him up on his offer. While the detectives were trying to make a connection between the slayings of Charles Whitehorn and Anna Brown, Comstock passed on tidbits that he collected from his network of informants. There was talk that Whitehorn's widow, Hattie, had been after her husband's money, talk that she'd been jealous of his relationship with another woman. Was it possible that this woman was Anna Brown? And if so, was Whitehorn the father of her baby?

The detectives began to follow Hattie Whitehorn around the clock. But nothing came of it.

By February 1922, nine months after the murders of Charles Whitehorn and Anna Brown, the investigations seemed to have hit a dead end. Pike, the detective Hale had hired, had moved on. Sheriff Freas was also no longer heading up the cases. He had been forced from office after a jury had found him guilty of failing to enforce the laws against gambling and bootlegging.

Then, on a frigid night that same month, William Stepson, a twenty-nine-year-old Osage champion steer roper, received a call that prompted him to leave his house in Fairfax. He returned home to his wife and two children several hours later, but he was visibly ill. Stepson had always been in remarkable shape, but within hours he was dead. Authorities, upon examining his body, believed that someone he had met while he was out had slipped him a dose of poison, possibly strychnine, which was extremely lethal.

By the time of Stepson's death, scientists had invented many tools to detect poison in a corpse. Yet in much of the country, including Osage County, there were no coroners trained in forensics, and testing for toxic substances was rarely done. Poisoning was thus a perfect way to commit murder. Unlike a gunshot, it doesn't make a sound. And the symptoms mimicked natural diseases like cholera or a heart attack. During Prohibition, there were so many accidental deaths caused from wood alcohol and other bootleg whiskeys that a killer could poison a person's glass of moonshine without ever arousing suspicions.

William Stepson

On March 26, 1922, less than a month after Stepson's death, an Osage woman died of a suspected poisoning. Once again, no thorough blood test was performed. In another incident, Joe Bates, an Osage man in his thirties, got some whiskey from a stranger, and after taking a sip, began frothing at the mouth before collapsing. He, too, had died of what authorities described as some strange poison. He left behind a wife and six children.

That August, as the number of suspicious deaths continued to climb, many Osage convinced Barney McBride, a wealthy fifty-five-year-old white oilman, to go to Washington, D.C., and ask federal authorities to investigate. McBride had been married to a Creek Indian, who had died, and was raising his stepdaughter. He had taken a strong interest in American Indian affairs and was trusted by the Osage. A reporter described him as a "kind-hearted, white-haired man." Given that he also knew many officials in Washington, he was considered an ideal messenger.

When McBride checked in to a rooming house in the capital, he found a telegram from an associate waiting for him. "Be careful," it said. McBride carried with him a Bible and a .45-caliber revolver. In the evening, he stopped at an Elks Club to play billiards. When he headed outside, someone seized him and tied a burlap sack tightly over his head. The next morning, McBride's dead body was found in Maryland, stabbed and beaten. All his clothes had been taken, except for his socks and shoes, which held a card with his name. The forensic evidence suggested that there had been more than one attacker, and police suspected that his killers had followed him from Oklahoma.

The news quickly reached Mollie and her family. The killing—which the *Washington Post* called "the most brutal in crime annals in the District"—appeared to be more than simply a murder. It had the hallmarks of a message, a warning. In a headline, the *Post* noted what seemed to be increasingly clear: CONSPIRACY BELIEVED TO KILL RICH INDIANS.

6

The Million Dollar Elm

EVEN WITH THE MURDERS, THE GREATEST OIL BARONS IN the world kept on coming. Every three months, at ten in the morning, these oilmen pulled into the train station in Pawhuska in their own luxurious railcars.

They came for the auction of leases that would allow them to drill for oil in a part of the Osage's vast underground reservation. The bidding for a single lease, which typically covered a 160-acre tract, had skyrocketed. In good weather, the auctions were held outdoors, on a hilltop in Pawhuska, in the shade of a large tree known as the Million Dollar Elm. Spectators would come from miles away. Ernest sometimes attended the events, and so did Mollie and other members of the tribe. "There is a touch of color in the audiences, too, for the Osage Indians . . . often are stoical but interested spectators," the Associated Press reported, using stereotypes.

An auctioneer named Colonel Ellsworth E. Walters, who was known as Colonel, presided over all the Osage sales, and he would eventually step under the tree. A master showman, he urged bidders on with folksy sayings like "Come on boys, this old wildcat is liable to have a mess of kittens."

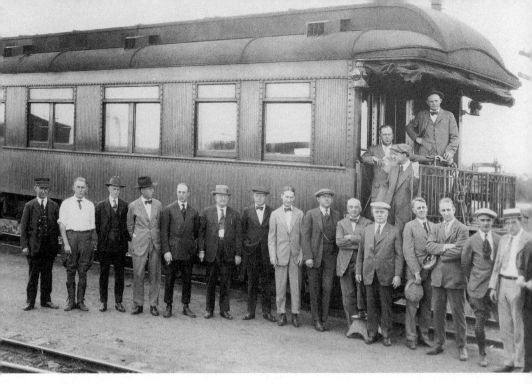

Frank Phillips (on bottom step) and other oilmen arrive in Osage territory in 1919.

Jean Paul Getty, who attended several Osage auctions, recalled how one oil lease could change a man's fate: "It was not unusual for a penniless wildcatter, down to his last bit and without cash or credit with which to buy more, to . . . bring in a well that made him a rich man." At the same time, a wrong bid could lead to ruin. "Fortunes were being made—and lost—daily," Getty said.

After a break for lunch, the more valuable leases were auctioned, and the crowd's gaze always turned toward the oil magnates, whose power rivaled, if not surpassed, that of the railroad and steel barons of the nineteenth century.

Some of them had begun to use their clout to bend the course of history. In 1920, Harry Sinclair, E. W. Marland, and other oilmen helped finance Warren Harding's successful presidential campaign. With Harding in the White House, a historian noted, "the oil men licked their chops." Sinclair used a bogus company to funnel a bribe of more than $200,000 to Harding's secretary of the interior—the cabinet member who oversees the management and conservation of federal lands and natural resources. Another oilman had his son deliver to the secretary $100,000 in a black bag.

In exchange for this secret money, the secretary allowed the oil barons to tap the navy's priceless oil reserves. Sinclair received the only lease to an extremely valuable oil reserve in Wyoming, which was known as Teapot Dome because of the shape of a sandstone rock nearby. The head of Standard Oil warned a former Harding campaign aide, "I understand the Interior Department is just about to close a contract to lease Teapot Dome, and all through the industry it smells. . . . I *do* feel you should tell the President that it *smells*."

The secret payoffs were as yet unknown to the public, and at the Million Dollar Elm, the oil barons were treated as princes of capitalism. During the bidding, tensions between them sometimes boiled over. Once, Frank Phillips and rival oilman Bill Skelly began to fight, rolling on the ground like rabid racoons, while Sinclair nodded at Colonel and walked off triumphantly with the lease.

On January 18, 1923, five months after the murder of McBride, many of the big oilmen gathered for another auction. Because it was winter, they met in the Constantine Theater, in Pawhuska. As usual, Colonel started with the least expensive leases.

Throughout the day, bids for new tracts steadily grew in value: from the minimum of $500 to $10,000 . . . $50,000 . . . $100,000 . . .

Downtown Pawhuska in 1906, before the oil boom

Pawhuska was transformed during the oil rush.

Colonel quipped, "Wall Street is waking up."

Tract 13 sold for more than $600,000, to Sinclair.

Colonel took a deep breath. "Tract 14," he said, which was in the middle of the rich Burbank field.

The crowd hushed. Then a mild voice rose from the middle of the room: "Half a million." It was a representative from Gypsy Oil Company, an affiliate of Gulf Oil, who was sitting with a map spread on his knees, not looking up as he spoke.

"Who'll make it six hundred thousand?" Colonel asked.

Colonel was known for his ability to detect even the slightest nod or gesture from bidders. At auctions, Frank Phillips and one of his brothers used almost unnoticeable signals—a raised eyebrow or a flick of a cigar. Frank joked that his brother had once cost them about $100,000 by swatting at a fly.

Colonel knew his audience and pointed at a gray-haired man with an unlit cigar clamped between his teeth. He was representing a group of investors and made an almost invisible nod.

"Seven hundred," cried Colonel, quickly pointing to the first bidder. Another nod.

"Eight hundred," Colonel said.

He returned to the first bidder, the man with the map, who said, "Nine hundred."

Another nod from the gray-haired man with the unlit cigar. Colonel belted out the words: "One million dollars."

Still, the bids kept climbing. "Eleven hundred thousand, now twelve," Colonel said. "Eleven—now twelve—now twelve."

Finally, no one spoke. Colonel stared at the gray-haired man, who was still chewing on his unlit cigar. A reporter in the room remarked, "One wishes for more air."

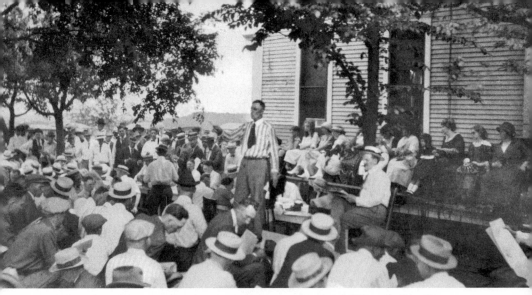

Colonel Walters conducting an auction under the Million Dollar Elm

No one moved or uttered another word.

"Sold!" Colonel shouted. "For one million one hundred thousand dollars."

Each new auction seemed to surpass the previous one for the record of the highest single bid and the total amount of money collected. The highest total collected at an auction climbed to nearly $14 million. A reporter from *Harper's Monthly Magazine* wrote, "Where will it end? Every time a new well is drilled the Indians are that much richer." The reporter added, "The Osage Indians are becoming so rich that something will have to be done about it."

A growing number of white Americans expressed alarm over the Osage's massive wealth—an outrage that was stoked by the press. Journalists told stories, often wildly exaggerated, of Osage who discarded grand pianos on their lawns or replaced old cars with new ones after getting a flat tire.

The accounts rarely, if ever, mentioned that numerous Osage had skillfully invested their money or that some of the spending by the Osage might have reflected ancestral customs that linked grand displays of generosity with tribal stature. Certainly during the Roaring Twenties, a time marked by what the novelist F. Scott Fitzgerald called "the greatest, gaudiest spree in history," the Osage were not alone in their excess spending. Marland, the oil baron who found the Burbank field, had built a twenty-two-room mansion in Ponca City, then abandoned it for an even bigger one. His new house had fifty-five rooms (including a ballroom with a gold-leaf ceiling and Waterford crystal chandeliers), twelve bathrooms, seven fireplaces, three kitchens, and an elevator lined with buffalo skin. The grounds contained a swimming pool, polo fields, a golf course, and five lakes with islands.

The press claimed that whereas one out of every eleven Americans owned a car, virtually every Osage had eleven of them.

Yet in only a few years, Marland would be forced to leave his mansion. He was so broke that he couldn't even afford his lighting bill. His architect recalled, "The last time I saw him, I think he was just sitting on a nail keg of some kind out there northeast of town. It was raining and he had on a raincoat and rain hat but he was just sitting there kind of dejected. Two or three men were working his portable drilling rig and hoping they might find oil. So I just walked off with a lump in my throat and tears in my eyes."

Unlike Marland and other wealthy Americans, many Osage could not spend their money as they pleased because of their appointed financial guardians. (One guardian falsely claimed that an Osage adult was "like a child six or eight years old, and when he sees a new toy he wants to buy it.") The decision to appoint a guardian—to make an American Indian, in effect, a half citizen—was nearly always based on the amount of American Indian ancestry the person had, or what a bigoted state supreme court justice referred to as "racial weakness."

Members of Congress would gather in wood-paneled committee rooms examining in great detail the Osage's spending, as if the country's security were at stake. At a House of Representatives subcommittee hearing in 1920, lawmakers combed through a report about the tribe's spending habits, including those of Mollie's family. The investigator cited with displeasure "Exhibit Q": a bill for $319.05 that Mollie's mother, Lizzie, had racked up at a butcher shop.

The investigator pleaded with Congress to take action. "Every white man in Osage County will tell you that the Indians are now running wild," he said, adding, "The day has come when we must begin our restriction of these moneys or dismiss from our hearts and conscience any hope we have of building the Osage Indian into a true citizen."

A few congressmen and witnesses tried to stop the scapegoating of the Osage. At a later hearing, even a judge who served as a guardian acknowledged that rich American Indians spent their wealth no differently than white people with money did. "There is a great deal of humanity about these Osages," he said. William Hale also argued that the government should not be making the Osage's financial decisions for them.

But in 1921, Congress passed even harsher laws controlling how the Osage could spend their money. Guardians would not only continue to oversee their wards' finances, but under the new law, the Osage Indians with guardians would also be "restricted," which meant that each of them could withdraw no more than a few thousand dollars per year from his or her trust fund. It didn't matter if these Osage needed their money to pay for education or a sick child's hospital bills.

"We have many little children," the last hereditary chief of the tribe, who was in his eighties, explained in a statement issued to the press. "We want to raise them and educate them. We want them to be comfortable, and we do not want our money held up from us by somebody who cares nothing for us." He continued, "We want our money now. . . . It is an injustice to us all. We do not want to be treated like a lot of little children." As a full-blooded Osage, Mollie was among those whose funds were restricted, though at least her husband, Ernest, was her guardian.

It wasn't only the federal government that was meddling in the tribe's financial affairs. The Osage found themselves surrounded by predators—"a flock of buzzards," as one member of the tribe complained at a council meeting. Corrupt local officials sought to devour the Osage's fortunes. Stickup men were out to rob their bank accounts. Merchants demanded that the Osage pay "special" prices—that is, higher ones.

At one congressional hearing, another Osage chief, a man named Bacon Rind, testified that the whites had "bunched us down here in the backwoods, the roughest part of the United States, thinking 'we will drive these Indians down to where there is a big pile of rocks and put them there in that corner.'" Now that the pile of rocks had turned out to be worth millions of dollars, he said, "everybody wants to get in here and get some of this money."

7

This Thing of Darkness

IN THE FIRST DAYS OF FEBRUARY 1923, THE WEATHER turned violently cold. Icy winds cut across the plains, and howled through the ravines, and rattled tree branches. The prairie became as hard as stone, birds disappeared from the sky, and the sun looked pale and distant.

One day, two men were out hunting four miles northwest of Fairfax when they spotted a car at the bottom of a rocky ravine. Rather than approaching it, the hunters returned to Fairfax and told police. A deputy sheriff and the town marshal went to investigate. In the dying light, they walked down a steep slope toward the vehicle. Curtains, as vehicles often had back then, covered the windows, and the car looked like a black coffin. On the driver's side, there was a small opening in the curtain, and the deputy saw a man slumped behind the steering wheel. "He must be drunk," the deputy said. But as he yanked open the driver's door, he spotted blood—on the seat and on the floor. The man had been shot and killed. There was no gun present, ruling out suicide. "He had been murdered," the deputy later noted.

Henry Roan

Since the brutal slaying of the oilman Barney McBride, nearly six months had passed without the discovery of another suspicious death. Yet as the two lawmen stared at the man in the car, they realized that the killing hadn't stopped after all. This time the lawmen had no trouble identifying the victim: Henry Roan, a forty-year-old Osage Indian who was married with two children. He'd once worn his hair in two long braids before being forced to cut them off at boarding school, just as he'd been made to change his name from Roan Horse.

Even without the braids, his long, handsome face and tall, lean body evoked the image of an Osage warrior.

The lawmen returned to Fairfax, where they alerted the justice of the peace. They also made sure that Hale was told. As the mayor of Fairfax recalled, "Roan considered W. K. Hale his best friend." Roan was one of the Osage whose financial allowance had been officially limited, and he had often asked Hale to advance him cash. "We were good friends and he sought my aid when in trouble," Hale later recalled, adding that he'd given his friend so many loans that Roan had listed him as the beneficiary on his $25,000 life-insurance policy.

A couple of weeks before his death, Hale said, Roan had phoned him, distraught because his wife was having an affair. Hale went to visit Roan and tried to console him.

Several days later, Roan was still upset about his wife and asked Hale if he could borrow a few dollars to get a drink of moonshine. Hale advised: "Henry, you better quit that. It's hurting you." And he warned him that the Prohibition men were "going to get" him.

"I am not going to bring any to town," Roan said. "I will hide it out."

Roan then disappeared, until his body turned up.

Once more, the dreadful rituals began. The deputy and the marshal returned to the ravine, and Hale went with them. By then, the crime scene was dark, and the men lined up their vehicles on the hill and shone their headlights down into the depths below.

Hale remained on top of the hill and watched as the coroner's inquest began. One of the Shoun brothers concluded that the time of Roan's death was around ten days earlier. The doctors noted the position and condition of the body. They also noted the broken glass strewn on the hood and on the ground beyond. They listed the things Roan carried: "$20 in greenback, two silver dollars, and . . . a gold watch." And the lawmen detailed the nearby tread marks in the frozen mud from another car—presumably the assassin's.

Word of the murder rekindled the sense of prickly dread. The *Osage Chief* stated on its front page, HENRY ROAN SHOT BY UNKNOWN HAND.

The news especially jolted Mollie. In 1902, more than a decade before meeting Ernest, she and Roan had been briefly married. There are few surviving accounts detailing their relationship, but it was likely an arranged marriage: two young people pressed together to preserve a vanishing way of life. Mollie was only fifteen at the time. Because the marriage had been contracted according to Osage custom, there was no need for a legal divorce, and they simply went their own ways. Still, they remained bound by this short relationship that had apparently ended with no bitterness and perhaps even some hidden warmth.

Many people in the county turned out for Roan's funeral. The Osage elders sang the traditional songs for the dead, only now the songs seemed as if they were meant for the living, for those who had to endure this world of killing. Hale served again as a pallbearer, holding aloft the casket of his friend.

Mollie had always assisted the police, but as they began looking into Roan's death, she became uneasy. She had never told Ernest, her jealous second husband, about her Osage wedding with Roan. Ernest had offered Mollie support during these terrible times, and their third child, a girl named Anna, had recently been born. If Mollie were to let the police know of her connection to Roan, she would have to admit to Ernest that she'd deceived him all these years. So she decided not to say a word—not to her husband or the authorities. Mollie had her secrets, too.

After Roan's death, electric lightbulbs began to appear on the outside of Osage houses, dangling from rooftops and windowsills and over back doors, their collective glow conquering the dark. An Oklahoma reporter observed, "Travel in any direction that you will from Pawhuska and you will notice at night Osage Indian homes outlined with electric lights, which a stranger in the country might conclude to be an ostentatious display of oil wealth. But the lights are burned, as every Osage knows, as protection against the stealthy approach of a grim specter—an unseen hand. . . . The perennial question in the Osage land is, 'who will be next?' "

The murders had created a climate of terror that ate at the community. People suspected neighbors, suspected friends. Charles Whitehorn's widow said she was sure that the same parties who had murdered her husband would soon "do away with her." A visitor staying in Fairfax later recalled that people were overcome by "paralyzing fear," and a reporter observed that a "dark cloak of mystery and dread . . . covered the oil-bespattered valleys of the Osage hills."

Despite the growing risks, Mollie and her family pressed on with their search for the killers. Bill Smith confided in several people that he was getting "warm" with his detective work. One night, he was with Rita at their house, in an isolated area outside Fairfax, when they thought they heard something moving just outside. Then the noise stopped. A few nights later, Bill and Rita heard the jostling again. They were certain that intruders were nearby, rattling objects, probing, then vanishing. Bill told a friend, "Rita's scared," and Bill seemed to have lost his confidence, too.

Less than a month after Roan's death, Bill and Rita fled that home, leaving behind most of their belongings. They moved into an elegant two-story house, with a porch and a garage, near the center of Fairfax. (They'd bought the house from the doctor James Shoun, who was a close friend of Bill's.) Several of the neighbors had watchdogs, which barked at the slightest disturbance. Surely these animals would signal if the intruders returned. "Now that we've moved," Bill told a friend, "maybe they'll leave us alone."

Not long afterward, a man appeared at the Smiths' door. He told

Bill that he'd heard he was selling some farmland. Bill informed him that he was mistaken. The man, Bill noticed, had a wild look about him, the look of an outlaw, and he kept glancing around the house as if he were casing it.

In early March, the dogs in the neighborhood began to die, one after the other. Their bodies were found slumped on doorsteps and on the streets. Bill was certain that they'd been poisoned. He and Rita found themselves in the grip of tense silence. He confided in a friend that he didn't "expect to live very long."

On March 9, a day of swirling winds, Bill drove with a friend to the bootlegger Henry Grammer's ranch, which was on the western edge of the reservation. Bill told his friend that he needed a drink of moonshine. The Roan investigation had produced one revelation: before disappearing, Henry Roan had said that he was going to get whiskey at Grammer's ranch. This was the same place, coincidentally or not, where Mollie's sister Anna often got her whiskey, too.

Grammer was a rodeo star who had performed at Madison Square Garden and been crowned the steer-roping champion of the world. He was also an alleged train robber, a kingpin bootlegger with connections to the Kansas City Mob, and a blazing gunman.

Yet the legal system seemed unable to hold him for long, even though he was also a convicted

Henry Grammer received a three-year sentence after he killed a man in Montana.

murderer. And as Grammer's bootlegging empire grew, he had an army of bandits under his control.

Bill and his friend arrived at Grammer's ranch in the gathering dusk. Hidden in the surrounding woods were five-hundred-gallon copper stills for brewing whiskey. Grammer had set up his own private power plant so that his gangs could work all day and all night—the light of the moon was no longer needed to secretly make moonshine.

Finding that Grammer was away, Bill asked one of the workers for several jars of whiskey. He took a few swigs. Then he and his friend drove back to Fairfax, passing the strings of lightbulbs—the 'fraid lights, as they were called—that shivered in the wind.

Bill dropped his friend off, and when he got home, he pulled his car into the garage. Rita was in the house with Nettie Brookshire,

Rita Smith and her servant Nettie Brookshire at a summer retreat

a nineteen-year-old white servant who often stayed over. They soon went to bed.

Just before three in the morning, a man who lived nearby heard a loud explosion. The force of the blast radiated through the neighborhood, bending trees and signposts and blowing out windows. In a Fairfax hotel, a night watchman sitting by a window was showered with broken glass and thrown to the floor. In another room of the hotel, a guest was hurled backward. Closer to the blast, doors on houses were smashed and torn apart; wooden beams were cracked like bones. A witness who had been a boy at the time later wrote, "It seemed that the night would never stop trembling."

Mollie and Ernest felt the explosion, too. "It shook everything," Ernest later recalled. "At first I thought it was thunder." Mollie, frightened, got up and went to the window and could see something burning in the distant sky, as if the sun had burst violently into the night. Ernest stood with his wife, the two of them looking out at the eerie glow.

Then Ernest slipped on his trousers and ran outside. People were stumbling from their houses, groggy and terrified, carrying lanterns. They fired guns in the air as a warning signal and as a call for others to join the rush of people moving, on foot and in cars, toward the site of the blast. As people got closer, they cried out, "It's Bill Smith's house! It's Bill Smith's house!" Only there was no longer a house. Nothing was left but heaps of charred sticks, twisted metal, and shredded furniture, which Bill and Rita had bought just days earlier from the Big Hill Trading Company. Strips of bedding were hanging from telephone wires, and pulverized debris floated through the toxic black air. Even Bill's car had been demolished. Clearly, someone had planted a bomb under the house and detonated it.

Rita and Bill Smith's house before the blast—

and then after

Flames consumed the remaining fragments of the house and gusted into the sky, a nimbus of fire. Volunteer firemen were carrying water from wells and trying to put out the blaze. And people were looking for Bill and Rita and Nettie. "Come on men, there's a woman in there," one rescuer cried out.

The justice of the peace had joined the search, and so had Mathis and the Shoun brothers. Even before bodies were found, the Big Hill undertaker had arrived with his hearse. A rival undertaker showed up as well, the two hovering like predatory birds.

The searchers scoured the ruins. James Shoun, having once owned the house, knew where the main bedroom had been situated. He combed in the vicinity, and that's when he heard a voice calling out. Others could hear it, too, faint but distinct: "Help! . . . Help!" A searcher pointed to a smoldering mound. Firemen doused the area with water, and amid the steaming smoke, everyone began clawing the rubble away. As they worked, the voice grew louder. Finally, a face began to take shape, blackened and tormented. It was Bill Smith. David Shoun later recalled that in all his years as a doctor, he'd never seen a man in such agony: "He was halloing and was in awful misery." James Shoun tried to comfort Bill, telling him, "I won't let you suffer."

As the group of men cleared the debris, they could see that Rita was lying beside him in her nightgown. She looked as if she were still peacefully sleeping, in a dream. But when they lifted her up, they saw she had no more life in her. When Bill realized that she was dead, he let out a torturous cry. "Rita's gone," he said over and over.

Ernest, wearing a bathrobe that someone had handed him to cover himself, was looking on. He was unable to turn away from the horror. The Big Hill undertaker asked him for permission to remove Rita's body, and Ernest agreed. What would Mollie say when she learned that another sister had been murdered? Now Mollie, once expected to die first because of her diabetes, was the only one left.

The searchers couldn't find Nettie. The justice of the peace determined that the young woman, who was married and had a child, had been "blown to pieces."

The doctors and the others lifted Bill Smith up as he grabbed for breath. They carried him toward an ambulance and took him to the Fairfax Hospital. He was the lone survivor, but before he could be questioned, he lost consciousness.

It took a while for local lawmen to arrive at the hospital because they had been in Oklahoma City for a court case. "The time of the deed was also deliberate," an investigator later noted, because it was done when officers "were all away." After hearing the news and rushing back to Fairfax, lawmen set up floodlights at the front and rear exits of the hospital, in case the killers planned to finish off Bill there. Armed guards kept watch, too.

Wavering between life and death, Bill would sometimes mutter, "They got Rita, and now it looks like they've got me."

After nearly two days, Bill regained consciousness. He asked about Rita. He wanted to know where she was buried. David Shoun said, "Bill, have you any idea who did it?" But the doctor later told authorities that Bill never revealed anything relevant. On March 14, four days after the bombing, Bill Smith died—another victim of what had become known as the Osage Reign of Terror.

❋

A Fairfax newspaper published an editorial demanding that the law "leave no stone unturned to ferret out the perpetrators and bring them to justice." A firefighter at the scene had told Ernest that those responsible for this "should be thrown in the fire and burned."

In April 1923, the governor of Oklahoma, Jack C. Walton, sent his top state investigator, Herman Fox Davis, to Osage County. Many Osage had come to believe that local police were working with the killers, so only an outsider like Davis could cut through the corruption and solve the growing number of cases. Yet within days, Davis was spotted hanging around with some of the county's notorious criminals. Another investigator then caught Davis taking a bribe from the head of a local gambling ring in exchange for letting him run his illegal businesses. It soon became clear that the state's special investigator was himself a crook.

In June 1923, Davis pleaded guilty to bribery and received a two-year sentence, but a few months later he was pardoned by the governor. Then Davis and several conspirators robbed—and killed—a well-respected attorney. This time, Davis received a life sentence. In November, Governor Walton was impeached and removed from office, partly for having abused his pardon power and partly for having received bribes from the oilman E. W. Marland.

Amid this terrible corruption, W. W. Vaughan, a fifty-four-year-old attorney who lived in Pawhuska, tried to act with decency. He had worked closely with the private investigators struggling to solve the Osage murder cases. One day in June 1923, Vaughan received an urgent call from a friend of George Bigheart, the forty-six-year-old nephew of the legendary chief James Bigheart. Suffering from suspected poisoning, Bigheart had been rushed to a hospital in

Oklahoma City. His friend said that Bigheart had information about the Osage murders but would speak only to Vaughan, whom he trusted. When Vaughan asked about Bigheart's condition, he was told to hurry.

Before leaving, Vaughan told his wife, who had recently given birth to their tenth child, about a hiding spot where he had stashed evidence that he had been gathering on the Osage murders. If anything should happen to him, he said, she should take it out immediately and turn it over to the police. She would also find money there for her and the children.

When Vaughan got to the hospital, Bigheart was still awake and aware. There were others in the room, and Bigheart motioned for them to leave. He then shared his information, including incriminating documents. Vaughan remained at Bigheart's side for several hours until he died. Then Vaughan telephoned the new Osage County sheriff to say that he had all the information he needed and that he was rushing back on the first train. The sheriff asked him if he knew who had killed Bigheart. Oh, he knew more than that, Vaughan said.

He hung up and went to the station, where he was seen boarding an overnight train. When the train arrived at his stop the next day, though, there was no sign of him. The *Tulsa Daily World* reported, MYSTERY CLOAKS DISAPPEARANCE OF W. W. VAUGHAN OF PAWHUSKA.

The Boy Scouts, whose first troop in the United States was organized in Pawhuska in 1909, joined the search for Vaughan. Bloodhounds hunted for his scent. Thirty-six hours later, Vaughan's body was spotted lying by the railroad tracks thirty miles north of Oklahoma City. He'd been thrown from the train. His neck was broken, and he'd been stripped, just like the oilman Barney McBride.

W. W. Vaughan with his wife and several of their children

The documents Bigheart had given him were gone, and when Vaughan's widow went to his hiding spot, she found that it had been cleaned out.

The justice of the peace was asked by a prosecutor if he thought that Vaughan had known too much. The justice replied, "Yes, sir, and had valuable papers on his person."

The official death toll of the Osage Reign of Terror had climbed to at least twenty-four members of the tribe. Among the victims were two more men who had tried to help with the investigation. One, a prominent Osage rancher, was thrown down a flight of stairs. The other, a lawyer, was shot on his way to share information with state officials about the case. News of the murders began to spread. The world's richest people per capita were becoming the world's most murdered.

All efforts to solve the mystery had failed. Because of anonymous threats, the justice of the peace was forced to stop holding inquests into the latest murders. He was so terrified that merely to discuss the cases, he would retreat into a back room and bolt the door. The new county sheriff didn't even pretend to investigate the crimes. "I didn't want to get mixed up in it," he later admitted.

In 1923, after the Smith bombing, the Osage tribe began to urge the federal government to send investigators who had no ties to state officials and would hopefully be untainted by all the corruption. The tribe issued a statement calling for immediate action to stop what one member called the "most foul series of crimes ever committed in this country."

While the tribe waited for the federal government to respond, Mollie lived in dread, knowing that she was the likely next target in the apparent plot to eliminate her family. She couldn't forget the night, several months before the explosion, when she had been in bed with Ernest and heard a noise outside her house. Someone was breaking into their car. Ernest comforted Mollie, whispering, "Lie still," as the thief roared away in the stolen vehicle.

When the bombing occurred, William Hale had been in Texas, and upon his return he saw the charred wreckage of the house— "a horrible monument," as one investigator called it. Hale promised Mollie that somehow he'd avenge her family.

One day, Hale's pastures were set on fire, the blaze spreading for miles. To Mollie, even the King of the Osage Hills seemed vulnerable. And after pursuing justice for so long, she retreated behind the closed doors and the shuttered windows of her house. She stopped entertaining guests and attending church. It was as if the murders had shattered even her faith in God.

Mollie with her sisters Rita (left), Anna (second from left), and Minnie (far right)

Her diabetes also appeared to be worsening. The Office of Indian Affairs received a note from someone who knew Mollie, saying that she was "in failing health and is not expected to live very long." Ill and consumed by fear, she gave her third child, Anna, to a relative to be raised.

Time ground on. There are few official records of Mollie's existence during this period. There is no record of how she felt when agents from the little-known Bureau of Investigation, which would be renamed the Federal Bureau of Investigation (FBI) in 1935, finally arrived in town. There's also no record of what she thought of doctors like the Shoun brothers constantly coming and going and injecting her with what was said to be a new miracle drug: insulin. It was as if, after being forced to play a tragic hand, she'd dealt herself out of history.

Then, in late 1925, the local priest received a secret message from Mollie. Her life, she said, was in danger. An agent from the Office of Indian Affairs soon picked up another report: Mollie wasn't dying of diabetes at all; she, too, was being poisoned.

CHRONICLE TWO

The Evidence Man

8

Department of Easy Virtue

ONE DAY IN THE SUMMER OF 1925, TOM WHITE, THE special agent in charge of the Bureau of Investigation's field office in Houston, received an urgent order from headquarters in Washington, D.C. The new boss man, J. Edgar Hoover, asked to speak to him right away—in person. White quickly packed. Hoover demanded that his staff wear dark suits and sober neckties and black shoes polished to a gloss. He wanted his agents to be a specific type: Caucasian, lawyerly, professional. Every day, he seemed to issue a new order—a new "Thou Shall Not"—and White put on his big cowboy hat with an air of defiance. When Tom White arrived in the nation's capital, he made his way through the noise and lights to bureau headquarters. He'd been told that Hoover had an "important message" for him, but he had no idea what it was.

White was an old-style lawman. He had served in the Texas Rangers near the turn of the century, and he had spent much of his life roaming on horseback across the southwestern frontier, a Winchester rifle or a pearl-handled six-shooter in hand, tracking fugitives and murderers and stickup men. He was six feet four and had the eerie calm of a gunslinger. Even when dressed in a stiff suit, he seemed to have sprung from a mythic age. Years later, a bureau agent who had worked for White wrote that he was "as God-fearing as the mighty defenders of the Alamo," adding, "He had a majestic tread, as soft and silent as a cat. . . . He commanded the utmost in respect and scared the daylights out of young Easterners like me who looked upon him with a mixed feeling of reverence and fear."

White had joined the Bureau of Investigation in 1917. He knew that the brotherhood of old frontier lawmen to which he belonged was vanishing. Though he wasn't yet forty, he was in danger of becoming a relic in a Wild West traveling show, living but dead.

President Theodore Roosevelt had created the bureau in 1908, hoping to fill a hole in federal law enforcement. When White first entered the bureau, it still had only a few hundred agents and only a smattering of field offices. Its authority over crimes was limited, and agents handled a hodgepodge of cases. Their investigations included banking violations; the shipment of stolen cars across state lines; escapes by federal prisoners; and crimes committed on American Indian reservations.

Like other agents, White was supposed to be strictly a fact-gatherer. "In those days we had no power of arrest," White later recalled. Agents were also not allowed to carry guns. But when he was on a dangerous bureau assignment, White sometimes tucked a six-shooter in his belt. Together with his younger brother J. C. "Doc," he was part of a small group who were known inside the bureau as the Cowboys.

Tom White was struggling to master new scientific methods, such as how to read fingerprints. Yet he had been upholding the law since he was a young man, and he had honed his skills as an

Tom White

investigator. He could see patterns and logically organize a scattering of facts. He had also experienced wild gunfights, but unlike his brother Doc—who, as one agent said, had a "bullet-spattered career"—Tom had a habit of *not* wanting to shoot. And he was proud that he'd never put anyone into the ground. There was a thin line, he felt, between a good man and a bad one.

White had seen many people he worked with at the bureau cross that line. During President Harding's term in the early 1920s, Harding had packed the Justice Department with officials who bent all the rules. The Department of Justice had become known as the Department of Easy Virtue.

In 1924, a congressional committee revealed that the oil baron Harry Sinclair had bribed his way to a valuable lease to drill in the Teapot Dome federal petroleum reserve. This crime and the investigation it spurred showed just how rotten the system of justice was in the United States at the time. As Congress began looking into the matter, the crooked attorney general used all his power to block the investigation. Members of Congress were spied on. Their offices were broken into and their phones tapped. This corruption within the president's inner circle gave Teapot Dome the distinction of being the worst presidential scandal until Watergate, fifty years later.

By the summer of 1924, President Harding had died in office and his successor, Calvin Coolidge, had appointed a new attorney general, Harlan Fiske Stone. Stone concluded that the only way to create a national police force free from political influence and corruption was to rebuild the bureau from top to bottom. To the surprise of many of the department's critics, Stone selected J. Edgar Hoover, the twenty-nine-year-old deputy director of the bureau, to serve as acting director while he searched for a permanent replacement. Though Hoover wasn't directly involved in Teapot Dome, he had been in charge of a rogue intelligence division, which had unethically spied on people merely because of their political beliefs. Hoover had also never been a detective, never been in a shoot-out or even made an arrest.

But he had long wanted to become the director, so he carefully hid from Stone how involved he had been in the illegal surveillance operations. And he began to eagerly make some of the changes Stone requested to reform the bureau. In a memo, he told Stone that he had raised the qualifications for new agents, requiring them to have some legal training or knowledge of accounting.

In December 1924, Stone officially gave Hoover the job he so desperately wanted. Hoover would rapidly reshape the bureau into a modern force. During his nearly fifty-year reign as director, however, he would use the agency not only to combat crime but also to commit terrible abuses of power.

Tom White now arrived at headquarters, which was then housed on two rented floors in a building on the corner of K Street and Vermont Avenue. Hoover had been getting rid of many of the frontier lawmen from the bureau, and as White headed to Hoover's office, he could see the new breed of agents—the college boys who typed faster than they shot. Old-timers mocked them as "Boy Scouts."

White was led into Hoover's office, where there was a massive wooden desk and a map on the wall showing all the bureau's field offices. And there, before White, was the boss man himself. Hoover was then slim and boyish-looking.

White and his cowboy hat towered over Hoover, who was so sensitive about his lack of height that he rarely promoted taller agents to headquarters. He later installed a raised dais behind his desk to stand on. But if Hoover was intimidated by the sight of this

J. Edgar Hoover at the Bureau of Investigation in December 1924

giant Texan, he didn't show it. He told White that he needed to discuss a matter of the utmost urgency with him. It had to do with the Osage murders. White knew that the case was one of the bureau's first major homicide investigations, but he was unfamiliar with its details. He listened as Hoover spoke in short bursts—a strategy that Hoover had created in his youth to overcome a bad stutter.

In the spring of 1923, after the Osage Tribal Council had passed the resolution seeking the Justice Department's help, an agent from the bureau had been sent to investigate the murders, which by then totaled at least twenty-four Osage. The agent spent a few weeks in Osage County before concluding that "any continued investigation is useless." Other agents were also sent to investigate, all to no avail. The Osage had been forced to pay for part of the cost of the federal investigation with their own money—an amount that would eventually reach $20,000, the equivalent today of nearly $300,000. Despite the money spent, once Hoover was in charge, he hoped to dump the case back on state authorities to avoid being blamed for the failure. Yet before he could, the bureau had blood on its hands.

A few months earlier, agents had persuaded the new governor of Oklahoma to release the outlaw Blackie Thompson, a convicted bank robber, so that he could work undercover for the bureau to gather evidence on the Osage killings. But while the agents were supposed to be keeping Blackie under close watch, they'd lost him in the Osage Hills. He then robbed a bank and killed a police officer.

It took months for authorities to catch Blackie. Hoover had managed to keep the bureau's role in the affair out of the press. But behind the scenes, there was a growing political uproar. The state attorney general had sent Hoover a telegram saying that he held the bureau "responsible for failure" of the investigation. Attorney John Palmer, the tribe's well-known advocate, sent an angry letter to a U.S. senator, implying that the bureau's investigation had been tainted by corruption.

When Hoover met with White, his grip on power was not yet firm, and he knew that even a whiff of scandal coming so soon after Teapot Dome could end his career.

Hoover needed White—one of his few experienced agents and one of the Cowboys—to resolve the case of the Osage murders and thereby protect Hoover's job. "I want you," Hoover said, to "direct the investigation."

He ordered White to take command of the Oklahoma City field office. White knew that relocating to Oklahoma would be a great burden to his wife and two young children. But he understood the stakes of the mission, and he told Hoover, "I am human enough and ambitious enough to want it."

White had no doubt what would happen if he didn't succeed. Previous agents on the case had been banished to distant outposts or cast out from the bureau entirely. He was also aware that several of those who had tried to catch the killers had themselves been killed. From the moment he walked out of Hoover's office, he was a marked man.

9

The Undercover Cowboys

AFTER TAKING OVER THE OKLAHOMA CITY FIELD OFFICE in July 1925, Tom White reviewed two years' worth of files on the Osage killings. Murder cases that are not solved quickly are often never solved. Evidence dries up; memories fade. More than four years had passed since the killings of Anna Brown and Charles Whitehorn. Frequently, the only way to crack such cases is to find a missed clue hidden within the original records.

The files on the Osage murders contained history in its rawest form: random bits of data vacuumed up, like a novel whose pages were out of order. White scoured this randomness for a hidden design. Though his experiences on the frontier made him used to dealing with violent death, he found the brutality detailed in the reports breathtaking. Previous agents had concentrated on the six cases that seemed most likely to be solved: the bombing deaths of Rita Smith; her husband, Bill Smith; and their servant Nettie Brookshire; and the fatal shootings of Anna Brown, Henry Roan, and Charles Whitehorn.

White struggled to find links among all the two dozen murders, but a couple of things were clear: rich Osage Indians were being targeted, and three of the victims—Anna Brown, Rita Smith, and their mother, Lizzie—were blood related. Surprisingly, agents hadn't spoken to Lizzie's surviving daughter, Mollie Burkhart. Investigators were taught to see the world through the eyes of others. But how could White possibly understand what this woman had seen—from being born in a lodge on the wild prairie to being catapulted into a fortune to being terrorized as her family and other Osage were picked off one by one? The files offered few insights about Mollie's life, mentioning only that she was ill with diabetes and had isolated herself in her house.

A few details in the files seemed important. Repeat killers tend to stick to a routine, yet the Osage murders were carried out in a bewildering variety of methods. This, along with the fact that victims' bodies had turned up in different parts of the state and country, suggested that this was not the work of a single killer. Instead, whoever was behind the crimes must have hired henchmen. The nature of the murders also gave some insight into the mastermind. The person was not an impulsive killer but someone intelligent enough to understand toxic substances and patient enough to carry out his diabolical vision over years.

As White studied the data in the reports, he concluded that the information from private eyes and local lawmen was based on little more than what they'd overheard. Given the corruption everywhere in Osage County, he thought that these sources might be intentionally spreading lies to cover up the real plot. White realized that the greatest problem with the earlier investigations was not that agents had failed to uncover any leads; it was that there were *too* many leads. Agents would develop one, then simply drop it, or fail to confirm the facts or disprove the facts. Even when agents seemed to be moving on the right track, they couldn't find any evidence that would be admissible in a court of law.

White had to learn many new techniques in his quest to be a modern evidence man. But the most useful one was timeless: coldly, carefully separating rumors from facts that he could prove. White now needed to build a case based on what he called an "unbroken chain of evidence."

He began to recruit a team of agents. Witnesses were reluctant to cooperate because of prejudice, corruption, or, as an agent put it, an "almost universal fear of being 'bumped off.'" And so most of the agents would have to work undercover, while White would serve as the public face of the investigation.

Hoover had kept in the bureau a handful of other experienced Cowboys, and White decided that they were the only ones who could infiltrate wild country, shadow suspects, go days without sleep, maintain cover under pressure, and handle deadly weapons if necessary. As White put together a squad of Cowboys, he didn't include his brother Doc. They always avoided being assigned to the same cases to protect their family from potentially losing two members at once.

White first recruited a former New Mexico sheriff, who, at fifty-six, became the oldest member of the team. The shy sheriff was skilled at taking on undercover identities, having pretended to be everything from a cow rustler to a counterfeiter. White then hired a stocky, talkative blond-haired former Texas Ranger, who, according to a supervisor, was best suited for situations "where there is any element of danger." In addition, White brought on an experienced deep-cover operative who looked more like an insurance salesman—perhaps because it was his former profession.

One agent from the earlier investigation, White decided, should be kept on: John Burger. He had a deep knowledge of the case—from the suspects to the trails of evidence—and he had developed a wide network of informants that included many outlaws. Because Burger was already well known in Osage County, he could work openly with White. So would another agent, Frank Smith, a Texan who listed his interests as: "Pistol and rifle practice—Big game hunting—Game fishing—Mountain climbing—Adventures—Man hunting."

Finally, White brought in John Wren—possibly the only American Indian in the bureau. Wren was part Ute—from a tribe that had flourished in what is today Colorado and Utah. He had a twirled mustache and black eyes and was a gifted investigator, but he had recently been fired from the bureau for failing to meet new bureaucratic regulations and write up written reports. "Some of his work can only be described as brilliant," a special agent in charge said, but he "will not commit it to paper." In March 1925, Hoover had rehired Wren but only after warning him to measure up to the new standards. White knew that Wren would bring an essential perspective to the team.

Some of the previous agents on the case, including Burger, had shown the kind of prejudice toward the Osage that was then commonplace. In a joint report, Burger and another agent had stated, "The Indians, in general, are lazy, pathetic, cowardly, dissipated," and Burger's colleague insisted that the only way to make "stubborn Osage Indians talk and tell what they know is to cut off their allowance . . . and if necessary, throw them in jail." Such contempt

White's team included a former Texas Ranger who was said to be suited for "any element of danger."

had deepened the Osage's distrust of federal agents and hurt the investigation. But Wren had capably handled many cases on American Indian reservations.

White told Hoover which men he wanted, and those not already assigned to the Oklahoma office received urgent orders, in code, from headquarters: "PROCEED UNDER COVER IMMEDIATELY REPORTING TO AGENT IN CHARGE TOM WHITE." Once the team had been assembled, White grabbed his gun and set out for Osage County—another traveler in the mist.

10

Eliminating the Impossible

ONE AFTER THE OTHER, THE STRANGERS SLIPPED INTO Osage County. The former sheriff showed up pretending to be an elderly, quiet cattleman from Texas. Then the talkative former Texas Ranger appeared, also disguised as a rancher. Not long afterward, the former insurance salesman opened a business in downtown Fairfax, selling real policies. Finally, Agent John Wren arrived as an "Indian medicine man" who claimed to be searching for his relatives.

White had advised his men to keep their covers simple so they didn't give themselves away. The two posing as cattlemen soon cozied up to William Hale, who considered them fellow Texas cowboys. He introduced them to many of the leading townsfolk. The insurance salesman dropped by the houses of various suspects, pretending he wanted to sell them policies. Agent Wren made his own connections, attending tribal gatherings and getting information from Osage who might not otherwise talk to a white lawman.

The undercover team was now in place, but it was hard for White to know where to focus the investigation. The records from the coroner's inquest into the death of Anna Brown had mysteriously vanished. "My desk was broken into and the testimony disappeared," the justice of the peace in Fairfax said.

Virtually no evidence had been saved from the various crime scenes, but in the case of Anna, the undertaker had secretly kept one object: her skull. White examined it and concluded, as earlier investigators had, that the bullet must have come from a small-caliber gun—a .32, or perhaps a .38 pistol. He also noticed that there was no exit wound, meaning that the bullet should have been found in her body during the autopsy. Someone on the scene—a conspirator or even the killer—must have swiped it.

The justice of the peace admitted that he'd had such suspicions as well. He was pressed on the matter: Was it possible that, say, the two doctors, David and James Shoun, had taken it?

"I don't know," he said.

When David Shoun was questioned, he insisted that he and his brother had "made a diligent search" for the bullet. James Shoun protested similarly. White was convinced that somebody had altered the crime scene. But, given the number of people at the autopsy, it seemed impossible to say who the culprit was.

To separate the facts from the rumors in the bureau's case files, White settled on a simple but elegant approach: he would methodically try to confirm each suspect's alibi. As Sherlock Holmes famously said, "When you have eliminated the impossible, whatever remains, however improbable, must be the truth."

White reviewed the previous federal investigation with the help of John Burger. Agent Burger had worked on the case for a year and a half, and by drawing on his findings, White was able to quickly rule out many of the suspects, including Anna's ex-husband, Oda Brown. His alibi checked out, and it became clear that Brown's accuser had made up his story hoping to bargain for better prison conditions. Further investigation eliminated other suspects, too.

Agent John Burger

White then explored the rumor that Rose Osage had killed Anna out of jealousy over her boyfriend, Joe Allen. (Rose and Joe had since married.) According to the statement the Kaw Indian woman had given to a private detective, Rose had confessed to her to being the murderer. The Fairfax town marshal also shared with agents that he had found a dark stain on the back seat of Rose's car, which looked like blood.

Agent Burger informed White that when he had brought Rose and Joe to the sheriff's office for questioning, she insisted that she'd had nothing to do with Anna's killing. "I never had a quarrel or fight with Anna," she stated. Agent Burger then confronted Joe, whom he described as "very self-contained, sullen and wicked appearing." Another investigator had separately asked Joe, "Were you thick with Annie?"

"No, I was never," he said.

Joe had given the same alibi that Rose did: on the night of

May 21, 1921, they had been together in Pawnee, seventeen miles southwest of Gray Horse, and had stopped at a rooming house. The owner of the rooming house supported Joe and Rose's claims. The investigators noticed, however, that the stories told by Rose and Joe were almost exactly the same, as if they had rehearsed them.

Rose and Joe were released, and afterward Agent Burger decided to seek the help of an informant—the bootlegger and drug dealer Kelsie Morrison, who seemed like he would be an ideal source of information. He'd once been married to an Osage woman and was close to Rose and other suspects. Before Agent Burger could recruit Morrison, though, he needed to find him.

Morrison had fled Osage County after attacking a local Prohibition officer. Burger and other agents found out that he was hiding in Dallas, Texas, using the fake name of Lloyd Miller. The agents sprang a trap. They had a registered letter sent to the post office box listed under Miller's name, then they nabbed Morrison when he went to get it. "We interviewed 'Lloyd Miller' who for about an hour denied that he was Kelsie Morrison but finally admitted that he was," Agent Burger reported.

The feds cut a confidential deal with Morrison. They wouldn't arrest him for assault if he would work as an informant on the Osage murder cases. There was a risk that he might slip away, so before releasing him, Agent Burger made sure that Morrison had gone through a rigorous process known as Bertillonage. Devised by the French criminologist Alphonse Bertillon in 1879, it was the first scientific method for identifying repeat criminals. Agent Burger took eleven of Morrison's body measurements. Among them were the length of his left foot, the width and length of his head, and the diameter of his right ear.

Agent Burger also took Morrison's mug shot, another of Bertillon's innovations. In 1894, the journalist Ida Tarbell wrote that any prisoner who passed through Bertillon's system would be forever "spotted."

But Bertillon's system was already being displaced by a more efficient method of identification that was revolutionizing the world of scientific detection: fingerprinting. In some cases, a suspect could now be placed at the scene of a crime even without a witness present. When Hoover became the Bureau of Investigation's acting director, he created the Identification Division to hold the fingerprints of arrested criminals from around the country. Such scientific methods, Hoover proclaimed, would assist "the guardians of civilization in the face of the common danger."

Agent Burger had Morrison's fingertips dabbed in ink. "We have

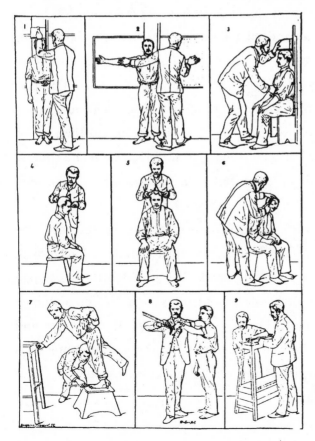

Bertillon's measurement system

his picture, description, measurements and fingerprints in the event we have cause to apprehend him," he informed headquarters.

He then gave Morrison some spending money. Morrison promised to visit Rose Osage and Joe Allen, as well as known local criminals, to see what he could learn about the murders. Morrison warned that if anyone discovered he was working for the feds, it would mean his death.

Morrison soon reported back that he had spoken to Rose about Anna's murder and asked her, "Why'd you do it?" And she replied, "I did not kill Anna." In a memo, Agent Burger noted of his prized informant, "If he is not bumped off too soon he can do us a lot of good."

White now reviewed all the information that had been gathered by Morrison and the agents regarding Rose Osage and Joe Allen. Rose and Joe had a confirmed alibi, and Rose had proclaimed her innocence to Morrison. So the Kaw Indian's statement that Rose had earlier confessed to her seemed puzzling. One detail, in particular, was curious. According to the Kaw Indian's account, Anna was in the car when Rose shot her, and her body was then left at Three Mile Creek. But the evidence from the crime scene showed that Anna had been killed at the creek. Her body had never been moved.

It seemed that the original witness must be lying and that Rose and Joe were innocent. When agents interrogated the Kaw Indian, it didn't take much for her to crack. She admitted that Rose had never told her any such story about the killing. In fact, a strange white man had come to her house, written up the statement, and forced her to sign it, even though none of it was true. White realized that the conspirators were not only erasing evidence—they were manufacturing it.

11

The Third Man

BY THE END OF JULY 1925, TOM WHITE HAD TURNED HIS full attention to the last of the listed suspects in Anna Brown's murder: Bryan Burkhart, Mollie's brother-in-law. White reviewed Bryan's statement from 1921. On the night Anna disappeared, Bryan claimed he had taken her straight home from Ernest and Mollie's house, dropping her off between 4:30 and 5:00 p.m. Bryan said he then headed into Fairfax, where he was seen with William Hale, his brother Ernest, and his visiting uncle and aunt, who went with him to the theater. There wouldn't have been time for him to go to the creek, shoot Anna, and return to town before the show started. His alibi seemed airtight.

To confirm details of that night, Agent Burger and a colleague had earlier traveled to Campbell, a town in northern Texas, to question Ernest and Bryan's aunt and uncle. The agents sped past the old trails that cowboys had once followed—trails that were now replaced by cattle cars pulled by shrieking locomotives. Agents discovered that Hale had grown up in a wooded grove only a few miles from Campbell. His mother had died when he was three years old. The King of the Osage Hills was burdened by a past, too.

In Campbell, agents stopped at the austere house of Bryan's uncle and aunt. The uncle was away, but the aunt invited the investigators inside and launched into a racist rant about how Ernest had married Mollie, one of those wealthy Osage Indians. Burger asked her about the night Anna disappeared. Oh, she'd heard the whispers about how Bryan was responsible for Anna's death, she said, but none of it was true; after dropping Anna off, Bryan had joined the rest of the party in Fairfax.

The uncle suddenly appeared at the front door. He seemed displeased to find a pair of federal agents inside his home. He was reluctant to speak, but he confirmed that Bryan had met them in Fairfax. He added that after the show he and his wife had spent the evening in the same house with Bryan and that he was there the whole time—and simply couldn't have been the murderer. The uncle then made it clear that he wanted the agents to get out.

In August 1925, White sent his undercover operatives to the town of Ralston to investigate a lead that had not been properly followed up. On the night Anna Brown disappeared, case records showed, she might have been spotted in a car by a group of white men who were sitting in front of a hotel on Ralston's main street. Previous investigators, including local lawmen and the private eyes, had spoken to these valuable witnesses and then seemingly buried what they had learned. At least one of the witnesses had since vanished, and White was convinced that, as one agent had noted in a report, such people were being "paid by suspects to go away and stay away."

White and his men tried to track down some of the other witnesses who had been outside the hotel, including an elderly farmer who had been questioned earlier by an agent. During that initial interview, the farmer had seemed to be suffering from dementia: he had stared at the agent blankly. After a while, though, he had perked up. His memory was just fine, he explained. He'd simply wanted to make sure that the investigators were who they said they were. Talking to the wrong person about these murders, he'd said, was liable to get one planted in the ground.

The farmer now spoke to White and his men. According to testimony that the farmer later gave under oath, he remembered that evening well, because he'd often discussed it with friends of his who gathered regularly at the hotel. "We old fellows have a lot of

The former New Mexico sheriff who played the role of a cattleman on White's team

time in town and that is where we sit down," he said. He recalled that the car had stopped by the curb, and through its open window he could see Anna—she was right there in front of him. She said hello, and someone in the group said back, "Hello, Annie."

The farmer's wife, who had been with him in Ralston that night, was also certain that the woman in the car was Anna. Asked if there had been anyone else with Anna, the farmer's wife replied, "Yes, sir."

"Who?"

"Bryan Burkhart."

Bryan, she said, had been driving the car and wearing a cowboy hat. Another witness said that he also saw Bryan with Anna in the car. "They went straight west from there right on through town and I don't know where they went from there," the witness recalled.

It was the first proven crack in Bryan's alibi. He might have taken Anna home, but he'd eventually gone back out with her. As an agent wrote in a report, Bryan "perjured himself when he swore before the coroner's inquest at Fairfax . . . that he had left Anna safely at her home in Fairfax between 4:30 and 5 p.m."

White needed to establish where the two had gone after leaving Ralston. Piecing together details from previous informants as well as from witnesses found by the undercover team, White was able to create a time line. They found that Bryan and Anna had stopped at a nearby speakeasy, an illegal bar, and stayed there until about 10:00 p.m. Then they headed to another, several miles north of Fairfax, where Bryan's uncle was spotted with them. So perhaps the uncle had been lying to Agent Burger to cover not only for Bryan but for himself as well. The owner of the place told agents that Bryan and Anna had been there until about 1:00 a.m.

Accounts of where Bryan and Anna went after that grew murkier. One witness said that they'd stopped, alone, at another speakeasy closer to Fairfax. Others reported seeing Bryan and Anna leave the speakeasy in the company of a "third man" who wasn't the uncle. "Third man is said to

Bryan Burkhart

have been present with Anna Brown and Bryan Burkhart," Agent Burger noted.

The last sighting of Bryan and Anna together that the investigators heard about had been at approximately 3:00 a.m. A witness who knew them both said that she'd heard a car stop near her house in Fairfax. A man whom she believed to be Bryan shouted, "Stop your foolishness, Annie, and get into this car."

After that, there was no trace of Anna—she'd become a ghost. Bryan's neighbor, though, spotted him returning home at sunrise. Bryan later told the neighbor not to say a word to anybody and gave him money to keep quiet.

Bryan had become White's prime suspect. But, as with many mysteries, each answer to a question opened up another question. If Bryan had killed Anna, what was his motive? Was he involved in the other murders? And who was the third man?

12

A Wilderness of Mirrors

BY THE END OF THAT SUMMER, TOM WHITE BEGAN TO suspect that there was a mole inside the investigation, someone stealing information and working against them. When one of his agents was questioning a seedy local attorney, the attorney had a shocking knowledge of the inner workings of the case. He admitted that he'd "seen part of the reports made by the Bureau . . . and had an opportunity to see more of them."

The bureau's probe had long been plagued by information leaks and sabotage. A U.S. attorney also discovered that the reports given to him by the bureau had vanished from his office. The breaches threatened the lives of agents and created doubts, with officials questioning each other's loyalty. One federal prosecutor demanded that no copy of his report be "handed to any representative of the State of Oklahoma."

Perhaps most damaging, two private eyes tried to expose the bureau's main informant, Kelsie Morrison. These private eyes leaked to several local officials that Morrison was working with the bureau, then went so far as to hold him on a trumped-up robbery charge. Blocking the investigation, Agent John Burger noted, appeared to be these private detectives' only goal, adding, "Someone must be paying them to do this."

An agent reported that Morrison seemed "frightened out of his wits" after being released from jail. During one of their meetings, Morrison pleaded with agents to get whoever did the killings before they got him. Agent Burger warned Morrison, "Look out for double crossing and traps."

White sometimes met with his team at night in the countryside, the men huddling in the dark like fugitives. Agents in the past had sensed that they were being followed, and White gave his men this advice in case their cover was blown: "Keep your balance, avoid any rough stuff if possible." Making it clear that they should carry weapons, against the bureau's official guidelines, he added, "But if you have to fight to survive, do a good job."

White found himself wandering through a wilderness of mirrors—his work felt more like spycraft than a criminal investigation. There were moles and double agents and possibly triple agents.

No one seemed more suspicious than the private eye called Pike, who had been hired by William Hale back in 1921 to solve the Osage murders but left the case without seeming to make any progress. A man in Osage County had approached Agent Burger and introduced himself as a go-between for Pike. The go-between said that Pike had withheld a crucial piece of information that he had discovered—he knew the identity of the third man who'd been spotted with Bryan and Anna around the time that she was killed.

Agent Burger wrote that Pike apparently "has known and talked with this third man." But the go-between made it clear that Pike would share this information under only one condition: that he be paid a king's ransom. "It is quite apparent there is some crooked work afoot," Agent Burger wrote in a report.

Agents demanded, through the go-between, that Pike come forward. But again he refused, determined to get money and obstruct justice. Agents then launched a manhunt for Pike, whose last known address was in Kansas City. Agent Burger wrote, "He changed his Kansas City address soon after it became known that we were working on him. We feel sure he has been paid to skip."

Not long after, Pike was caught while allegedly committing highway robbery in Tulsa. To save himself, he gave agents the name of a local gambler. Agents could confirm that the gambler had been at one of the speakeasies with Bryan and Anna on the night of May 21, 1921. But further investigation proved that the gambler had gone home too early to be the third man.

It seemed as if the agents had once more been duped. But they continued to work on Pike, to pressure him. Over time, he began to reveal, little by little, a shocking angle to the case. He'd never really been hired to solve the murder of Anna Brown. In fact, he'd been asked to hide Bryan's whereabouts on the night of the crime.

Pike told agents that he was supposed to make up evidence and to produce false witnesses—to "shape an alibi," as he put it. What's more, he claimed that his orders had come directly from William Hale.

Pike explained that Hale took pains never to say out loud that Bryan had been involved in Anna's killing but that it was clear to him from what Hale was asking him to do. If Pike was telling the truth, it meant that Hale—a seeming champion of law and order who had held himself up as Mollie Burkhart's most loyal protector—had been lying all these years about Anna's murder.

Pike could not answer what White wanted to know most: Was Hale merely protecting Bryan, or was he part of a more villainous plot? But Pike told agents one more thing that was startling. When he met with William Hale and Bryan Burkhart, there was sometimes another person there: Ernest Burkhart. Pike added that Ernest was careful never to "discuss this case or talk it over with him in the presence of Mollie Burkhart."

Tom (standing to the left) and his brothers, including Doc (on the donkey) and Dudley (far right)

Emmett showed remarkable consideration toward the people in his custody and insisted on making arrests without brandishing his six-shooter. Tom noticed that he always treated people the same way, no matter whether the prisoners were Black or white or Mexican. At the time, lynchings, particularly of Blacks in the South, were often carried out by white mobs. These killings, frequently by hanging, were one of the most terrible failures of the American legal system. Whenever Emmett heard that locals were planning to throw a "necktie party," he would rush out to try to stop it. "If a mob attempts to take" a Black prisoner from the sheriff, a reporter noted in one case, "there will be trouble."

Emmett refused to put young, nonviolent prisoners in the jail alongside older, more dangerous convicts, and because there was no other place for them, he let them stay in his own house, living with his children. One girl remained with them for weeks on end. Tom never knew why she was in jail, and his father never discussed it.

Tom often puzzled over why criminals did what they did. Some of the prison's inmates seemed bad through and through, the devil born in them. Some seemed mentally ill, seeing things that other people couldn't see. Many of the prisoners, though, seemed to have been driven to a desperate act—often something violent and despicable—and afterward they were full of regret, seeking redemption. In some ways, these convicts were the most frightening for Tom to think about, for they showed that badness could take hold of anyone.

Tom watched his father work. At all hours of the day, including on Sundays, Emmett would be summoned to hunt suspected criminals. Emmett grabbed his gun, canvassed any witnesses to the crime, then mounted his horse and went in pursuit. He also kept a pack of bloodhounds, which he sometimes used in the chase.

Every time the sheriff headed out into the dark, the bloodhounds howling, Tom had to live with the awful uncertainty that his father might never return—that, like Tom's mother, he might disappear from this world forever.

Tom's father oversaw the county jail, in Austin

The first hanging that Tom witnessed was carried out in January 1894. The duty of performing an execution, which hadn't occurred in the county for a decade, fell to the sheriff. On the day of the execution, Tom, who was twelve years old, stood on a tier inside the jail. No one shooed him away, and he could see the condemned man being led by his father to the scaffolding, time measured in each step and breath. Then a sound of astonishment and horror rippled through the crowd. Tom's father had been determined to make the killing mercifully swift, but despite his best efforts, things went wrong and the man suffered terribly.

Perhaps because Tom witnessed this—and other executions—or perhaps because he had seen the effect of the ordeal on his father, or perhaps because he feared that the system could doom an innocent man, Tom grew to oppose the death penalty, what was then sometimes called "judicial homicide." And he came to see the law as a struggle to tame the violent passions not only in others but also in oneself.

In 1905, when Tom was twenty-four, he joined the Texas Rangers. Created in the nineteenth century as a volunteer citizen militia to fight American Indians on the frontier and, later, Mexicans along the border, the Rangers had grown into a kind of state police force. American Indians and Mexicans had long despised the Rangers for their brutal shoot-first methods. But among white Texans they were widely mythologized. Tom's brother Dudley entered the force the same year as Tom, and their brother Doc soon joined them. Another of their brothers, Coley, followed even more closely in their father's footsteps, later becoming the sheriff of Travis County. Doc recalled the simple advice that his father gave him upon becoming a lawman: "Get all the evidence you can, son. Then put yourself in the criminal's place. Think it out. Plug up those holes, son."

Tom learned to be a Ranger by following the example of the most skilled officers. If you observed carefully, you could learn how to track a horse through the brush. You picked up little tricks: turning over your boots each morning in case a scorpion or some other critter had crept inside, and shaking out your blanket to check for rattlesnakes before lying down at night. You discovered how to avoid quicksand and how to locate streams in otherwise parched land. You understood that it was better to ride a black horse and dress in black, so as not to be scoped by a gunman in the night.

Tom became increasingly skilled at dealing with what he called "rascality": cow rustlers, horse thieves, scalawags, rumrunners, stagecoach robbers, desperadoes, and other lawbreakers. During his time as a Ranger, he investigated several murders. His brother Doc recalled, "We had nothing—not even fingerprints. We had to use mostly witnesses, and they were sometimes hard to come by." Even more troublesome, some Rangers had no patience for the letter of

In back row, from left to right, are Tom's brothers, Doc, Dudley, and Coley. In front are Tom's father, his grandfather, and Tom. (top)

A group of Texas lawmen that includes Tom White (No. 12) and his three brothers, Doc (No. 6), Dudley (No. 7), and Coley (No. 13) (bottom)

the law. One member of Tom's company would seek out the most ruthless bad man in town and then provoke a fight so he could kill him. Tom, who believed that a lawman could usually "avoid killing if you didn't lose your head," later told a writer that he had heated discussions with this Ranger. To Tom, it didn't seem right for any man to play judge, jury, and executioner.

In 1908, while Tom White was stationed in Weatherford, a town east of Abilene, he met a young woman named Bessie Patterson. She was petite, at least beside him, and she had short brown hair and sincere eyes. Tom, who'd spent much of his life in male com-

pany, was taken with her. While he was a man of stillness, she was outspoken and a whirl of motion. His job, however, was ill suited for marriage. Doc's captain once said, "An officer who hunts desperate criminals has no business having a wife and family."

Many of the Rangers with whom Tom had served died young in the line of duty. Tom saw both inexperienced and vet-

Tom's brother Dudley

eran officers die. He saw irresponsible lawmen die and careful ones, too. Before long, Tom decided to leave the Rangers altogether and marry Bessie. They settled in San Antonio, where the first of their two sons was born. Tom became a railroad detective, and the steady wage made it possible to raise a family. Tom was a dedicated family man, but like his father he was attracted to the darkness, and in 1917 he took the oath to become a special agent of the Bureau of Investigation. He swore, "I will support and defend the Constitution of the United States against all enemies. . . . So help me God."

In July 1918, not long after Tom joined the bureau, his brother Dudley went with another Ranger to arrest two men who had deserted from the U.S. military and were hiding in a remote wooded area in East Texas known as the Big Thicket. At three in the morning, the darkness was suddenly ablaze with gunfire. The deserters had ambushed them. Dudley's partner was shot twice, and as he lay bleeding, he could see Dudley standing and firing one of his six-shooters. Then Dudley was falling, as if someone had undercut his legs, his body smashing against the ground. A bullet had struck him near the heart, killing him.

Tom was overcome by the news; his brother—who was married and had three children under the age of eight—had seemed unstoppable to Tom. The two deserters were caught and charged with murder. Tom's father attended each day of their trial until both men were convicted. By then, Tom White had returned to work at the Bureau of Investigation.

14

Dying Words

IN SEPTEMBER 1925, AS TOM WHITE TRIED TO DETERMINE what secrets William Hale and his nephews Ernest and Bryan were hiding, he wondered if one person had previously uncovered them: Bill Smith. It was Smith who had first suspected that Lizzie was poisoned. And he was the one who had investigated whether there was a larger conspiracy connected to the family's oil wealth. If Smith was killed because of what he had learned, that information might be the key to unlocking the hidden world.

After the explosion destroyed Bill and Rita Smith's house, agents asked Bill's nurse in the hospital whether he had mentioned anything about the murders. She said that Bill often muttered names in his feverish sleep, but she had been unable to make them out. Sometimes when he woke up, she added, he seemed worried that he might have said something in his sleep—something that he shouldn't have. Shortly before Bill died, the nurse recalled, he had met with his doctors, James and David Shoun, and with his lawyer. The doctors had asked the nurse to leave the room. It was clear that they didn't want her to overhear their conversation with Bill, and she suspected that he gave some sort of statement indicating who was responsible for blowing up his house.

White, already suspicious of the Shouns, owing to the missing bullet in the Anna Brown case, began to question each person who had been in the hospital room with Bill. Later, federal prosecutors also questioned these men. According to a written record of these interrogations, David Shoun said that he and his brother had called the lawyer, believing that Bill might name his killers, but nothing came of it. "If Bill Smith had an idea who blowed him up, he never said," the doctor recalled.

One of the prosecutors pressed him about why it had been so important for the nurse to leave the room. Shoun explained that nurses "often leave when the doctors come in."

"If she says that you asked her to step out, she lies?"

"No, sir. If she says that, I did." David Shoun said he would swear a dozen times that Bill never identified his killers. Pointing to his hat, he added, "Bill Smith gave me that hat, and he is my friend."

James Shoun was equally sure, telling the prosecutor, "He never did say who blew him up."

When Bill Smith's lawyer was questioned, he, too, insisted that he had no idea who was responsible for blowing up the Smiths' house. "Gentlemen, it is a mystery to me," he said. But as he was being grilled, he revealed that in the hospital Bill Smith had said, "You know, I only had two enemies in the world," and he told him that those enemies were William K. Hale, the King of the Osage Hills, and his nephew Ernest Burkhart.

The investigators asked James Shoun about this, and eventually he told them the truth: "I would hate to say positively that he said . . . that Bill Hale blew him up, but he did say Bill Hale was his only enemy."

"What did he say about Ernest Burkhart?" a prosecutor asked.

"He said they were the only two enemies he knew of."

The Shouns were close to Hale and the Burkharts, having been their families' physicians. Not long after the conversation at the hospital, one of the Shoun brothers asked the nurse to visit Bryan Burkhart at his house because Bryan was ill. She agreed to do so, and while she was there, Hale showed up. He talked privately with Bryan, then approached the nurse. After some conversation, he asked her if Bill Smith had named his killers before he died. The nurse told him, "If he did I would not be telling it." Hale seemed to be trying to find out whether she knew anything and, perhaps, to be warning her not to reveal a word if she did.

As White and his agents dug deeper, they began to suspect that the doctors had set up the private meeting with Bill Smith not to get information about who blew up the house but for another, ulterior motive. During the hospital meeting, James Shoun was put in charge of distributing Rita Smith's money and property after her death. Such a position was highly sought after by whites, for it paid extremely high fees and gave the person in charge the chance to skim off some of the money.

It was now clear why the doctors had called not the sheriff or a prosecutor but Bill Smith's personal attorney. They had asked him to bring the paperwork for Bill to sign before he died.

Another prosecutor asked David Shoun if Bill was even alert

enough to make such a decision. "Did he know what he was signing?"

"I suppose he did; he was supposed to be rational."

"You are a doctor, was he rational?"

"He was rational."

"And he made arrangements for your brother to be appointed for his wife's estate?"

"Yes, sir." After further questioning, he admitted, "A very wealthy estate."

The more White investigated the flow of oil money from Osage headrights, the more he found layer upon layer of corruption. Although some white guardians and administrators tried to act in the best interests of the tribe, countless others used the system to swindle the very people they were supposed to be protecting. Many guardians would buy items from their own stores at much higher prices. (One guardian bought a car for $250 and then resold it to his ward for $1,250.) Or guardians would make all of

The Osage chief Bacon Rind protested that "everybody wants to get in here and get some of this money."

their wards' purchases from certain stores and banks, and would receive secret payments in return for the favor. Or guardians would claim to be buying homes and land for their wards while really buying these for themselves. Or guardians would outright steal.

One government study estimated that before 1925, guardians had stolen at least $8 million directly from the accounts of their Osage wards. "The blackest chapter in the history of this State will be the Indian guardianship over these estates," an Osage leader said, adding, "There has been millions—not thousands—but millions of dollars of many of the Osages dissipated and spent by the guardians themselves."

This so-called Indian business, as White discovered, was an elaborate criminal operation. Supposedly upstanding businessmen and ranchers and lawyers and politicians turned out to be crooked guardians. Meanwhile, lawmen, prosecutors, and judges covered up the swindling, and sometimes even acted as corrupt guardians and administrators themselves. In 1924, the Indian Rights Association released a report documenting how rich American Indians in Oklahoma were being "shamelessly and openly robbed in a scientific and ruthless manner."

The report also showed how judges gave guardianships to faithful friends as a reward for their support at the polls. Judges were known to say to citizens, "You vote for me, and I will see that you get a good guardianship."

A white woman married to an Osage man described to a reporter how the locals would plot: "A group of traders and lawyers sprung up who selected certain Indians as their prey. They owned all the officials. . . . These men had an understanding with each other. They cold-bloodedly said, 'You take So-and-So, So-and-So and So-and-So and I'll take these.' They selected Indians who had full headrights and large farms."

The Indian Rights Association reported the case of a widow whose guardian had secretly stolen most of her possessions. Then the guardian lied to the woman, saying that she had no more money left. "For her and her two small children, there was not a bed nor a chair nor food in the house," the investigator said. When the widow's baby got sick, the guardian still refused to turn over any of her money, though she pleaded for it. "Without proper food and medical care, the baby died," the investigator said.

The Osage were aware of such schemes but had no way to stop them. After the widow lost her baby, evidence of the fraud was brought before a county judge, only to be ignored. "There is no hope of justice so long as these conditions are permitted to remain," the investigator concluded. "The human cry of this . . . woman is a call to America." An Osage, speaking to a reporter about the guardians, stated, "Your money draws 'em and you're absolutely helpless. They have all the law and all the machinery on their side. Tell everybody, when you write your story, that they're scalping our souls out here."

15

The Hidden Face

ONE DAY IN SEPTEMBER 1925, THE UNDERCOVER OPERA-
tive who was pretending to be an insurance salesman stopped at a
gas station in Fairfax and struck up a conversation with a woman
working there. When the operative told her that he was looking to
buy a house in the vicinity, she mentioned that William Hale "controlled everything" in these parts. She said that she'd purchased
her own home from Hale, which was on the edge of his pasture.
One night, she recalled, thousands of acres of Hale's land had been
set on fire. Nothing was left behind but ashes. Most people didn't
know who had started the blaze, but she did: Hale's workers, on his
orders, had torched the land for the insurance money—$30,000
in all.

This wasn't the only suspicious connection to Hale that White's
team investigated. White also tried to learn more about how
Hale had become the beneficiary of Henry Roan's $25,000 life-
insurance policy. After Roan turned up dead in 1923, Hale had the
most obvious motive. Yet the sheriff never investigated Hale, nor
had other local lawmen.

White tracked down the insurance salesman who had initially tried to sell the policy in 1921. Hale had always insisted that Roan, one of his closest friends, had made him the beneficiary because of all the loans he'd given Roan over the years. But the salesman told a different story.

As the salesman recalled it, Hale had pushed for the policy, telling him privately "that's just like spearing fish in a keg." Hale even promised to pay extra for a policy that would give him more money if Roan died.

The salesman had told Hale that because he wasn't part of Roan's family, he could become his beneficiary only if he had lent Roan money. Hale had said, "Well, he owes me a lot of money, he owes me ten thousand or twelve thousand dollars."

White found it hard to believe that this debt was real. If Roan had really owed Hale that amount of money, Hale could have just shown proof of the debt to Roan's wealthy estate, and they would have paid him back. Hale had no need to get an insurance policy on his friend's life—a policy that wouldn't pay Hale anything unless Roan, who was then only in his late thirties, suddenly died.

Roan was evidently unaware of what Hale was really up to, believing that his supposedly closest friend was just helping him out. But there remained one obstacle to Hale's scheme. A doctor had to examine Roan—a heavy drinker—and sign off on him as a safe risk for the insurance company. Hale shopped for doctors until he found a man in Pawhuska willing to recommend Roan. James Shoun also vouched for him.

White discovered that the first insurance company had rejected the application. But Hale didn't give up. He just approached a second insurance company. The application asked if Roan had previously been turned down by a competitor. The answer "no" was filled in. An insurance agent who reviewed the application later told authorities, "I knew the questions in it had been answered falsely."

On this second try, Hale had produced a loan document to prove that he was owed $25,000 by Roan—the exact amount of the insurance policy. The document appeared to be signed by Roan and was dated "Jany, 1921." This was important, because it showed that the note was signed in January before efforts to get the insurance began. This made the loan document seem real, giving Hale the right to the $25,000.

But White thought the document seemed fishy. Agents later showed it to a handwriting and document expert to analyze. This was a new method in the field of criminal investigation. Though not flawless, it could be helpful when done carefully.

The expert detected that the date initially typed on the document had said "June" and that someone had then carefully rubbed out the u and the e. The u was then replaced with an a, and the e with a y, so that the date read "Jany."

White suspected that Hale had faked the document while trying to get the insurance policy and changed it after realizing that he had blundered on the date. Later, a federal official questioned the man who Hale claimed had typed up the document. He denied ever having seen it. Asked if Hale was lying, he said, "Absolutely."

The second insurance company approved the policy after Hale took Roan to the Pawhuska doctor again for the required medical examination. The doctor recalled asking Hale, "Bill, what are you going to do, kill this Indian?"

Hale, laughing, said, "Hell, yes."

After Hale served as a pallbearer at Roan's funeral, White learned, local lawmen did more than ignore Hale as a murder suspect. They tried to blame the crime on another man, named Roy Bunch. White and his agents spoke to Bunch, who maintained his innocence. He also told them that, after Roan's murder, Hale had come to him and said, "If I were you, I'd get out of town."

"Why should I run?" Bunch said. "I didn't do it."

"People think you did," Hale said.

He offered Bunch money to help him flee. Afterward, Bunch spoke to a friend, who persuaded him not to take off, because it would have only made him look guilty.

White and his men thoroughly investigated Bunch and ruled him out as a suspect. And the person who seemed most focused on framing Bunch was Hale, the King of the Osage Hills.

Though White had gathered some evidence against Hale in the murder of Roan, there were still huge holes in the case. There was no proof—no fingerprints, no trustworthy eyewitnesses—that Hale had shot Roan or that he had ordered one of his nephews or another henchman to do so. And while the suspicious life-insurance policy seemed to tie Hale to Roan's murder, it did not provide a motive for the other Osage killings.

Yet as White studied the Roan case further, one detail stood out. Before Hale got the life-insurance policy on Roan, he had tried to buy Roan's headright—his share in the tribe's mineral trust, which was more precious than any diamonds or gold. Hale knew that the law prevented anyone from buying or selling a headright, but he'd been confident that pressure from powerful whites would soon eliminate this obstacle. The law had not been changed, however, and White suspected that this setback had prompted Hale to come up with the insurance murder scheme.

There was one legal way that someone could obtain a headright: inheritance. And as White examined estate records for many of the murder victims, it was clear that with each new death, more and more headrights were being directed into the hands of one person—Mollie Burkhart. And it just so happened that she was married to Hale's nephew Ernest, a man who, as an agent wrote in a report, "is absolutely controlled by Hale." Kelsie Morrison, the bootlegger and bureau informant, said to agents that both Ernest and Bryan Burkhart did exactly what their uncle told them to do. Morrison added that Hale was "capable of anything."

White studied the pattern of deaths in Mollie's family. They now seemed part of a ruthless plan. Anna Brown, divorced and without children, had left nearly all her wealth to her mother, Lizzie. Because Lizzie had assigned most of her headright to her surviving daughters, Mollie and Rita, she became the next logical target. Then came Rita and her husband, Bill Smith. White realized that the unusual method of the final killing—a bombing—had a vicious logic. The wills of Rita and Bill spelled out that if they died at the same time, much of Rita's headright would go to her surviving sister, Mollie. Here, the mastermind had made one mistake. Because Bill unexpectedly outlived Rita by a few days, he had inherited much of her wealth, and upon his death the money went to one of his relatives instead of Mollie. Still, most of the family's

13

A Hangman's Son

THE FIRST TIME THAT TOM WHITE SAW A CRIMINAL hanged, he was just a boy, and the executioner was his father. In 1888, his father, Robert Emmett White, was elected sheriff of Travis County, Texas, which included Austin, then a city of fewer than fifteen thousand people. A towering man with a dense mustache, Emmett, as Tom's father liked to be called, was poor, stern, hardworking, and pious. Tom was born in 1881 and was the third of five children. The nearest schoolhouse—which had one room and a single teacher for eight grades—was three miles away, and to get there, Tom and his siblings had to walk.

When Tom was six, his mother died, leaving his father to raise Tom and his siblings, all of whom were under the age of ten.

As sheriff, Emmett White was in charge of the county jail, in Austin, and he moved with his children into a house next door. The building resembled a fortress, with barred windows and cold stone passageways and tiered cells. Tom later recalled, "I was raised practically right in the jail. I could look down from my bedroom window and see the jail corridor and the doors to some of the cells."

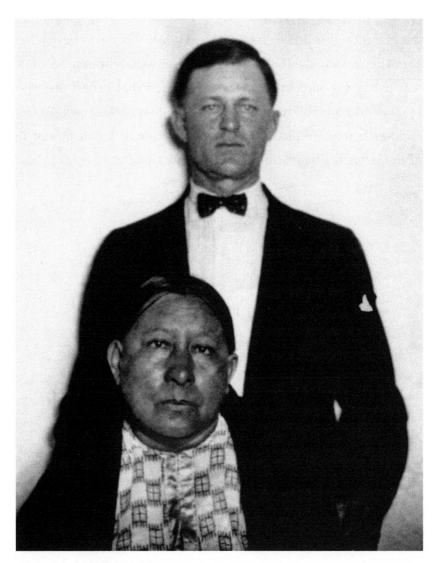

Ernest and Mollie Burkhart

headrights had been funneled to Mollie Burkhart, whose wealth was controlled by Ernest. And Hale, White was convinced, was secretly managing this fortune through his loyal nephew.

White couldn't determine whether Ernest's marriage to Mollie— four years before Anna's murder—had been part of the plot from the beginning or if Hale had convinced his nephew to betray her after they married. In either case, the plan was so brazen, so sinister, that it was hard to believe. It demanded that Ernest live with Mollie and have children with her, all while scheming against her and her family. He hid, as Shakespeare wrote of a conspirator in *Julius Caesar*, his "monstrous" face behind a smile.

16

The Quick-Draw Artist, the Yegg, and the Soup Man

TOM WHITE AND HIS MEN FELT A GROWING SENSE OF progress. A Justice Department prosecutor sent J. Edgar Hoover a note, saying that in the few months since White began leading the investigation, "many new angles of these cases were successfully developed" and a "new and enthusiastic spirit seemed to pervade the hearts of all of us."

Still, White faced the same problem with the investigation of Mollie Burkhart's murdered family that he did with his inquiry into Henry Roan's death. There was no physical evidence or witnesses to prove that William Hale had carried out or ordered any of the killings. And without an airtight case, White knew that he'd never be able to bring down this man who hid behind layers of respectability and who seemed to have power over the sheriff's office, prosecutors, judges, and some of the highest state officials.

In a stark report, agents noted that:

- Scott Mathis, the Big Hill Trading Company owner and guardian of Anna Brown and Lizzie, was "a crook and evidently in the power of Hale"

- an associate of Mathis's served as a "spy for Bill Hale and the Big Hill Trading Company, and does all the framing for them in their crooked deals in skinning the Indians"

- the chief of police in Ponca City had "taken money from Bill Hale"

- the chief of police in Fairfax "will do nothing against Hale whatsoever"

- a local banker and guardian "will not talk against the Hale faction, for the reason that Hale has too much on him"

- the mayor of Fairfax, "an arch crook," was Hale's close friend

- a longtime county prosecutor was part of Hale's political machine and was "no good" and "crooked"

- even a federal official with the Office of Indian Affairs was "in the power of Bill Hale and will do what Hale says."

White realized that his struggle for justice was only beginning. As a bureau report would put it, Hale "seemingly could not be punished."

Hoover, meanwhile, was growing impatient. He wanted the investigation to highlight the more modern bureau, which he ran with ruthless efficiency. He also wanted to increase his own power in Washington.

During the fall of 1925, White tried to reassure Hoover that he'd gather enough evidence to convict Hale and his accomplices. White sent Hoover a memo reporting that an undercover operative was on Hale's ranch at that very moment, spying. White was feeling pressure not just from Hoover. In the short time that he had been on the case, he had seen the lights burning each night around the homes of the Osage. He had seen that members of the community were afraid to let their children go into town alone. And he had seen more and more residents selling their homes and moving to distant states or even other countries, like Mexico and Canada. The desperation of the Osage was unmistakable, as was their lack of trust in the investigation. What had the U.S. government done for them? Why did they, unlike other Americans, have to use their own money to fund a Justice Department investigation? Why had nobody been arrested? An Osage chief said, "I made peace with the white man and lay down my arms never to take them up again and now I and my fellow tribesmen must suffer."

White had come to understand that racist and corrupt white citizens would not point a finger at one of their own in the killing of American Indians. So he decided to change his strategy and instead try to find a source among the wildest, most dangerous group of Oklahomans: the outlaws of the Osage Hills. Reports from agents and informants like Kelsie Morrison suggested that several of these desperadoes had knowledge about the murders. These men might not be any less racist. But because some of them had recently been arrested or convicted of crimes, White would at least hold some leverage over them. The name of one outlaw, in particular, kept coming up: Dick Gregg, a twenty-three-year-old stickup man who used to run with the Al Spencer Gang and who was now in a Kansas penitentiary serving a ten-year sentence for robbery.

Gregg had once told Agent John Burger that he knew something about the murders but wouldn't give him any details, insisting that he couldn't betray a confidence. In a report, Agent Burger noted in frustration, "Gregg is 100 percent criminal and will tell as little as he can."

A. W. Comstock, the attorney and guardian, was one of the few whites in town willing to help investigators. He knew Gregg's father well and provided legal advice for the family. Comstock used his relationship with Gregg's father to help persuade the young outlaw to cooperate with the bureau.

Eventually, White met with Gregg himself. White liked to take mental notes about the criminals he met, in order to fix them in his memory—a skill honed from his time on the frontier when he could not rely on mug shots or fingerprints. Decades later, when White was asked to describe Gregg, he wrote with remarkable precision: "A

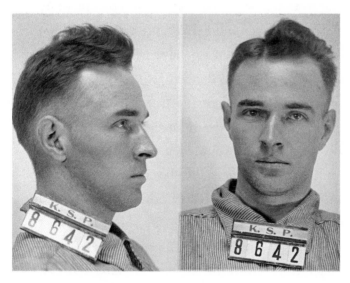

Dick Gregg had been a member of the Al Spencer Gang.

very small man, I should say 5′6″ and weighed 125 lbs, fair complexion, blue eyes and light brown hair. A good-looking youngster." Gregg's pretty looks were deceiving, according to a prosecutor, who wrote that he was "a cold cruel calculating type of criminal" who "would not hesitate to commit murder." Still, in White's view, Gregg belonged to that category of outlaw who was not born bad and who might even have "gone places" with proper training.

A. W. Comstock with an Osage Indian

Though Gregg was known for his nerve as a stickup man, he was reluctant to cross Hale. If word got out, Gregg worried his life would be in danger. But, hoping to shave time off his robbery sentence, he agreed to tell White and other agents what he knew. Sometime in the summer of 1922, he recalled, the outlaw Al Spencer told him that Hale wanted to meet with the gang.

So Spencer, Gregg, and several associates headed to one of Hale's pastures near Fairfax. Hale rode up fiercely on his horse, emerging from the tall prairie grasses. The group sat by the edge of a creek and shared some whiskey. Then Hale asked Spencer to step aside with him, and offered Spencer and his gang at least $2,000 to bump off a couple—an old man and his "blanket," meaning an American Indian woman. Spencer asked Hale whom he wanted dead. "Bill Smith and his wife," he said. Spencer told Hale that he might be cold-blooded but he wouldn't kill a woman for money. As he put it, "That's not my style." Hale said he hoped that Gregg, at least, would go through with the plan. But Gregg agreed with Spencer.

White thought that Gregg was being "on the level" and that his refusal to kill for hire showed him to be "an outlaw with some honor." But though Gregg's testimony offered the clearest indication yet that Hale had ordered the murders, it was of limited legal value. After all, the statement was coming from a crook seeking to shorten his sentence, and Spencer, the one person who could back up Gregg's testimony, had since been gunned down by a posse of lawmen.

Gregg said that agents should find Curley Johnson, an outlaw who ran with the stickup man Blackie Thompson. "Johnson knows all about the Smith blow-up and will squeal if made to do so," Gregg promised. But Johnson, it turned out, was also dead and buried. Less than a year earlier, he'd died suddenly—word was, of poisoned alcohol.

White's desperate search for a witness soon led him to Henry Grammer, the rodeo star and gunslinging bootlegger who, every year or so, seemed to draw his pistol on another man because of a dispute. Though Grammer and Hale generally moved in different social circles, White established that they'd known each other for years, from the time when Hale had first appeared in Osage territory, at the turn of the century.

In a rodeo contest in 1909, they'd competed together with the Osage Cowboys against the Cherokee Cowboys. CHEROKEES NO MATCH FOR THE OSAGE ROPERS, declared the *Muskogee Times-Democrat*. By 1925, Hale had shed his past. But there remained a faded photograph from the contest, showing Hale and Grammer sitting proudly on their horses, holding coiled ropes.

Just before the Smith house blew up, Hale had told friends that he was heading out of town to attend the Fat Stock Show in Fort Worth, Texas. White looked into Hale's alibi and was told that Grammer had gone with him.

A witness had overheard Hale talking to Grammer before the murders, murmuring something about being ready for "that Indian

William Hale (fourth from left) and Henry Grammer (third from left) competing in a roping contest in 1909

deal." Like the other potential witnesses against Hale, however, Grammer was dead. On June 14, 1923, three months after the Smiths' house was demolished, Grammer was killed when his Cadillac spun out of control and flipped over.

Finally, a yegg—a safecracker—gave White and his team the name of another witness to the bombing plot: Asa Kirby, a gold-toothed outlaw who had been an associate of Grammer's. The yegg said that Kirby was the "soup man"—the expert in explosives—who had designed the bomb. But it turned out that Kirby couldn't testify, either. A few weeks after Grammer's fatal car crash, Kirby had broken into a store in the middle of the night to steal a stash of diamonds, only to find that the shopkeeper had been tipped off beforehand and was lying in wait with his 12-gauge shotgun. In an instant, Kirby was blasted into the world beyond. The person who had tipped off the shopkeeper about the robbery, White was hardly surprised to learn, was William K. Hale.

By foiling the heist, Hale had strengthened his reputation for upholding law and order. But another outlaw told White that Hale had actually set up the robbery—that he'd told Kirby about the diamonds and suggested the ideal time to break in. It was, evidently, a plot within a plot, and White was left with a suspiciously long list of dead witnesses.

He asked about Grammer's car accident and was told by people who knew him that they believed the Cadillac's steering wheel and brakes had been tampered with. Curley Johnson's widow, meanwhile, was sure that her husband had been murdered—intentionally poisoned by Hale and his henchmen. And when White learned about a potential witness in the Roan murder case, he discovered that this person had been beaten to death. Anyone who had evidence

William Hale

against Hale, it seemed, was being eliminated. The yegg said that Hale was "taking care of too many people," adding, "I might be taken care of myself."

Having failed to locate any living witnesses, White found himself stymied, and Hale seemed aware that agents were on to him.

"Hale knows everything," Kelsie Morrison had told agents. But there were signs that the informant might be playing both sides. Agents learned that Morrison had told a friend he had all the dope on the murders and had saved Hale's "damned neck till now."

Hale had begun spreading around his money and favors to solidify his power. In a report, Agent John Wren wrote that Hale was offering gifts of clothing, providing loans, and even "giving ponies away to young boys."

One of the undercover operatives reported that Hale seemed to be mocking investigators. Hale had boasted to him, "I'm too slick and keen to catch cold."

White would see Hale on the streets of Fairfax—the embodiment of what White and his brothers, and their father before them, had spent their lives chasing. He carried himself, White thought, "like he owned the world."

One day, as the strain on White intensified, as each promising lead dead-ended, he took his rifle and disappeared into the countryside to hunt something he could actually catch. Spotting a duck, he aimed and fired until the air was laced with smoke.

17

The State of the Game

OUT OF THE BLUE, TOM WHITE RECEIVED A TIP. IN LATE October 1925, he was meeting with the governor of Oklahoma to discuss the case one-on-one. Afterward, an aide to the governor told White, "We've been getting information from a prisoner at McAlester"—the state penitentiary—"who claims to know a great deal about the Osage murders. His name is Burt Lawson. Might be a good idea to talk to him."

Desperate for a new lead, White and Agent Frank Smith rushed over to McAlester. They didn't know much about Lawson, other than that he was from Osage County and that he had had several brushes with the law. In 1922, he had been charged with murdering a fisherman but was let off after claiming that the fisherman had first come at him with a knife. Less than three years later, Lawson was convicted of second-degree burglary and sentenced to seven years.

White liked to interview people in a place they weren't familiar with in order to unsettle them, and so he had Lawson taken to a room off the warden's office. White studied the man who appeared before him: short, portly, and middle-aged, with long ghostly-white hair.

After a moment, White said to him, "We understand from the governor's office you know something about the Osage murders."

"I do," Lawson said.

He explained that in 1918 he began working as a ranch hand for Bill Smith, and that he grew to know Hale and his nephews Ernest and Bryan Burkhart. In a signed statement, Lawson said, "Some time around the early part of 1921 I discovered an intimacy between my wife and . . . Smith, which finally developed in breaking up my family and caused me to leave the employment of Smith." Ernest knew of Lawson's hatred of Smith, and about a year later he visited him. Lawson recalled that Ernest "turned to me and said, 'Burt, I have got a proposition I want to make to you.' I remarked, 'What is it, Ernest?' Ernest said, 'I want you to blow up and kill Bill Smith and his wife.'"

When Lawson wouldn't agree to do it, he said Hale came to see him and promised him $5,000 in cash for the job. Hale told him that he could use the explosive liquid nitroglycerin and that all he had to do was place a fuse under the Smiths' house. "Hale then pulled from his pocket," Lawson recalled, "a piece of white fuse about three feet and said, 'I will show you how to use it.' He then took his pocketknife and cut off a piece about six inches long . . . then took a match from his pocket and lighted the end."

Lawson still said no, but after he was arrested for killing the fisherman, Hale visited him again and said, "Burt, you will be needing some attorneys pretty soon and I know you haven't got any money to pay them with, and I want that job pulled."

Lawson said, "All right, Bill, I'll pull it."

One night not long after, Lawson recalled, another deputy sheriff opened his cell and led him to Hale, who was in a car outside. Hale drove Lawson to a building in Fairfax, where Ernest was waiting. Hale told Ernest to get "the box," and Ernest brought out a wooden container. Inside was a jug filled with nitroglycerin; a long, coiled fuse was attached to the spout.

After carefully loading the box into the car, the three of them made their way to the Smiths' house. "I got out and took the box and fuse, and Hale and Ernest drove on away," Lawson recounted. "I then went in the back way and into Smith's cellar, and placed the box in the far corner of the cellar, then laid the fuse out like Hale told me. . . . I then sat down in the dark and waited." Lawson continued, "I saw the lights turned on. I suppose they all undressed and went to bed for pretty soon the lights went out. I sat there for quite a while, I had no way to tell what time it was, but I would figure it was about three quarters of an hour, and after I thought they were all asleep, I lighted a short piece of fuse. . . . As soon as the long end began to smoke, I beat it as fast I could." He said he could hear the house breaking apart as he ran. Hale and Ernest picked him up in a spot nearby and returned him to the jail, where the deputy sheriff snuck him back into his cell. Before Hale left, he'd warned Lawson, "If you ever cheep this to anybody we will kill you."

White and Agent Smith felt a rush of excitement. There were still questions. Lawson had not mentioned the involvement of Asa Kirby, the soup man. But Kirby could have prepared the bomb for Hale without interacting with Lawson. White would need to tie up these loose ends, but at last a witness had emerged who could directly place Hale in the center of the plot.

On October 24, 1925, three months after White took over the

case, he sent Hoover a telegram, unable to hide a sense of triumph: "Have confession from Burt Lawson that he placed and set off the explosive that blew up Bill Smith's home; that he was persuaded, prompted and assisted to do it by Ernest Burkhart and W. K. Hale."

Hoover was elated. Via telegram, he quickly sent White a message: "Congratulations."

※

As White and his men worked to verify the details in Lawson's confession, they felt a growing urgency to get Hale and his nephews off the streets. The attorney and guardian A. W. Comstock had begun to receive threats to his life. He was now sleeping in his office, in downtown Pawhuska, with his .44-caliber revolver by his side. "Once, when he went to open the window, he found sticks of dynamite behind the curtain," a relative recalled. He was able to dispose of them, but, the relative added, "Hale and his bunch were determined to kill him."

White was also very concerned about the fate of Mollie Burkhart. He was suspicious of the reports he had received saying that she was sick with diabetes. Hale had successfully arranged, body by body, for Mollie to inherit the majority of her family members' wealth. Yet the plot seemed unfinished. Hale had access to Mollie's fortune through Ernest, but his nephew did not yet directly control it, and would do so only if Mollie died and left it to him. A servant in Mollie's house had told an agent that one night Ernest had muttered to her while drunk that he was afraid something would happen to Mollie. Even Ernest seemed terrified of the plan's ultimate end.

John Wren, the Ute agent, had recently spoken to Mollie's priest, who said that Mollie had stopped coming to church, which was unlike her. He had heard she was being forcibly kept away by family members. The priest was so alarmed that he had broken his vow of confidentiality. Soon after, the priest reported that he had received a secret message from Mollie. She was afraid that someone was trying to poison her. Given that poisoned whiskey had been one of the killers' preferred methods, the priest sent word back warning Mollie "not to drink any liquor of any kind under any circumstances."

But Mollie's diabetes seemed to have provided an even more devious way to deliver the poison. She had been told she needed insulin, and some of the town's doctors, including the Shoun brothers, had been giving her injections. Instead of improving, Mollie seemed to be getting worse. Government officials working for the Office of Indian Affairs were concerned that Mollie was slowly being poisoned. A Justice Department official had noted that her "illness is very suspicious, to say the least." It was urgent, the official went on, to "get this patient to some reputable hospital for diagnosis and treatment free from the interference of her husband."

By the end of December 1925, White felt that he could no longer wait, even though he had not finished confirming many details in Lawson's confession, and there remained certain contradictions. Nevertheless, White rushed to get arrest warrants for Hale and Ernest Burkhart for the murders of Bill and Rita Smith and their servant Nettie Brookshire. The warrants were issued on January 4, 1926. Because agents could not make arrests at the time, they fanned out with U.S. marshals and other lawmen, including Sheriff Freas, who had been reelected after getting kicked out of office for allowing gambling and bootlegging.

Several lawmen quickly found Ernest Burkhart at his favorite dive, a pool hall in Fairfax, and brought him to the jail in Guthrie, eighty miles southwest of Pawhuska. Hale, however, could not be found. Agent Wren learned that he had ordered a new suit of clothes and that he had said he was planning to leave town at a moment's notice. Authorities feared that Hale had disappeared for good when he suddenly strolled into Sheriff Freas's office. He looked as if he were heading to a formal party. He wore a perfectly pressed suit, shoes shined to a gleam, a felt hat, and an overcoat with his diamond-studded Masonic lodge pin fastened to the lapel. "Understand I'm wanted," he said, explaining that he was there to turn himself in—no need to send the fellows out on a search party.

As he was taken to the jail in Guthrie, he was confronted by a local reporter.

Hale's deep-set eyes burned, and he moved, in the words of the reporter, "like a leashed animal."

The reporter asked him, "Have you a statement to make?"

"What are you?" Hale demanded, not used to being questioned.

"A newspaperman."

"I'll not try my case in the newspapers, but in the courts of this county."

Hoping Hale might at least talk about himself, the reporter asked, "How old are you?"

"I'm fifty-one years of age."

"How long have you been in Oklahoma?"

"Twenty-five years, more or less."

"You are pretty well known, aren't you?"

"I think so."

"Have large numbers of friends?"

William Hale in front of the Guthrie jail

"I hope so."

"Wouldn't they like to have a statement from you, even though you merely say 'I am innocent'?"

"I'll try my case in the courts, not in the newspapers. Cold to-night, isn't it?"

Hale was led away by authorities. If he had momentarily been uneasy, he was confident by the time White spoke to him—even cocky, seemingly convinced that he remained untouchable. Hale insisted that White had made a mistake. It was as if White were the one in trouble, not him.

White suspected that Hale would never admit his sins, certainly not to a lawman and perhaps not even to God, whom he so often spoke of. Ernest Burkhart was their only chance for a confession. A prosecutor working with White put it more bluntly, "We all picked Ernest Burkhart the one to break."

Ernest Burkhart was brought into a room on the third floor of a federal building in Guthrie, which was being used as a makeshift interrogation area. The agents called it "the box." Burkhart was wearing the same clothes that he'd had on when he was arrested, and White thought that he looked like a "small-town dandy." He moved about nervously and licked his lips.

White and Agent Frank Smith questioned him. "We want to talk to you about the murder of Bill Smith's family and Anna Brown," White said.

"I don't know a thing about it," Burkhart insisted.

White explained that they had talked to a man named Burt Lawson in the penitentiary, who said differently—said that Burkhart knew a good deal about the murders. The mention of Lawson did not seem to faze Burkhart, who insisted that he'd never had any dealings with him.

"He says you were the contact man in setting up the Smith house explosion," White said.

"I lying," Burkhart said emphatically.

A ubt seized White: What if Lawson *was* lying and had simply picked up information from other outlaws in prison who had heard rumors about the case? Perhaps Lawson was lying in the hopes that prosecutors would reduce his jail time in exchange for his testimony. Or maybe the whole confession had been a setup by Hale—another one of his plots within a plot. White still didn't know quite *what* to believe. But if Lawson was lying about anything, getting a confession from Burkhart was even more crucial; otherwise, the case would collapse.

For hours, in the hot, claustrophobic box, White and Smith went over the evidence that they'd gathered on each of the murders, trying to trip up Burkhart. White thought that he saw some element of remorse in him, as if he wanted to unburden himself, to protect his wife and children. Yet whenever White or Smith mentioned Hale, he stiffened in his chair, more afraid of his uncle, it seemed, than he was of the law.

"My advice to you is to tell it all," White said, almost pleadingly.

"There's nothing to tell," Burkhart said.

After midnight, White and Smith gave up and returned Burkhart to his cell.

By the next day, White's case ran into even more trouble. Hale announced that he could prove positively that he had been in Texas at the time of the explosion, for he had received a telegram there and signed for it. If this was true—and White was inclined to believe that it was—then Lawson had indeed been lying all along. In White's desperation to get Hale, he'd committed the ultimate sin for an evidence man—he'd believed what he wanted to believe.

White knew that he had only hours before Hale's lawyers would produce the record of this telegram and spring Hale, along with Burkhart, from jail—and before word got out that the bureau had humiliated itself. This news would surely reach Hoover, and as one of Hoover's aides said, "If he didn't like you, he destroyed you." Hale's lawyers promptly tipped off a reporter who ran a story about Hale's "perfect" alibi, noting, "He's not afraid."

Desperate, White turned to the man who had embarrassed Hoover during the bureau's early investigation: Blackie Thompson, the outlaw who had been released from prison as an informant, only to murder a police officer. Since being caught, he'd been locked up at the state penitentiary, a black mark on the bureau's reputation.

Yet, from the bureau's early reports on the case, White suspected that Blackie might have key information about the murders. Without telling Hoover, White had the outlaw moved to Guthrie. If anything went wrong, if Blackie escaped or hurt a soul, White's career would be over. When Blackie arrived at the federal building, he was in chains and flanked by a small army. On a nearby rooftop, White had placed a rifleman, who kept Blackie in his scope through a window.

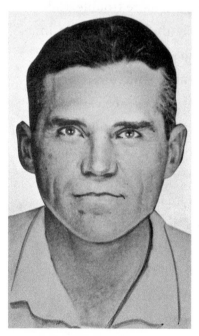

The outlaw Blackie Thompson

Blackie was still hostile, sullen, and mean, but when White asked him about Hale and Ernest Burkhart's role in the Osage murders, his mood seemed to change. After all, Blackie had once complained that Hale and Burkhart "want everything for nothing."

Agents told Blackie that they couldn't cut a deal with him to reduce his sentence, and he spoke grudgingly at first about the murders. But gradually he revealed more and more. He said that Burkhart and Hale had once approached him and his old buddy Curley Johnson to kill Bill and Rita

Smith. As part of the payment, they had proposed that Blackie steal Burkhart's car, and one night, while Burkhart was at home in bed with Mollie, Blackie had taken it from their garage. Blackie had later been picked up by the law for car theft and never went through with any of the killings.

It wasn't clear if Blackie would ever agree to testify in court to these matters, but White hoped that he now had enough information to save the case. He left Blackie surrounded by guards and rushed with Agent Smith to interrogate Burkhart again.

Back in the box, White told Burkhart, "We're not satisfied with the answers you gave us last night. We believe there's a good deal you didn't tell us."

"All I know is what's common talk," Burkhart said.

White and Agent Smith played their last card: they told Burkhart that they had another witness who would testify to his part in the scheme to kill Bill and Rita Smith. Burkhart, knowing that he had been bluffed once, said that he didn't believe them.

"Well, I can go get him if you don't think we have got him," Agent Smith said.

"Bring him in," Burkhart said.

White and Smith went and got Blackie and escorted him into the room. While the gunman on the roof kept Blackie in his scope through the window, the outlaw sat across from Burkhart, who looked stunned.

Agent Smith turned to Blackie and said, "Blackie, have you told me . . . the truth concerning the propositions made by Ernest Burkhart to you?"

Blackie replied, "Yes, sir."

Agent Smith added, "To kill Bill Smith?"

"Yes, sir."

"Did you tell me the truth when you told me Ernest gave you an automobile as part payment of that job?"

"Yes, sir."

Blackie, evidently enjoying himself, looked squarely at Burkhart and said, "Ernest, I have told them everything."

Burkhart appeared defeated.

After Blackie was taken away, White thought that Burkhart was ready to confess and turn on Hale, but each time Burkhart came close to doing so, he stopped himself. Around midnight, White left Burkhart in the custody of the other agents and returned to his hotel room. There were no more tricks to play. Exhausted and despairing, he collapsed on his bed and fell asleep.

Not long after, White was jolted awake by the phone. Facing the prospect that something else had gone wrong, he picked up the receiver and heard the urgent voice of one of his agents. "Burkhart's ready to tell his story," he said. "But he won't give it to us. Says it's got to be you."

When White entered the box, he found Burkhart slumped in his seat, tired and resigned. Burkhart told White that he hadn't killed all those people, but he knew who had. "I want to tell," he said.

White reminded Burkhart of his rights, and Burkhart signed a paper that said, "After being so warned, and with no promises having been made me of immunity from prosecution, and of my own free will and accord, I now make the following statement."

Burkhart began speaking about William Hale—about how he

had worshipped him as a boy, how he had done all types of jobs for him, and how he had always followed orders. "I relied on Uncle Bill's judgment," he said. Hale was a schemer, Burkhart said, and though his uncle hadn't shared with him the details of all his plots, he had shared his murderous plan to kill Rita and Bill Smith. Burkhart said that he had protested when Hale had told him of his intention to blow up the whole house and everyone in it, including his own relatives. He said Hale responded, "What do you care? Your wife will get the money."

Burkhart admitted that he went along with Hale's plan, as he always did. Hale had first approached the outlaws Blackie Thompson and Curley Johnson to do the deadly job. (In a later statement, Burkhart recalled, "Hale had told me to see Curley Johnson, and to find out how tough he was, and if he wanted to make some money, and told me to tell Johnson the job was to bump a squaw-man"—referring to Bill Smith.) Then, when Johnson and Blackie couldn't do the job, Hale sought out Al Spencer. After Spencer refused, Hale spoke to the bootlegger and rodeo star Henry Grammer, who promised to provide a man for the job. "Just a few days before the blow-up happened, Grammer told Hale that Acie"—Asa Kirby—"would do it," Burkhart recalled. "That is what Hale told me."

Burkhart said that Burt Lawson had nothing to do with the explosion, explaining, "You have got the wrong pig by the tail." (Later, Lawson admitted to White, "All that story I told was a lie. All I know about the Smith blow-up was just what I heard in jail. . . . I done wrong and lied.") Burkhart also said that Grammer had gone with Hale to Fort Worth so they would both have an alibi. Before leaving, Hale told Burkhart to send a message to John Ramsey, a cow thief and bootlegger who worked for Henry Grammer. The message was for Ramsey to tell Kirby that it was time to carry out "the job." Burkhart did as Hale asked and was home with Mollie on the night of the explosion.

"When it happened I was in bed with my wife," he recalled. "I saw a light on the north side. My wife went to the window and looked out." She said that she thought somebody's house was on fire. "As soon as she said that I knew what it was."

Burkhart also provided crucial details about how Hale had arranged the murder of Henry Roan for the insurance money. "I know who killed Henry Roan," Burkhart said, and he identified Ramsey—the cow thief—as the triggerman.

The case had broken wide open. White placed a call to Agent John Wren, who was out in the field. "There's a suspect up there named John Ramsey," White told him. "Take him into custody right away."

Ramsey was soon picked up and brought into the box. He wore overalls over his tall, thin frame. His black hair was greasy, and he walked with a slight limp. A reporter said he seemed "like a nervy and, perhaps, a dangerous man."

According to the accounts of White and other agents, Ramsey looked at the agents warily, insisting he didn't know a thing. Then White laid Burkhart's signed statement in front of him, and Ramsey stared at the paper, as if trying to tell its authenticity. Just as White and Smith had presented Blackie to Burkhart, they now brought in Burkhart to confirm his statement to Ramsey. And Ramsey threw up his hands and said, "I guess it's on my neck now. Get your pencils."

Ramsey told the lawmen that sometime in early 1923, Grammer approached him and told him Hale had "a little job he wanted done." When Ramsey asked what it was, Grammer said that Hale needed an Osage knocked off. Ramsey eventually agreed to take the job, and he lured Roan down into the canyon, promising him whiskey. "We sat on the running board of his car and drank," Ramsey recounted. "The Indian then got in his car to leave, and I then shot him. . . . I suppose I was within a foot or two of him when I shot him. I then went back to my car and drove to Fairfax."

White observed the way Ramsey kept saying "the Indian," rather than Roan's name. Then, as if to justify his crime, Ramsey added that even now "white people in Oklahoma thought no more of killing an Indian than they did in 1724."

White had answers about Roan's murder, but he still had questions about the murder of Mollie's sister Anna Brown. Ernest Burkhart remained cagey about the role of his brother Bryan, not wanting to point a finger at him. But he revealed the identity of the mysterious third man who had been seen with Anna shortly before her death. It was someone whom the agents knew all too well: Kelsie Morrison, their undercover informant, who had supposedly been working with the agents to *identify* the third man. Morrison had not just been a double agent who had funneled information back to Hale and his henchmen. It was Morrison, Ernest said, who had fired the fatal shot that killed Anna Brown.

While the authorities went to round up Morrison, they also made sure that a doctor went to check on Mollie Burkhart, who was still quite ill from what was suspected poisoning under the care of the Shoun brothers.

Burkhart never admitted having any knowledge that Mollie was being poisoned. Perhaps this was the one sin that he couldn't bear to admit. Or perhaps Hale had not trusted him to kill his own wife.

The Shoun brothers were brought in and interrogated over what, exactly, they had been treating Mollie with. One of the prosecutors who was working with White asked James Shoun, "Weren't you giving her insulin?"

"I may have been," he said.

The prosecutor grew impatient. "Wasn't she taken away from you and taken to the hospital at Pawhuska? Weren't you administering insulin to her?"

Shoun said that maybe he'd misspoken: "I don't want to get balled up and don't want to get in bad."

The prosecutor asked again if he'd given injections to her. "Yes, I gave her some," he said.

"For what?"

"For sugar diabetes."

"And she got worse?"

"I don't know."

"And she got so bad she was taken away from you and taken to a hospital at Pawhuska, and she got better immediately under the care of another doctor?"

James Shoun and his brother denied any wrongdoing, and White could not prove who was responsible for the poisoning.

When Mollie was feeling better, she was questioned by authorities. She was not one who liked to be seen as a victim, but for once she admitted that she was scared and bewildered. At times, she relied on an interpreter to help with her English—a language that now seemed to convey secrets beyond understanding.

An attorney helping the prosecution explained to her, "We are all your friends and working for you." He told her that her husband, Ernest, had confessed that he knew something about these murder cases and that Hale had apparently planned all of them, including the bombing of her sister Rita's house.

"Bill Hale and your husband are kin-folks, are they not?" he added.

"Yes, sir," she replied.

At one point, the attorney asked her if Hale was at her house around the time of the explosion.

"No, he was not there. Just my husband and my children was all that was at home."

"No one came there that night?"

"No."

"Was your husband at home all evening?"

"Yes, all evening."

He asked her if Ernest had ever told her anything about Hale's plot. She said, "He never told me anything about it." All she wanted, she said, was for the men who did this to her family to be punished.

"It makes no difference who they are?" the attorney asked.

"No," she said firmly. But she couldn't, *wouldn't*, believe that Ernest had been involved in such a plot. Later, a writer quoted her saying, "My husband is a good man, a kind man. He wouldn't have done anything like that. And he wouldn't hurt anyone else, and he wouldn't ever hurt me."

Now the attorney asked her, "You love your husband?"

After a moment, she said, "Yes."

Once armed with the statements of Ernest Burkhart and John Ramsey, Tom White and Agent Frank Smith confronted William Hale. White sat across from this gentlemanly-looking figure who, he was convinced, had killed nearly all the members of Mollie's family and who had killed witnesses and co-conspirators. And White had discovered one more disturbing development; according to several people close to Anna Brown, Hale had had an affair with Anna and was the father of her unborn baby. If true, it meant that Hale had killed his own child.

White tried to contain the violent feelings inside him as Hale greeted him and Agent Smith with the same politeness that he had demonstrated while being arrested. Ernest Burkhart had once described Hale as the best man you "ever saw until after you found him out and knowed him," adding, "You could meet and you'd fall in love with him. Women were the same way. But the longer you stayed around him, he'd get to you. He'd beat you some way."

White did not waste time. As he later recalled, he told Hale, "We have unquestioned signed statements implicating you as the principal in the Henry Roan and Smith family murders. We have the evidence to convict you."

Even after White detailed the overwhelming evidence against him, Hale seemed untroubled, as if he still held the upper hand. Kelsie Morrison had earlier told agents that Hale was certain that "money will buy the protection or acquittal of any man for any crime in Osage County."

White could not foresee the bitter, sensational legal battle that was about to unfold—one that would be debated in the U.S. Supreme Court and would nearly destroy his career. Still, hoping to tie up the case as neatly and quickly as possible, he made one last attempt to persuade Hale to confess. "We don't think you want to expose [your family] to a long trial and all its sordid testimony, the shame and embarrassment," White said.

Hale stared at White with gleeful zeal. "I'll fight it," he said.

18

A Traitor to His Blood

THE REVELATIONS OF THE ARRESTS AND THE HORROR OF the crimes held the nation in their grip. The press wrote about "an evidently well-organized band, diabolic in its ruthlessness, to destroy with bullet, poison, and bomb the heirs to the oil-rich lands of the Osage"; about crimes that were "more blood-curdling than those of the old frontier days"; and about the federal government's effort to bring to justice the alleged "King of the Killers."

Tom White had been consumed with the cases involving Henry Roan and Mollie Burkhart's family members. He and his men had not yet been able to connect Hale to all twenty-four Osage murders or to the deaths of the attorney W. W. Vaughan and the oilman Barney McBride. Yet White and his team were able to show how Hale benefited from at least two of these other killings. The first was the suspected poisoning of George Bigheart, the Osage Indian who, before dying, had passed on information to Vaughan. White learned from witnesses that William Hale had been seen with Bigheart just before he was rushed to the hospital and that after his death, Hale made a claim on Bigheart's estate for $6,000, presenting a forged creditor's note to show he was owed the money. Ernest Burkhart revealed that Hale, before filling out the note, had practiced making his handwriting look like Bigheart's.

Hale was also tied to the apparent poisoning of Joe Bates, another Osage Indian, in 1921. After Bates suddenly died, Hale had produced a suspicious deed to his land. Bates's widow later wrote a letter to the Office of Indian Affairs, saying, "Hale kept my husband drunk for over a year. Hale would come to the house and ask him to sell his inherited shares in land. Joe always refused no matter how drunk he was. I never believed that he sold that land, he always told me he would not even up to a few days before his death. . . . Well, Hale got the land."

Despite the brutality of the crimes, many whites couldn't get enough details about the story. Under the headline OLD WILD WEST STILL LIVES IN LAND OF OSAGE MURDERS, a wire service sent out a nationwide bulletin that the story, "however depressing, is nevertheless blown through with a breath of the romantic, devil-may-care frontier west that we thought was gone." A newsreel about the murders, titled *The Tragedy of the Osage Hills,* was shown at cinemas. "The true history of the most baffling series of murders in the annals of crime," a handbill for the short film said. "A Story of Love, Hatred and Man's Greed for Gold. Based on the real facts as divulged by the startling confession of Burkhart."

Amid the sensationalism, the Osage were focused on making sure that Hale and his conspirators did not find a way to wriggle free, as many feared they would. Bates's widow said, "We Indians cannot get our rights in these courts and I have no chance at all of saving this land for my children."

On January 15, 1926, the Society of Oklahoma Indians issued a resolution that said,

> **Members of the Osage Tribe of Indians have been foully murdered for their headrights . . .**
>
> **Whereas, the perpetrators of these alleged crimes deserve to be vigorously prosecuted and, if convicted, punished to the full extent of the law . . .**
>
> **THEREFORE, BE IT RESOLVED by this Society that we commend the federal and state officials for their efforts in trying to ferret out and prosecute the criminals guilty of these atrocious crimes.**

Yet White knew that America's courts, like its policing agencies, were full of corruption. Many lawyers and judges were on the take. Witnesses were coerced. Juries were bribed or threatened.

Hale held enormous influence over Oklahoma's fragile legal institutions. As a reporter who visited the region noted, "Townspeople, from low to high, speak of him with bated breath. His influence and that of his associates is felt everywhere."

Because of Hale's power, a federal prosecutor warned that it was "not only useless but positively dangerous" to try him in the state legal system. But much of the surface land where the Osage murders had occurred, including the slaying of Anna Brown, was no longer under the tribe's control. These cases, Justice Department officials concluded, had to be tried by the state. Only if a murder occurred on Osage Indian territory could federal authorities prosecute it.

As officials scoured the various cases, they thought that they'd found at least one murder that did happen on tribal land: Henry Roan was killed on an Osage allotment that hadn't been sold to whites.

Prosecutors working with White decided to move forward with this case first, and Hale and John Ramsey were charged in federal court with Roan's murder. They faced the death penalty.

The prosecution team making the government's case against Hale was impressive. It included two high-ranking officials in the Justice Department, as well as a young, newly appointed U.S. attorney, Roy St. Lewis.

A local attorney named John Leahy, who was married to an Osage woman and had been hired by the Osage Tribal Council, was also part of the team.

Hale had his own team of lawyers—some of the "ablest legal

Prosecutor Roy St. Lewis reviewing the voluminous Osage murder case files

talent of Oklahoma," as one newspaper put it. Among them was Sargent Prentiss Freeling, a former Oklahoma attorney general and a strong supporter of states' rights. To defend John Ramsey, Roan's alleged shooter, Hale hired an attorney named Jim Springer. Under Springer's counsel, Ramsey quickly took back his confession, insisting, "I never killed anyone." According to Ernest Burkhart, Hale had previously assured Ramsey "not to worry, that he—Hale—was on the inside and had everything fixed from the road-overseer to the Governor."

Back in early January 1926, while a grand jury was still deciding whether to charge Hale with a crime, one of Hale's cronies—a pastor—was accused of perjury, lying in court. A little later, another Hale associate was arrested for trying to get witnesses drunk so they couldn't testify. As the trial neared, crooked private eyes began trailing witnesses and even trying to make them disappear. The bureau put out an alert about one private eye who agents feared might have been hired as an assassin.

A gunman was hired to assassinate Kelsie Morrison's former wife, Katherine Cole, an Osage woman who had agreed to testify against Hale. The gunman later recalled, "Kelsie said that he wanted to make some arrangement to get shed of Katherine, his wife, because she knew too much about the Anna Brown murder deal. Kelsie said that he would give me a note to Bill Hale and that Hale would fix the arrangements." Hale paid the gunman and told him to "get her out drunk and get rid of her." But at the last minute, the gunman wouldn't go through with it. And after being picked up on a robbery charge, he told police about the plan. Still, the plots continued.

White, who had ordered his men to work in pairs for security, received a tip that a former member of the Al Spencer Gang had shown up in Pawhuska to kill federal agents. White told Agent Smith, "We'd better head this off," and armed with .45 automatics, they confronted the man at a house where he was staying.

"We hear you've threatened to run us out of town," White said.

The outlaw said, "I'm just a friend of Bill Hale's. Just happened in town, is all."

White later told Hoover, "Before this man could put into execution any of his 'dirty' work, he left . . . as he was given to understand that it would be healthier for him some other place."

White was extremely concerned about Ernest Burkhart's safety. Hale later informed one associate that Burkhart was the only witness he was afraid of. "Whatever you do, you get to Ernest," Hale told the associate. Otherwise, he said, "I'm a ruined man."

On January 20, Burkhart had not yet been charged because the government was waiting to see how much he was going to cooperate. But he told White that he was sure he was going to be "bumped off."

"I'll give you all the protection the government can afford," White promised him. "Whatever is necessary."

White arranged for Agent John Wren and another member of his team to secretly take Burkhart out of the state and guard him until the trial. White later told Hoover, "We think that it is likely that they will endeavor to kill Burkhart. Of course, every precaution is being taken to prevent such a step, but there are many ways that this could be done, for friends of Ramsey and Hale could probably slip poison to him."

Mollie, meanwhile, still didn't believe that Ernest was "intentionally guilty." And when he did not return home for days, she became frantic. Her whole family had been killed, and now it appeared as if she'd lost her husband, too. An attorney assisting the prosecution asked whether she'd feel better if agents brought her to see Ernest.

"That is all I wanted," she said.

Afterward, White and Mollie met. He promised her that Ernest would be back soon. Until then, White said, he would make sure that they could write to each other.

After Mollie received a letter from Ernest saying that he was well and safe, she replied, "Dear husband, I received your letter this morning and was very glad to hear from you. We are all well and Elizabeth is going back to school." Mollie noted that she was no longer so sick. "I feel better now," she said. Clinging to the illusion of their marriage, she ended, "Well Ernest I must close my short letter. Hoping to hear from you soon. Good by from your wife, Mollie Burkhart."

On March 1, 1926, White and the prosecution received a devastating setback. The judge agreed with the defense that even though Henry Roan's murder had occurred on an individual Osage allotment, this was not the same as tribal lands, and therefore the case could be tried only in state court. Prosecutors appealed the decision to the U.S. Supreme Court, but with a ruling not expected for months, William Hale and John Ramsey would have to be released. "It appeared that Bill Hale's lawyers—just as his friends predicted—had clipped the government's tail feathers good," one writer observed.

Hale and Ramsey were celebrating in the courtroom when they were approached by Sheriff Freas. He shook hands with Hale, then said, "Bill, I have a warrant for your arrest." White and prosecutors had worked with the Oklahoma attorney general to keep Hale and Ramsey behind bars by filing state charges against them for the bombing murders.

White and the prosecutors had no choice but to begin the state case in Pawhuska, the Osage County seat and a Hale stronghold. "Very few, if any, believe that we can ever be able to get a jury in Osage County to try these parties," White told Hoover. "Trickeries and all methods of deceit will be resorted to."

At a preliminary hearing, on March 12, Osage men and women, many of them relatives of the victims, crammed into the courtroom to bear witness. Hale's wife, his eighteen-year-old daughter, and his many vocal supporters clustered behind the defense table. Journalists jostled for space. "Seldom if ever has such a crowd gathered in a court room before," a reporter from the *Tulsa Tribune* wrote. "Here are well-groomed business men, contesting standing room with roustabouts. There are society women sitting side by side with Indian squaws in gaudy blankets. Cowboys in broad brimmed hats and Osage chiefs in beaded garb drink in the testimony. Schoolgirls crane forward in their seats to hear it. All the cosmopolitan population of the world's richest spot—the Kingdom of the Osage—crowd to catch the drama of blood and gold."

Many people in the gallery gossiped about an Osage woman who was sitting on one of the benches, quiet and alone. It was Mollie Burkhart, cast out from the two worlds that she'd always straddled. Whites, loyal to Hale, shunned her, while many Osage ostracized her for bringing the killers among them and for remaining loyal to

Ernest. Reporters portrayed her as an "ignorant squaw." The press hounded her for a statement, but she refused to give one. Later, a reporter snapped her picture, her face defiantly composed, and a "new and exclusive picture of Mollie Burkhart" was sent around the world.

Hale and Ramsey were escorted into the courtroom. Though Ramsey appeared indifferent, Hale acknowledged his supporters confidently. "Hale is a man of magnetic personality," the *Tribune* reporter wrote. "Friends crowd about him at every recess of court and men and women shout cheerful greetings."

In jail, Hale had jotted down these lines from a poem as he remembered them:

Judge Not! The clouds of seeming guilt may dim thy brother's fame,
For fate may throw suspicion's shade upon the brightest name.

White sat down at the prosecution table. In an instant, one of Hale's lawyers said, "Your honor, I demand that T. B. White over there, head of the federal Bureau of Investigation in Oklahoma City, be searched for firearms and excluded from this courtroom."

Hale's supporters hooted and stamped their feet. White stood, opening his coat to show that he wasn't armed. "I will leave if the court orders it," he said. The judge said that this wouldn't be necessary, and the crowd quieted as White sat back down.

The hearing proceeded uneventfully until that afternoon, when a man entered the courtroom who had not been seen in Osage County for weeks: Ernest Burkhart. Mollie watched her husband as he walked unsteadily down the long aisle to the stand. Hale glowered at his nephew, whom one of Hale's lawyers called a "traitor to his own blood." Moments before, Burkhart had confided to a prosecutor that if he testified, "they'll kill me." And as Burkhart sat in the witness chair, it was clear that whatever strength he had mustered to reach this point was fading.

A lawyer for Hale rose and demanded to speak privately with Burkhart. "This man is my client!" he said. The judge asked Burkhart if this individual was really his attorney, and Burkhart, with one eye on Hale, said, "He's not my attorney . . . but I'm willing to talk to him."

White and the prosecutors watched in disbelief as Burkhart stepped down from the stand and went with Hale's lawyers into the judge's chambers. Five minutes drifted by, then ten, then twenty; at last, the judge ordered the bailiff to retrieve them. Finally, one of Hale's lawyers, Sargent Prentiss Freeling, emerged from the chamber and said, "Your Honor, I'd like to ask the court to allow Mr. Burkhart until tomorrow to confer with the defense." The judge agreed, and Hale went over to his nephew and murmured something, the plot unfolding this time right in front of White. As Burkhart left the courtroom, White tried to catch his attention, but Burkhart was swept away by a mob of Hale's supporters.

The next morning in court, one of the prosecutors made the announcement that White and everyone in the buzzing gallery were expecting: Ernest Burkhart refused to testify for the state. In a memo to Hoover, White explained that Burkhart's "nerve went back on him and, after he was allowed to see Hale and once more be placed under his domination, there was no hope of his testifying." Instead, Burkhart took the stand as a defense witness. One of Hale's lawyers asked him if he'd ever spoken to Hale about the murder of Roan or any other Osage Indian.

"I never did," Burkhart murmured.

When the lawyer asked if Hale had ever requested that he hire someone to kill Roan, Burkhart said, "He never did."

Step by step, in a quiet monotone voice, Burkhart changed his story. Prosecutors tried to salvage their case by filing separate charges against Burkhart, naming him as a co-conspirator in the bombing of the Smiths' house. They scheduled his trial first, hoping for a conviction they could use against Hale and Ramsey. But the two most important pillars of evidence against Hale—the confessions of Burkhart and Ramsey—had crumbled. White recalled that in the courtroom "Hale and Ramsey gave us triumphant grins," adding, "The King on top again."

19

The Double Agent

WHEN THE TRIAL OF ERNEST BURKHART BEGAN, IN LATE
May, White found himself in the midst of another crisis. Hale took
the stand and testified, under oath, that during his interrogation,
White and his agents, including Frank Smith, had brutally tried
to coerce a confession from him. Hale said that the men from the
bureau had told him they had ways of making people talk. "I looked
back," Hale went on. "What caused me to look back was hearing a
pistol cock behind me. Just as I looked back, Smith jumped across
the room, grabbed me by the shoulder and shoved a big gun in
my face."

Hale said that Agent Smith had threatened to beat his brains
out and that White had told him, "We will have to put you in the
hot chair." Then, he said, the agents shoved him into a special
chair, attached wires to his body, and put a black hood over his
head and a device like a catcher's mask over his face. "They kept
talking about putting the juice to me and electrocuting me and did
shock me," Hale said.

Burkhart and Ramsey testified that they had received similar
abuse, which was the only reason they had made their confessions.

One morning in early June, Hoover was stunned to pick up the *Washington Post* and find, above the fold, the following headline:

PRISONER CHARGES USE OF ELECTRICITY BY JUSTICE AGENTS . . . ATTEMPT TO FORCE HIM TO ADMIT MURDERS TOLD ON STAND. . . .

While Hoover had no particular devotion to the niceties of the law, he did not seem to believe that White was capable of such tactics. What worried Hoover was scandal or, to use his preferred term, "embarrassment." He sent White an urgent telegram, demanding an explanation. Though White did not want to dignify the "ridiculous" allegations, he promptly responded, insisting that the charges were a "fabrication from start to finish as there was absolutely no third degree method used. I never used such tactics in my life."

White and his agents took the stand to deny the charges. Still, U.S. senator William B. Pine—a wealthy Oklahoma oilman and defender of the guardianship system—began to pressure government officials to fire White and his men from the bureau.

At Ernest Burkhart's trial, tempers could no longer be contained. When a defense attorney alleged that the government had committed fraud, a prosecutor shouted, "I'll meet the man who says it out in the courtyard." The two men had to be separated.

With the government's case in trouble, prosecutors eventually called a witness who, they believed, could sway the jury in their favor: Kelsie Morrison. The bootlegger and former bureau informant seemed to have only one guiding force—his own self-interest. When he had thought that Hale was more powerful than the U.S. government, he'd served as a double agent for the King of the Osage Hills. Once he was caught and realized that the government controlled his fate, he'd flipped sides and admitted his role in the conspiracy.

Now, as rain fell and thunder clapped outside the courtroom, Morrison testified that Hale had plotted to eliminate all the members of Mollie's family. Hale had told him that he wanted to get rid of "the whole damn bunch" so that "Ernest would get it all."

As for Mollie's sister Anna Brown, Morrison said that Hale had recruited him to "bump that squaw off" and had given him the weapon—a .380 automatic. Bryan Burkhart had acted as his accomplice, he said, adding that the two of them made sure that Anna was good and drunk before they drove out to Three Mile Creek. Morrison's wife at the time, Katherine Cole, was with them, he said, and he told her to stay in the car. Then he and Bryan grabbed hold of Anna. She was too drunk to walk, Morrison recalled, and so they carried her down into the ravine.

Anna Brown

Eventually, Bryan helped Anna sit up on a rock by the creek. "He raised her up," Morrison said. A defense attorney asked, "Pulled her up?"

"Yes, sir."

The courtroom was still. Mollie Burkhart looked on, listening.

The attorney continued, "Did you tell him in what position to hold her while you shot her?"

"Yes, sir."

"You stood there and directed him how to hold this drunken helpless Indian woman down in the bottom of that canyon while you got ready to shoot?"

"Yes, sir."

"Then when he got her just in the position you wanted him to have her, then you shot a bullet from this .380 automatic?"

"Yes, sir."

"Did you move her after you shot her?"

"No, sir."

Asked at one point what he had done after the shooting, Morrison replied, "I went home and ate supper."

Katherine Cole—who said she hadn't come forward right after the murder because Morrison had threatened to "stomp me to death"—confirmed his account. She said, "I stayed in the car alone about twenty-five or thirty minutes, until they returned. Anna Brown was not with them, and I never saw her alive again."

On June 3, in the middle of the trial, Mollie was called away. Her youngest daughter, Anna, whom a relative had been raising since

Mollie became seriously ill, had died. She was just four years old. Little Anna had not been well of late, and doctors believed her death was caused by illness because there seemed to be no evidence of foul play. But for the Osage, every death, every apparent act of God, was now in doubt.

Mollie attended the funeral. She had given her daughter to another family so that she would be safe. Now she watched as Little Anna, in her small plain box, disappeared into a grave. There were fewer and fewer Osage who knew the old prayers for the dead. Who would chant every morning at dawn for her?

After the burial, Mollie went straight to the courthouse—the cold stone building that seemed to hold the secrets to her grief and despair. She sat down in the gallery by herself, not saying a word, just listening to the testimony.

On June 7, several days after the death of his daughter, Ernest Burkhart was being escorted from the courtroom back to the county jail. When no one was looking, he slipped a note to a deputy sheriff. "Don't look at it now," he whispered.

Later, when the deputy unfolded the note, he discovered that it was addressed to John Leahy, the local prosecutor. It said simply, "See me tonight in the county jail. Ernest Burkhart."

The deputy passed the note to Leahy, who found Burkhart pacing restlessly in his cell. He had deep circles around his eyes, as if he hadn't slept for days. "I'm through lying, judge," Burkhart said, the words rushing out of him. "I don't want to go on with this trial any longer."

"Being with the prosecution, I'm in no position to advise you," Leahy said. "Why don't you tell your lawyers?"

"I can't tell them," Burkhart said.

Leahy looked at Burkhart, not sure if the coming confession was yet another trick. But Burkhart looked sincere. The death of his daughter, the haunting face of his wife each day at the trial, the realization that the evidence against him was piling up—it was too much to withstand.

"I'm absolutely helpless," Burkhart said. He pleaded with Leahy to ask Flint Moss, an attorney whom Burkhart knew, to come see him.

Leahy agreed, and on June 9 Burkhart returned to the courtroom after having spoken to Moss. This time, Burkhart did not sit at the defense table with Hale's team of attorneys. He walked to the bench and whispered something to the judge. Then he stepped back, breathing loudly, and said, "I wish to discharge the defense attorneys. Mr. Moss will now represent me."

There were protests from the defense, but the judge agreed to the request. Moss stood beside Ernest and pronounced, "Mr. Burkhart wishes to withdraw his plea of not guilty and enter a plea of guilty."

Gasps filled the courtroom. "Is this your desire, Mr. Burkhart?" the judge asked.

"It is."

"Have state or federal officials offered you immunity or clemency if you changed your plea?"

"No."

He had decided to throw himself at the mercy of the court, having earlier told Moss, "I'm sick and tired of all this. . . . I want to admit exactly what I did."

Burkhart now read a statement confessing that he'd delivered a message from Hale to Ramsey, saying to let Kirby know it was time to blow up the Smith house. "I feel in my heart that I did it because I was requested to do it by Hale, who is my uncle," he said. "The truth of what I did I have told to many men, and as I see it the honest and honorable thing for me to do was to stop the trial and acknowledge the truth."

The judge said that before he would accept the plea, he needed to ask a question: Had federal agents forced Burkhart to sign a confession at gunpoint or under threat of electrocution? Burkhart said that other than keeping him up late, the men from the bureau had treated him just fine. (Later, Burkhart said that some of Hale's attorneys had prodded him to lie on the stand.)

The judge said, "Then your plea of guilty will be accepted."

The courtroom erupted. The *New York Times* reported on the front page, BURKHART ADMITS OKLAHOMA KILLING: CONFESSES HE HIRED MAN TO DYNAMITE SMITH HOME . . . SAYS UNCLE HEADED PLOT.

After Ernest Burkhart's admission, the campaign to fire White and his men ended.

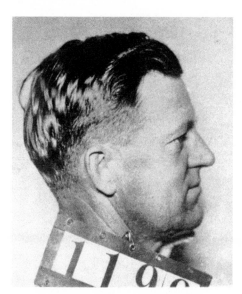

Ernest Burkhart's mug shot

Yet only a fraction of the case had been completed. Tom White and the authorities still had to convict the other henchmen, including Bryan Burkhart and John Ramsey. And, most treacherous of all, they still had to bring down William Hale.

White, after witnessing the shenanigans in Ernest's trial, was less certain that Hale could be convicted, but he received at least one encouraging bit of news. The U.S. Supreme Court had ruled that the place where Roan had been murdered was indeed on tribal lands. "That put us back in federal district courts," White noted.

On June 21, 1926, Ernest Burkhart was sentenced to life in prison and hard labor. Even so, the people around him saw relief on his face. Before being led away in irons to the state penitentiary, Burkhart turned and smiled weakly at Mollie. But her expression remained impassive, perhaps even cold.

20

So Help You God!

IN THE LAST WEEK OF JULY 1926, AS THE SUMMER HEAT reached infernal temperatures, the trial of William Hale and John Ramsey for the murder of Henry Roan began at the redbrick courthouse in Guthrie. "The stage is set: the curtain rises slowly on the great tragedy of the Osage—the long-awaited federal trial of two old-time cowboys," the *Tulsa Tribune* reported.

Tom White stationed extra guards at the jail after stopping attempts to break out the outlaws who were going to testify against Hale. Hale was being held on a separate tier from the cell housing Blackie Thompson, but he managed to pass him a note through a hole where a radiator pipe went through the ceiling. Blackie admitted to agents that Hale had asked him what he needed to "not testify against him." Blackie added, "I wrote one note that I would not testify against him if he would get me out." Hale wrote back, promising to arrange his escape in return for one more thing— that Blackie then kidnap Ernest Burkhart from prison and make him disappear so that he couldn't testify. "He wanted me to take Ernest Burkhart to Old Mexico," Blackie said, adding that Hale didn't "want Burkhart killed in this country where he would be found."

Given the abundance of evidence against Hale and Ramsey, White believed that the verdict would depend, in large part, on whether the witnesses and the jury became tainted. At Ernest Burkhart's trial, the first panel of possible jurors had been dismissed after evidence surfaced that Hale had tried to bribe them. Now, before selecting a jury, prosecutors questioned candidates to find out whether anyone had approached them. The judge then asked the twelve chosen jurors to swear that they would render a true verdict according to the law and the evidence—"so help you God!"

There was one question that the judge and the prosecutors and the defense never asked but was central to the proceedings: Would a jury of twelve white men ever punish another white man for killing an American Indian? A prominent member of the Osage tribe put the matter more bluntly: "It is a question in my mind

Hale (second from left) and John Ramsey (third from left) with two U.S. marshals

whether this jury is considering a murder case or not. The question for them to decide is whether a white man killing an Osage is murder—or merely cruelty to animals."

On July 29, as testimony was set to begin, crowds of spectators arrived early in order to get a seat. The temperature outside was ninety degrees, and it was hard to breathe in the courtroom. John Leahy, the prosecutor, rose to give his opening statement. "Gentlemen of the jury," he said. "William K. Hale is charged with aiding and abetting to the killing of Henry Roan, while John Ramsey is charged with the killing." Leahy outlined the alleged facts of the insurance murder plot in a matter-of-fact voice. One observer noted of Leahy that "the veteran of legal battles does not go in for fireworks or courtroom histrionics but he makes his points all the stronger for his quiet reserve." Looking on, Hale smiled ever so slightly, while Ramsey leaned back in his chair, fanning himself in the heat, a toothpick between his teeth.

On July 30, the prosecution called Ernest Burkhart to the stand. There was speculation that Burkhart would change his story again and return to the fold of his uncle. But this time, Burkhart answered the prosecution's questions honestly. He recalled that Hale and Henry Grammer had talked about how to eliminate Roan. The original plan was not for Ramsey to shoot Roan, Burkhart said. Instead, Hale was going to use one of his other main methods— a batch of poisoned moonshine. Burkhart's testimony finally made public what the Osage had long known: members of the tribe had been systematically killed with tainted alcohol.

In the case of Roan, Burkhart said, Hale ultimately decided to have him shot. But Hale was furious when he later learned that Ramsey had not followed instructions to fire the bullet to make it look like Roan had shot himself, and that he had failed to leave the gun at the scene. "Hale said to me if John Ramsey had done it the way I told him to nobody would have known but that Roan had attempted suicide," Burkhart recalled.

On August 7, the prosecution rested its case, and the defense soon called Hale to the stand. Addressing the jurors as "gentlemen," he insisted, "I never devised a scheme to have Roan killed. I also never desired his death."

Although Hale had made a compelling witness, White was confident that the government had proven its case. Not only did the prosecution have Burkhart's testimony, but White had testified to Ramsey's confession. And several witnesses had described how Hale had committed fraud to receive the money from Roan's insurance policy after his death. The prosecutor Roy St. Lewis called Hale "the ruthless freebooter of death." Another prosecutor told the jury, "The richest tribe of Indians on the globe has become the illegitimate prey of white men. The Indian is going. A great principle is involved in this case. People of the United States are following us through the press. The time has now come for you gentlemen to do your part."

On August 20, a Friday, the jury started its deliberations, discussing the evidence and trying to agree on a verdict. Hours went by. The next day, no agreement was reached, nor the day after that.

After nearly a week of stalemate, the judge called the jury and the attorneys into the courtroom. He asked the jurors, "Is there any possibility of an agreement on a verdict?"

The foreman rose and said, "There is none."

The judge asked if the prosecution had any remarks, and St. Lewis stood. His face was red, his voice trembling. "There are some good men on the jury and some that are not good," he said. He added that he had been informed that at least one, if not more, members of the panel had been bribed.

The judge considered this, then ordered that the jury be dismissed and the defendants held for a new trial.

White was stunned. More than a year of his work, more than three years of the bureau's work, with still no final decision. Another jury failed to reach an agreement when Bryan Burkhart was tried for the murder of Anna Brown. It seemed impossible to find twelve white men who would convict one of their own for murdering American Indians. The Osage were outraged, and there were murmurings about taking justice into their own hands. White suddenly had to send agents to protect Hale, this man whom he so desperately wanted to bring to justice.

Hale leaving the courthouse

The government, meanwhile, began preparing to retry Hale and Ramsey for the murder of Roan. As part of this effort, White was asked by the Justice Department to investigate the corruption that happened during the first trial. He soon uncovered that there had been a conspiracy to obstruct justice, including bribes and perjury. One witness said that the defense attorney Jim Springer had offered him money to lie on the stand, and when he refused, Springer aimed what appeared to be a gun in his pocket at him and said, "I will kill you."

In early October, a grand jury recommended filing charges against Springer and several witnesses for what it called flagrant attempts to obstruct justice. The grand jury issued a statement: "Such practices should not be endured, otherwise our courts will be a mockery, and justice defeated." Several witnesses were charged with crimes and convicted, but prosecutors decided not to charge Springer, because he would have demanded delaying the second trial of Hale and Ramsey until his own case was resolved.

Before the retrial of Hale and Ramsey for the murder of Roan began, White's men were assigned to safeguard the jury. The prosecutor St. Lewis said, "There will be no one to blame except ourselves if they succeed in fixing this jury."

The prosecution's case was essentially the same, though in more streamlined form. But to the surprise of everyone in the courtroom, Mollie was briefly called to the stand—by defense attorney Freeling.

"Will you state your name?" he asked her.

"Mollie Burkhart."

"Are you the present wife of Ernest Burkhart?"

"Yes, sir."

He then exposed a secret that she'd long kept from Ernest, asking, "Was Henry Roan your husband at one time?"

"Yes, sir," she said.

The prosecution protested that the question had nothing to do with this trial, and the judge agreed. Indeed, there seemed to be no point to the line of questioning other than to inflict more suffering upon Mollie. After she identified a photograph of Roan, she stepped down from the stand and returned to the gallery.

When Ernest Burkhart was on the stand, the prosecutor Leahy questioned him about his marriage to Mollie. "Your wife is an Osage Indian?" Leahy asked him.

"She is," Ernest replied.

At an earlier proceeding, Ernest was asked what his profession was, and he'd said, "I don't work. I married an Osage."

One of Hale's lawyers now asked Ernest if he'd pleaded guilty to murdering his wife's sister by blowing up her house while she was inside.

"That is right," he said.

Hoping to place all the blame for the killings on Ernest, Hale's lawyer recited the names of Mollie's murdered family members, one after the other. "Has your wife now any surviving relatives outside of the two children she has by you?"

"She has not."

There was a hush in the courtroom as Mollie looked on; her gaze could no longer be avoided.

After only eight days of testimony, both sides rested their cases. One of the prosecutors said in his closing statement, "The time now has come for you men to stand for law and order and decency, time to uncrown this King."

The judge advised the jury members that they must set aside sympathies or prejudices for either side. He warned, "There never has been a country on this earth that has fallen except when that point was reached . . . where the citizens would say, 'We cannot get justice in our courts.'"

On the evening of October 28, the jury began deliberating. By the next morning, word had spread that the jurors had reached a decision, and the courtroom filled with the familiar participants.

The judge asked the foreman if, indeed, the jury had reached a verdict. "Yes, sir," he replied, and handed him a sheet of paper.

The judge looked at it for a moment, then passed it on to the clerk. The courtroom was so quiet that the ticking of a clock on the wall could be heard. A reporter later observed, "Hale's face expressed a guarded eagerness; Ramsey's was a mask." Standing in front of the still room, the clerk read out that the jury had found John Ramsey and William K. Hale guilty of first-degree murder.

Hale and Ramsey appeared shocked. The judge said to them, "A jury has found you guilty of the murder of an Osage Indian, Mr. Hale and Mr. Ramsey, and it becomes my duty to pass sentence. Under the law the jury may find you guilty and that carries the death penalty in a first-degree murder case. But this jury has qualified it with life imprisonment." The jurors were willing to punish the men for killing an American Indian, but they would not hang them for it.

The judge told Hale and Ramsey, "Stand before the bench." Hale rose quickly, Ramsey hesitantly. The judge declared that he was sentencing them to the penitentiary for the "period of your natural lives." He then asked, "Have you anything to say, Mr. Hale?"

Hale stared straight ahead. "No, sir," he said.

"And you, Mr. Ramsey?"

Ramsey simply shook his head.

Reporters rushed out of the courtroom to file their stories, proclaiming, as the *New York Times* put it, "KING OF OSAGE HILLS" GUILTY OF MURDER. The attorney Leahy would hail the outcome as "one of the greatest indications of law and justice that has been realized in the country." Mollie welcomed the verdict, but no successful investigation, no system of justice, could bring back her family.

A year later, when Anna Brown's murder was prosecuted, Mollie attended the trial. By then, Kelsie Morrison had taken back his confession, shifting his allegiance yet again in the hope of getting money from Hale. Authorities had seized a note that Morrison had sent to Hale in prison, in which he had promised to "burn" down the authorities "if I ever get the Chance."

Prosecutors reluctantly gave Bryan Burkhart immunity, a guarantee he wouldn't be punished for his crimes if he told the truth. They believed that this was the only way to convict Morrison. While Bryan had gotten Anna drunk and helped set up the shooting, it was Morrison who'd pulled the trigger.

During the trial, Mollie listened again to the gruesome details of her sister's murder. Then Bryan recalled that a week after the shooting, he had returned to the scene of the crime with Mollie and her family to identify Anna's body. The memory had stayed with Mollie, but only now could she fully understand the scene. Bryan had been standing near her, staring down at his victim while faking grief.

"Did you go out to see this body?" an attorney asked Bryan.

"That is what we all went for," he said.

The shocked attorney asked him, "You knew Anna Brown's dead body was out there, didn't you?"

"Yes, sir."

Morrison had been among the onlookers. Ernest had been there, too, comforting Mollie, even though he had known that Anna's two killers were standing only a few feet away. Ernest had also known from the moment Rita and Bill Smith's house exploded who was responsible. He had known the truth when, later that evening, he had crept into bed with Mollie, and he had known the whole time she had been desperately searching for the killers.

By the time Morrison was convicted of Anna's murder, Mollie could no longer look at Ernest. She soon divorced him, and whenever her ex-husband's name was mentioned, she recoiled in horror.

For J. Edgar Hoover, the Osage murder investigation became a showcase for the modern bureau. As he had hoped, the case had demonstrated to many around the country the need for a national, more professional, scientifically skilled force. The *St. Louis Post-Dispatch* wrote of the murders, "Sheriffs investigated and did nothing. State's Attorneys investigated and did nothing. The Attorney General investigated and did nothing. It was only when the Government sent Department of Justice agents into the Osage country that law became a thing of majesty."

Hoover was careful not to mention the bureau's earlier bungling. He did not reveal that Blackie Thompson had escaped under the bureau's watch and killed a policeman, or that because of so many false starts in the probe, other murders had occurred. Instead, Hoover created a pristine origin story in which the bureau, under his direction, had risen from lawlessness to tame the last wild American frontier.

Recognizing that this new publicity could expand his power and instill a cult of personality, Hoover asked White to send him information that he could share with the press.

Hoover fed details to sympathetic reporters—so-called friends of the bureau. One headline about the case blared:

NEVER TOLD BEFORE!—
HOW THE GOVERNMENT WITH THE MOST GIGANTIC
FINGERPRINT SYSTEM ON EARTH FIGHTS CRIME
WITH UNHEARD-OF SCIENCE REFINEMENTS;
REVEALING HOW CLEVER SLEUTHS ENDED A REIGN OF
MURDER AND TERROR IN THE LONELY HILLS OF THE
OSAGE INDIAN COUNTRY, AND THEN ROUNDED UP
THE NATION'S MOST DESPERATE GANG

In 1932, the bureau began working with the radio program *The Lucky Strike Hour* to dramatize its cases. One of the first episodes was based on the Osage murders. The program ended with, "So another story ends and the moral is identical with that set forth in all the others of this series. . . . [The criminal] was no match for the Federal Agent of Washington in a battle of wits."

Though Hoover privately praised White and his men for capturing Hale and his gang and gave the agents a slight pay increase, he never mentioned them by name as he promoted the case. They did not quite fit the image he wanted for the bureau—a force made up of college-educated recruits. Plus, Hoover never wanted his men to overshadow him.

The Osage Tribal Council was the only governing body to publicly single out and praise Tom White and his team, including the undercover operatives. In a resolution, which cited each of them by name, the council said, "We express our sincere gratitude for the splendid work done in the matter of investigating and bringing to justice the parties charged." The Osage, meanwhile, had taken their own steps to protect themselves against future plots. They persuaded Congress to pass a new law that barred anyone who was not at least half Osage from inheriting headrights from a member of the tribe.

Soon after Hale and Ramsey were convicted, White faced an important decision. The U.S. assistant attorney general who oversaw the federal prison system had asked White if he would take over as warden of Leavenworth, in Kansas. The oldest federal penitentiary, it was then considered one of the country's most dreaded places to be imprisoned. There had been charges of corruption there, and the assistant attorney general had told Hoover that White was ideal for the job, saying: "I hate to give up the chances of getting a warden that I think will be as good as Mr. White."

Hoover did not want White to leave the bureau. He told the assistant attorney general that it would be a tremendous loss. Still, Hoover said, "I feel that I would be unfair to [White] if I should oppose his promotion. I have, as you know, the highest regard for him, personally and officially."

After some torment, White decided to leave the bureau. The Leavenworth job offered him greater pay and meant that he would no longer need to uproot his wife and sons. It also offered him a chance to preside over a prison, just as his father had, although on a far larger scale.

On November 17, 1926, when White was still settling into the job, two new inmates were brought up the prison's horseshoe driveway by U.S. marshals. As the inmates approached the entryway in shackles, White walked toward them. Their faces were pale from a lack of sunlight, but White recognized them immediately: William Hale and John Ramsey.

"Why, hello, Tom," Hale said to White.

"Hello, Bill," White answered.

Ramsey said to White, "Howdy."

White shook hands with both inmates, who were then led away to their cells.

Leavenworth Penitentiary

21

The Hot House

IT WAS LIKE WANDERING THROUGH THE CATACOMBS OF memory. As Tom White walked along the cell blocks, he could see many people from his past, their eyes peering out from behind bars, their bodies gleaming with sweat. He saw William Hale and John Ramsey. He ran into members of the old Al Spencer Gang. And he came upon the two deserters who had killed his older brother, Dudley, though White never mentioned the connection, not wanting to cause them any distress.

White lived with his family on the prison grounds. His wife was initially unable to sleep, wondering, "How do you raise two young boys in this kind of environment?" The challenges of managing the prison—which was designed to hold twelve hundred inmates but instead had three times that number—were overwhelming. In the summer, the temperatures inside rose as high as 115 degrees, which is why prisoners would later call Leavenworth the Hot House.

One day, when it was so nightmarishly hot that the milk in the prison's kitchen soured, a riot erupted in the mess hall. Red Rudensky, an infamous safecracker, recalled that there was "ugly, dangerous, killing hate" and that White rushed in to quell the unrest:

"Warden White showed his courage, and came within a few feet of me, although cleavers and broken, jagged bottles were inches from him."

White tried to improve conditions in the prison. A custodian who later worked under him recalled, "The Warden was strict with the inmates but would never stand for any mistreatment or heckling of them."

After arriving at Leavenworth, William Hale was assigned to work on the ward where prisoners who had the contagious disease tuberculosis were housed. Later, he toiled on the prison farm, where he tended pigs and other animals the way he had during his early days on the frontier.

In November 1926, a reporter wrote to White, fishing for gossip about Hale, but White refused to provide any, insisting that Hale would be "treated as other prisoners are treated."

Over the years, William Hale never admitted ordering any of the murders: not the killing of Henry Roan, for which he was convicted, or the countless other murders that evidence showed he had orchestrated. But during his trial, Hale had made a cold and revealing statement about a different time he had tried to swindle a headright: "It was a business proposition with me."

Though Hale followed prison regulations, he continued to scheme to secure his release. He allegedly arranged for an appeals court to be bribed. And when these efforts failed to win him freedom, he boasted of "his probable release through influence of friends."

Yet for the first time in ages, life in Osage County went on without his overwhelming presence. Mollie Burkhart began again to socialize and attend church. She eventually fell in love with a man named John Cobb, who was part white and part Creek. According to relatives, their love was genuine, and in 1928 they were married.

There was another dramatic change in Mollie's life. She and the Osage had fought to end the corrupt system of guardianships, and on April 21, 1931, a court ruled that Mollie was no longer a ward of the state, writing that: "IT IS FURTHER ORDERED, ADJUDGED AND DECREED BY THE COURT, that the said Mollie Burkhart, Osage Allottee No. 285, . . . is hereby restored to competency . . ." At the age of forty-four, Mollie could finally spend her money as she pleased, and was recognized as a full-fledged American citizen.

On December 11, 1931, White was in his warden's office when he heard a noise. He went to the door and found himself staring into the barrel of a gun. Seven of the most dangerous convicts— including two Al Spencer Gang members and a bandit who was nicknamed Boxcar, because of his giant size—were attempting to escape. The group was armed with a Winchester rifle, a sawed-off shotgun, and six sticks of dynamite, which had been smuggled into the prison. The convicts took White and eight members of his staff hostage and used them as shields as they pushed forward. Once outside the front gate, the prisoners released the other hostages and headed out to the main road with White—their "insurance policy," as they called him. The inmates stopped an approaching vehicle, forced the driver out, and pushed White inside, then sped away.

Mollie Burkhart

White's captors told him that there'd be nothing left of him to bury if anything went wrong. But everything was going wrong. The car slipped off the muddy road and got stuck, forcing the prisoners to flee on foot. Soldiers from Fort Leavenworth joined the manhunt. Planes were flying overhead. The escaped inmates ran into a farmhouse and seized an eighteen-year-old girl and her younger brother. White pleaded with the men, saying, "I know you're going to kill me. But don't kill these two—they aren't in it at all."

Boxcar and another inmate went to look for a second car, taking White with them. Suddenly, White could see that the girl had broken free and was running. The gang seemed ready to start shooting, and so White grabbed the barrel of the gun being held by one of his captors. That prisoner yelled at Boxcar, "Shoot him! He's got my gun." As Boxcar leveled his shotgun at White's chest, only inches away, White lifted his left forearm to shield himself. Then he heard a blast and felt a bullet drilling through his arm, through flesh and blood, the buckshot fragmenting and going into his chest. But White was standing. It was like a miracle; he had been shot to pieces, and yet he was still breathing in the cold December air. Then he felt the butt of the rifle smashing into his face and he crumbled, all 225 pounds of him, and fell into a ditch, left to die.

Nearly a decade later, in December 1939, acclaimed newspaper reporter Ernie Pyle stopped at La Tuna prison, near El Paso, Texas. He asked to meet the warden and was led in to see Tom White, who was then nearly sixty years old. "White asked me to stay for lunch,"

Pyle later wrote. "So I did, and we sat and talked, and finally he told me the story, as I was hoping all the time he would. The story about his left arm."

White described how, after being shot by Boxcar, he was found in the ditch and rushed to the hospital. For several days, it was uncertain whether he would live, and doctors thought about amputating his arm. But he survived, somehow, and he even kept his arm, though it still had bullet fragments lodged inside and now dangled uselessly. White didn't mention one detail to Pyle: the girl who had been taken hostage credited White with protecting her and her brother. "I am sure they intended to kill all of us, and only Warden White's bravery saved us," she said.

None of the convicts managed to get away. They believed that if you touched a prison official, especially a warden, it was better, as one of them remarked, never to "come back because if you do you are going to have a hard, hard time." And so when the authorities caught up with Boxcar and two other escapees, Boxcar shot his companions, then shot himself. The other inmates prepared to kill themselves with the dynamite, but before they could light the fuse, they were captured.

One of them later said, "The funny part is that when we got back to the institution they never laid a hand on us. Warden White . . . left strict orders, 'No hands on these people, leave them alone. Treat them just like the rest of the prisoners.'" He added, "Otherwise we'd have got our heads broken in."

When White had recovered, he took over as warden of La Tuna, a less strenuous job. Pyle wrote of the shooting, "It didn't make him afraid, but it made him jumpy, and kind of haunted." Pyle added, "I don't see how, after an experience like that, you could look upon any convict with anything but hatred. But Warden White isn't that way. He is thoroughly professional about his job."

Although J. Edgar Hoover used the Osage murder investigation as a showcase for the bureau, it was a series of sensational crimes in the 1930s that raised public fears and enabled him to turn the organization into the powerful force it is today. These crimes included the kidnapping of famous aviator Charles Lindbergh's baby and the Kansas City Massacre, where several lawmen were killed in a shoot-out while transporting the Al Spencer Gang member Jelly Nash.

In the wake of these incidents, Congress passed a series of reforms that gave the federal government its first comprehensive criminal code and the bureau a sweeping mission. Agents were now allowed to make arrests and carry firearms, and the department was soon renamed the Federal Bureau of Investigation. White's brother Doc was involved in many of the bureau's biggest cases during this period—from hunting for public enemies like John Dillinger, Ma Barker, and her son Fred. Tom White's son had also joined the bureau, making three generations of White lawmen.

Once Hoover took control of the bureau, he never let it go. And while presidents came and went, Hoover, now thick around the waist and with jowls like a bulldog, remained. "I looked up and there was J. Edgar Hoover on his balcony, high and distant and quiet, watching with his misty kingdom behind him, going on from President to President and decade to decade," a reporter for *Life* magazine wrote. His ironfisted control led to abuses of power over

Tom White   J. Edgar Hoover

the decades, but the many details would not be made public until after his death in 1972.

Despite Tom White's perceptiveness, he was blind to Hoover's flaws, including his prejudices, his use of the bureau for his own agenda, and his paranoid plots against an ever-growing list of perceived enemies, among them American Indian activists.

Over the years, White wrote to Hoover from time to time. But Hoover was too busy now and had to be prodded to take note of his former star agent. When White, at the age of seventy, stepped down as warden of La Tuna in 1951, Hoover sent him a card only after another agent reminded him how much White would "appreciate a personal note from the director on his retirement."

In the late 1950s, White learned that Hollywood was about to shoot a movie, *The FBI Story*, that would feature a segment on the Osage murders. White sent Hoover a letter, suggesting that the

Tom White and
Hoover

filmmakers might want to talk to him about the case. "I would be glad to afford the information as I know it from start to finish," White said. Hoover replied that he would "certainly bear you in mind," but he never followed up. Hoover made a cameo appearance in the 1959 movie, which further enshrined him in the public's imagination.

But even though the movie was popular, the Osage case was fading from memory, overshadowed by more recent celebrated cases. Soon, most Americans had forgotten it. White thought about writing a story to document the case. He wanted to record the crimes against the Osage and to make sure that the agents who had worked with him were not erased from history. They had all since died in obscurity and often in poverty.

Several years after the Osage murder investigation, John Wren, the Ute agent, was forced out of the bureau again. As he left, he cursed and threw items from his desk. His treatment, he later wrote to Hoover, had been "unjust, unfair and unwarranted."

Along with documenting the roles of other agents, White no doubt hoped to secure himself a small place in history, though he'd never say so himself. He wrote a few pages but soon recognized that he wasn't much of a writer. By 1958, he had teamed up with Fred Grove, an author of Western novels who was part Osage. As Grove worked on the book, White asked him, in a letter, if the narrative could be told in the third person. "I would like to keep the big 'I' out of it all I can, because I don't want it conveyed that I am the whole story," White explained. "If it had not been for the good agents I had on the job we could never have made it."

In a letter to Hoover, White asked if the bureau would release to him some of the old case files to help him prepare the book. He also asked whether Hoover would write a brief introduction. "I hope this will not be asking too much of you," White said. "I feel that this would be invaluable. . . . You and I are about the only ones of the originals left now." But his request for the files was denied.

White's body was beginning to fail him. He had arthritis. He tripped walking and injured himself. Even in his ailing state, White kept assisting Grove with the book, as if he were consumed by an unsolved case, until the manuscript was completed. In a letter to Grove, White wrote, "I am hoping that all the good luck in the world will come our way from a good publisher." But publishers found the account less than captivating. And though Grove would eventually release a fictionalized version called *The Years of Fear,* the original historical account was never published. "I am sincerely sorry this letter couldn't bring better news," one editor said.

On February 11, 1969, Doc died at the age of eighty-four on the ranch where he and Tom had grown up. In a letter, White shared the news with Hoover, noting that he and his four siblings had been "born on this land." He added wistfully, "And now I am the only one left."

In October 1971, Tom White collapsed from an apparent stroke. He was ninety and had no more miraculous escapes. On December 21, in the early-morning hours, he stopped breathing. A friend said, "He died as he had lived, quietly and with a calm dignity." An agent urged Hoover to send condolences to White's widow, so Hoover sent a bouquet of flowers, which was laid upon the casket as it disappeared into the ground.

For a while, before the Osage murders faded from history, White was remembered as a good man who had solved the case. Years later, the bureau would release several of its files on the Osage investigation in order to preserve the case in the nation's memory. But there was something essential that wasn't included in these and other historical records, something that White himself had missed. There was another layer to the case—a deeper, darker, even more terrifying layer, which the bureau had never exposed.

CHRONICLE THREE

The Reporter

22

Ghostlands

SO MUCH IS GONE NOW. GONE ARE THE BIG PETROLEUM companies and the forests of derricks as the vast oil fields have been increasingly depleted. Gone is the Million Dollar Elm. Gone are the railroads, including where Al Spencer and his gang pulled off the last train robbery in Oklahoma, in 1923. Gone, too, are the outlaws, many of whom died as spectacularly as they lived. And gone are virtually all the boomtowns that raged from morning until night. Little remains of them but shuttered buildings, colonized by bats and rodents and pigeons and spiders. In the case of Whizbang, there is nothing except stone ruins submerged in a sea of grass. Several years ago, a longtime resident of one of the boomtowns lamented, "Stores gone, post office gone, train gone, school gone, oil gone, boys and girls gone—only thing not gone is graveyard and it git bigger."

Pawhuska is filled with its share of abandoned buildings, but it is one of the few towns that remain. It has a population of thirty-six hundred. It has schools, a courthouse (the same one where Ernest Burkhart was tried), and several restaurants, including a

A now-shuttered bar in Ralston, the town where Bryan Burkhart took Anna Brown to drink the night she was killed

McDonald's. And Pawhuska is still the capital of the vibrant Osage Nation, which, in 2006, ratified a new constitution.

The nation maintains its own elected government and has twenty thousand members. The majority are scattered in other parts of Oklahoma and the United States, but around four thousand live in Osage County, above the underground reservation. The Osage historian Louis F. Burns observed that after "only shreds and tatters remained" of his people, they had risen "from the ashes of their past."

One summer day in 2012, after traveling from New York, where I live and work as a reporter, I visited Pawhuska for the first time. I was hoping to find information on the Osage murder cases, which, by then, were nearly a century old. Like most Americans, when I was in school, I never read about the murders in any books. It was as if these crimes had been erased from history. So when I stumbled upon a reference to the murders, I began to look into them. Since then, I had been consumed with trying to answer lingering questions, to fill in the gaps in the FBI's investigation.

In Pawhuska, I stopped at the Osage Nation Museum, where I had arranged to meet with its longtime director, Kathryn Red Corn. A woman in her seventies, with a broad face and short graying hair, she had a gentle, scholarly manner that hid an inner intensity. She showed me an exhibit of photographs of many of the 2,229 allotted members of the tribe, including several of her relatives, who had each received a headright in 1906. In one of the display cases, I spotted a photograph of Mollie Burkhart sitting happily with her sisters. Another photograph showed their mother, Lizzie. And everywhere I turned while touring the exhibit, I recognized another victim of the Reign of Terror. Here, a striking young George Bigheart in a cowboy hat. There, Henry Roan with his long braids. Over there, a dashing Charles Whitehorn wearing a suit and bow tie.

The most dramatic photograph in the museum spanned an entire side of the room. Taken at a ceremony in 1924, it was a panoramic view of members of the tribe alongside prominent local white businessmen and leaders. As I scanned the picture, I noticed that a section was missing, as if someone had taken scissors to it. I asked Red Corn what happened to that part of the photograph. "It's too painful to show," she said.

When I asked why, she pointed to the blank space and said, "The devil was standing right there."

She disappeared for a moment, then returned with a small, slightly blurred print of the missing panel.

The missing panel of the photograph that shows Hale (far left), dressed in a suit and cap and wearing glasses. The entire panoramic photograph—which includes Hale on the very far left—is shown on the title page at the beginning of the book.

It showed William K. Hale, staring coldly at the camera. The Osage had removed his image, not to forget the murders, as most Americans had, but because they cannot forget.

Red Corn told me that a few years ago, she was at a party in nearby Bartlesville when a man approached her. "He said that he had Anna Brown's skull," she recalled. It was evidently the part of Brown's skull that the undertaker had kept in 1921, and later given to bureau agents for analysis. Outraged, Red Corn told the man, "That needs to be buried here." She called the Osage chief, and Anna's skull was retrieved and, at a quiet ceremony, interred with her other remains.

Red Corn gave me the names of several Osage who she thought might have information about the murders. And she promised to later share with me a related story about her grandfather. "It's hard for us to talk about what happened during the Reign of Terror," she explained. "So many Osage lost a mother or a father or a sister or a brother or a cousin. That pain never goes away."

Over several weekends each June, the Osage hold their ceremonial dances, *I'n-Lon-Schka*. These dances take place in Hominy, Pawhuska, and Gray Horse—three areas where the Osage first settled when they came to the reservation in the 1870s. The Osage travel from all over to attend these events, which help preserve fading traditions and offer a chance to see old family and friends and cook out and reminisce. The historian Burns once wrote, "To believe that the Osages survived intact from their ordeal is a delusion of the mind. What has been possible to salvage has been saved and is dearer to our hearts because it survived. What is gone is treasured because it was what we once were. We gather our past and present into the depths of our being and face tomorrow. We are still Osage. We live and we reach old age for our forefathers."

During a later visit to the region, I headed to Gray Horse to see the dances and meet someone who had been profoundly affected by the murders. Almost nothing remained of the original settlement but some rotted beams and bricks buried in the wild grasses, which the wind ruffled in ghostly rhythms.

To accommodate the dances, the Osage had erected a pavilion with a mushroom-shaped metal roof and a circular earth floor surrounded by rows of wooden benches. When I arrived on a Saturday afternoon, the pavilion was crowded with people. Gathered in the center, around a sacred drum used to commune with Wah'Kon-Tah, were several male musicians and singers. Ringed around them were the "lady singers," as they are called, and in a circle farther out were dozens of male dancers, young and old, wearing leggings, brightly colored ribbon shirts, and bands of bells below their knees. Each of these dancers had on a headdress—typically made of an eagle feather, porcupine quills, and a deer tail—which stood up like a Mohawk.

At the sound of the drumming and singing, these dancers stepped in a counterclockwise circle to honor the rotation of the Earth, their feet pounding the soft ground, their bells jangling. As the drumming and choral singing intensified, the dancers crouched slightly and stepped more quickly, moving together with precision. One man nodded his head while another flapped his arms like an eagle. Others gestured as if they were scouting or hunting.

There was a time when women were not allowed to dance at these events, but they now joined in as well. Wearing blouses and broadcloth skirts and handwoven belts, they formed a slower-moving, dignified circle around the male dancers.

Many other Osage looked on from the benches, fanning themselves in the heat. Each bench bore the name of an Osage family, and as I walked around to the southern side of the pavilion, I found the one I was looking for: Burkhart.

Before long, an Osage woman walked toward me. In her early fifties, she wore a powder-blue dress and stylish glasses, and her long, glossy black hair was pulled back in a ponytail. Her expressive face seemed vaguely recognizable. "Hi, I'm Margie Burkhart," she said, putting out her hand. Margie is the granddaughter of Mollie and Ernest Burkhart. She serves on a board that directs health-care services for the Osage, and she had driven to the dances from her home in Tahlequah, seventy miles southeast of Tulsa, with her husband, Andrew Lowe, a Creek Seminole.

The three of us sat on the wooden bench and, while watching the dancers, spoke about Margie's family. Her father, now deceased, was James "Cowboy" Burkhart—the son of Mollie and Ernest. Cowboy and his sister, Elizabeth, also now dead, had witnessed the Reign of Terror from inside their father's house of secrets. Margie

Margie Burkhart, the granddaughter of Mollie and Ernest

said of Ernest, "He took away everything from my dad—his aunts, his cousins, his trust." Though Cowboy was haunted by the knowledge of what his father had done, he adored Mollie. "He always spoke fondly of her," Margie recalled. "When he was little, he'd get these real bad earaches, and he said she'd blow in his ears to make the pain go away."

After Mollie divorced Ernest, she lived with her new husband, John Cobb, on the reservation. Margie was told that it had been a good marriage, a period of happiness for her grandmother. On June 16, 1937, Mollie died. The death, which wasn't considered suspicious, received little notice in the press. The *Fairfax Chief* published a short obituary: "Mrs. Mollie Cobb, 50 years of age . . . passed away at 11 o'clock Wednesday night at her home. She had been ill for some time. She was a full-blood Osage."

Later that year, Ernest Burkhart was paroled and let out of prison early. The Osage Tribal Council issued a resolution, protesting that "anyone convicted of such vicious and barbarous crimes should not be freed to return to the scene of these crimes." The *Kansas City Times,* in an editorial, said, "The freeing of a principal in so cold-blooded a plot, after serving little more than a decade of a life sentence, seems to reveal one of the besetting weaknesses of the parole system."

Margie said that after Ernest got out, he robbed an Osage home and was sent back to prison. In 1947, while Ernest was still in jail, Hale was released, having served twenty years at Leavenworth. Parole board officials maintained that their ruling was based on the grounds of Hale's advanced age—he was seventy-two—and his record as a good prisoner. An Osage leader said that Hale "should have been hanged for his crimes," and members of the tribe were convinced that the board's decision was the result of Hale's last bit of political influence. He was forbidden to set foot again in Oklahoma, but according to relatives he once visited them and said, "If that damn Ernest had kept his mouth shut we'd be rich today."

Margie told me that she never met Hale, who died in 1962 in an Arizona nursing home. But she saw Ernest after he got out of prison again, in 1959. Barred from returning to Oklahoma, he had initially gone to work on a sheep farm in New Mexico, earning $75 a month. In 1966, hoping to return to Oklahoma, he applied for a pardon. His appeal, which went before a five-member review board in Oklahoma, was based at least partly on his cooperation with the bureau's investigation of the murders. (White had always credited Burkhart's confession as saving his case.) Despite intense protests from the Osage, the board ruled, three to two, in favor of a pardon, which the governor then granted.

Stooped and with thinning hair, Ernest went back to Osage County, where at first he stayed with his brother Bryan. "When I met Ernest, I had just become a teenager," Margie recalled. "I was very surprised he looked so grandfatherly. He was very slight with graying hair; his eyes looked so kind. He wasn't rough even after all those years in prison. And I couldn't fathom that this man had done all that . . ." Her voice trailed off amid the insistent beating of the drum. After a while, she continued, "It was so hard on my dad. He and Liz were ostracized by the tribe, and that hurt so much. They needed family and support, and they didn't have any."

The experience had made her father, Cowboy, angry at the world. Andrew, Margie's husband, pointed out that her aunt Elizabeth was also deeply affected. "She was kind of paranoid," he said.

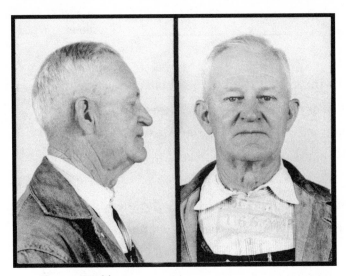

Ernest Burkhart

Cowboy and Elizabeth with their father, Ernest, whose
face was torn out of the photograph years later

Margie nodded and said, "Aunt Liz couldn't stay in one place and was always changing her address and phone number."

Ernest eventually moved into a mice-infested trailer just outside Osage County. Elizabeth showed little interest in seeing her father, but Cowboy occasionally visited. "I think a part of him longed for a father," Margie said. "But he knew what his father had done. He called him Old Dynamite."

When Ernest died, in 1986, he was cremated, and his ashes were given to Cowboy in a box. Ernest had left instructions with his son to spread them around the Osage Hills. "Those ashes were in the house for days, just sitting there," Margie recalled. "Finally, one night my dad got real mad and took the box and just chucked it over a bridge."

During a break in the dancing, as the sun began its descent in the sky, Margie and Andrew offered to show me around Gray Horse. The three of us got in her car, and she began driving down a narrow, dusty road. Not far from the pavilion was one of the few houses standing in Gray Horse. "That's where I grew up," Margie said. To my surprise, it was a small, spare wooden house, more like a cabin than a mansion. The Great Depression had wiped out many Osage fortunes, which had already been diminished by guardians and thieves.

Margie said that Mollie's fortune was no exception. The price of a barrel of oil, which had reached more than $3 during the boom years, plummeted to 65 cents in 1931, and each annual headright payment fell to less than $800. The following year, the *Literary Digest* published an article headlined OSAGE OIL WEALTH FADING. It reported, "These Indians became accustomed to lives of glorious ease. But now . . . their income from oil is rapidly disappearing, and that was practically all they had." Making the situation worse was the gradual depletion of the oil fields. In 1929, even before the stock market crash, a national newspaper story reported, "In five years, if the oil map continues to shift, the tribe may have to go back to work."

Over the next few decades, most of the boomtowns, including Gray Horse, began to die off. "When I was little, I could hear the oil wells pumping," Margie recalled. "Then one day they stopped." Today more than ten thousand wells remain scattered across the reservation, but they are generally what oilmen call "stripper" wells, each one generating less than fifteen barrels a day. When an auction for Osage oil leases was held in Tulsa in 2012, three leases sold for less than $15,000 in total. Margie, who inherited a little more than half of a headright from her father, still receives a quarterly check for her share in the mineral trust. The amount varies depending on the price of oil but recently has usually amounted to a few thousand dollars per year. "It certainly helps, but it's not enough to live on," she said.

The Osage have found new sources of revenue, including from seven casinos that have been built on their territory. (They were originally called the Million Dollar Elm Casinos.) They generate tens of millions of dollars for the Osage, helping to fund their government, educational programs, and health-care benefits. The Osage were also able to get back at least a portion of the oil funds mismanaged over decades by the U.S. government. In 2011, after an eleven-year legal battle, the government agreed to settle a lawsuit brought by the Osage for $380 million.

As we drove through Gray Horse, we came upon a clearing in the woods, where there was an old cemetery.

The graves of Mollie and her murdered family members

We got out of the car, and Margie paused in front of a tombstone bearing Mollie Burkhart's name. The epitaph said, "She was
a kind and affectionate wife and a fond mother and a friend to all."
Nearby were the plots for Mollie's murdered sisters; her murdered
brother-in-law, Bill Smith; her murdered mother, Lizzie; and her
murdered first husband, Henry Roan. Margie looked around at the
tombs and asked, "What kind of person could do this?"

Margie had earlier laid flowers around the graves, and she bent
down and straightened one. "I always try to decorate the stones,"
she said.

We resumed driving and cut along a dirt road through the prairie. Lush tall grasses spread as far as the eye could see, a rolling
green vista that was disturbed only by a few small rusted oil pumps

and by cattle grazing here and there. Earlier, when I drove to Gray Horse, I'd been startled by the sight of bison roaming through the prairie with their bowed heads and massive woolly bodies supported seemingly impossibly on narrow legs. In the nineteenth century, bison were extinguished from the prairie, but in recent years they have been reintroduced by conservationists. The media mogul Ted Turner had been raising bison on a forty-thousand-acre ranch between Fairfax and Pawhuska—a ranch that in 2016 was bought by the Osage Nation.

As Margie and her husband and I continued across the prairie, the sun floated above the rim of the earth before dying off with a burst of dazzling light.

We seemed to be driving aimlessly, riding up and down over the rolling land, like a ship adrift in the waves. Suddenly, at a peak, Margie jolted the car to a stop. In the distance was a ravine and, at the bottom, a meandering creek. "Over there, that's where they shot Anna," Margie said. "My dad took me horseback riding and showed me the spot. I was young and we only had our horses. It was kind of scary."

In 2009, an Osage woman named Elise Paschen published a poem called "Wi'-gi-e," which means "prayer" in Osage. Narrated from Mollie Burkhart's point of view, the poem is about the murder of Anna Brown:

> *Because she died where the ravine falls into water.*
> *Because they dragged her down to the creek.*
> *In death, she wore her blue broadcloth skirt.*
> *Though frost blanketed the grass she cooled her feet in the spring.*
> *Because I turned the log with my foot.*

Her slippers floated downstream into the dam.
Because, after the thaw, the hunters discovered her body.

The poem ends with these lines:

During Xtha-cka Zhi-ga Tze-the, the Killer of the Flowers Moon.
I will wade across the river of the blackfish, the otter, the beaver.
I will climb the bank where the willow never dies.

By the time Margie drove on, the prairie was shrouded in the dark of night. Only the beams from the headlights lit the dusty road. Margie said that her parents first told her what Ernest and Hale had done when she was a child. She said that occasionally *The FBI Story* would air on local television, and she and her family would watch it and cry.

As she spoke, I realized that the Reign of Terror had ravaged—and still ravaged—generations. A great-grandson of Henry Roan's once spoke of the legacy of the murders: "I think somewhere it is in the back of our minds. We may not realize it, but it is there, especially if it was a family member that was killed. You just have it in the back of your head that you don't trust anybody."

We emerged from the prairie and headed into downtown Fairfax. Although still officially a town, it seemed on the verge of oblivion. Year by year, its population had shrunk; now it was fewer than fourteen hundred. The main street was lined with the Western-style buildings that had been built during the boom, but they were abandoned. We paused by the largest storefront, its window darkened with grime and cobwebs. "That was the Big Hill Trading Company," Margie said. "When I was growing up, it was still in business.

It was huge and had these great wooden banisters and old wood floors. Everything smelled of wood." Now, even on a Saturday night, it was a "ghost town," as Margie put it.

She drove on and turned off the main street into a small residential area. A few of the old mansions remained, but they were deserted and decaying. Some were completely imprisoned in vines. At one point, Margie slowed down, as if searching for something.

"What are you looking for?" her husband asked.

"The place where the house was blown up."

"Isn't it back the other way?" he said.

"No, it's—ah, here it is," she said, pulling over by the lot, where another house had since been built.

Margie then mentioned something that I had not seen in any of the FBI records. Her father had told her that on the night of the explosion he and his sister and Mollie had been planning to spend the night at the Smiths' house. But Cowboy had a bad earache, and they had stayed home. "That's why they escaped," Margie said. "It was just fate." It took a moment for the implication to sink in. "My dad had to live knowing that his father had tried to kill him," Margie said.

For a while, we sat in the car in the darkness, trying to understand what could not be understood even after all these years. Finally, Margie shifted into drive and said, "Well, why don't we go back to the dances?"

23

A Case Not Closed

HISTORY IS A MERCILESS JUDGE. IT LAYS BARE OUR TRAGIC blunders and foolish missteps and exposes our deepest secrets, wielding the power of hindsight like a detective who seems to know the answer to the mystery from the beginning. As I combed through the historical records, I could see what Mollie Burkhart could not see about her husband. (An Osage had told me, "Who would believe that anyone would marry you and kill your family for your money?") I could see Tom White unable to recognize Burt Lawson's bogus confession or J. Edgar Hoover's sinister motives. And as I dug deeper into the Osage murder cases, I began to see certain holes in the bureau's investigation.

The authorities had insisted that once William Hale and his conspirators were given life sentences, they'd found the guilty parties. And after White had taken the job at Leavenworth, the cases were closed, closed with great triumph, even though the bureau had not yet connected Hale to all twenty-four murders. Was he really responsible for every one of them? Who, for example, had abducted the oilman Barney McBride in Washington, D.C., or thrown W. W. Vaughan off the speeding train?

Hale had relied on others to do his deadly work, but there was no evidence that Hale's usual henchmen had trailed McBride to the nation's capital or were with Vaughan on the train. Whoever had murdered these men had seemed to get away scot-free.

I could not find any new leads on the McBride case, but one day when I was doing research in Oklahoma City, I called Martha Vaughan, one of W. W. Vaughan's grandchildren. She was a social worker who lived in Sallisaw, Oklahoma, which is 160 miles from the state capital. She was eager to talk about her grandfather and offered to drive to see me. "Let's meet at the Skirvin Hotel," she said. "It'll give you a glimpse of some of the riches that oil brought to Oklahoma."

When I arrived at the hotel, I understood what she meant. Built in 1910 by the oilman W. B. Skirvin, it was once billed as the finest hotel in the Southwest, with a ballroom that seated five hundred people, and chandeliers imported from Austria, and pillars topped with busts of Bacchus, the Greek god of wine. In 1988, during a devastating oil downturn, the hotel closed and remained shuttered for years. But nearly two decades later, after undergoing a $55 million renovation, it reopened as part of the Hilton chain.

I waited for Martha in the lobby. When she arrived, she was with her cousin Melville Vaughan, a biology professor at the University of Central Oklahoma. "He knows a lot about Grandpa Vaughan," Martha said.

Melville was carrying two thick binders, and as we sat at the bar, he laid them before me. They were filled with research that over decades the family had obsessively collected about W. W. Vaughan's murder. The binders included faded newspaper clippings, Vaughan's death certificate, and an informant's statement to the FBI that Vaughan, shortly before being killed, had mentioned having collected "sufficient evidence to put Bill Hale in the electric chair."

Martha and Melville said that their grandfather's widow, Rosa, was left with ten children to raise and no income. They had to move from their two-story house into a storage garage. "They didn't have money to eat," Martha said. "The Osage banded together and basically helped feed the family." Some of Vaughan's children, including Martha's father, went to live with Osage families, where they grew up speaking Osage and learning the traditional dances. "My father felt safe among the Osage," Martha said.

She explained that though many members of her family believed that Hale had wanted Vaughan silenced, they suspected that there was more to the murder. They wondered who the assassin was and how the killing was carried out. Was Vaughan murdered before he was thrown off the train, or did the impact kill him? Someone with influence had made sure that the inquest was a sham—the cause of death was listed as "unknown."

For a while, we discussed elements of the case. Melville explained that his grandfather was big and strong, which meant that the assassin had to have been physically powerful or helped by accomplices. Vaughan, I recalled, had told his wife that he had stashed evidence on the murders—as well as money for the family—in a secret hiding place. I asked Melville and Martha how the killer could have found this hiding place. Martha said that there were only two possibilities: the killer either forced the information out of Vaughan before throwing him off the train, or the killer was someone whom Vaughan trusted enough to share such information.

Melville said that after Hale went to jail, a relative had tried to continue investigating the case. But he had received an anonymous threat that if he and the family pressed the matter any further, they'd all end up like W. W. Vaughan. After that, the family stopped digging.

Martha said, "I remember talking to my oldest uncle; my sister and I were visiting with him before he died. We said, 'Who did this to Grandpa Vaughan?' He mentioned the warning to the family and said not to go there. He was still frightened."

I asked if Rosa, or anyone else in the family, had ever mentioned any potential suspects besides Hale.

No, Martha said, but there was a man who'd stolen money from Grandpa Vaughan's estate after he died and whom Rosa then sued in civil court. I asked what the man's name was, and Martha said, "Something Burt."

"Yes, H. G. Burt," Melville said. "He was president of a bank."

I wrote down the name in my notebook, and when I looked up, I could see the eagerness in their eyes. I suddenly feared that I'd given them false hope. "It's been a long time," I said. "But I'll see what I can find out."

The southwest branch of the U.S. National Archives is in a warehouse in Fort Worth, Texas, that is bigger than most airport hangars. Inside, stacked in fifteen-foot-high rows, in climate-controlled conditions, are more than a hundred thousand cubic feet of records. They include transcripts from the U.S. District Courts of Oklahoma (1907–1969), logs on the deadly Galveston hurricane of 1900, materials on the assassination of John F. Kennedy, documents on slavery and Reconstruction, and reports from many of the

Bureau of Indian Affairs field offices. Within these mountains of files, I hoped to find a clue regarding the murder of W. W. Vaughan.

I had already reviewed court records about the lawsuit that Rosa Vaughan had filed against H. G. Burt. At first glance, the dispute, which began in 1923, seemed unremarkable. Vaughan and Burt, who was the president of a bank in Pawhuska, were considered close friends, and Vaughan had long acted as one of Burt's attorneys. According to Rosa, Burt owed her deceased husband $10,000, which she was seeking to get back.

Yet the devilry is in the details, and as I dug deeper, I discovered that the money in dispute was connected to another victim of the Reign of Terror, George Bigheart. Vaughan had also been Bigheart's attorney. And before Bigheart revealed critical information about the murders to Vaughan—and before he died of suspected poisoning at the hospital in Oklahoma City—he had sought a "certificate of competency" from authorities. With this document, he would no longer be designated a ward of the government, and he could spend his headright payments as he pleased. Vaughan had successfully helped him file his application, and for this and other legal services, Bigheart had planned to pay him as much as $10,000—a sum that is worth nearly $140,000 today. But Burt had somehow collected the money instead. Days later, both Bigheart and Vaughan were dead.

Rosa Vaughan's lawsuit against Burt was initially dismissed in state court. Martha had told me the family was sure that the jury had been rigged. The Oklahoma Supreme Court eventually reversed the decision on appeal and ordered Burt to turn over to Rosa Vaughan $5,000, plus interest.

"What kind of person tries to steal from a penniless widow with ten children?" Martha had said to me.

As I reviewed various records at the National Archives as well as information from other sources, I began to piece together a clearer portrait of Burt. Born in Missouri in 1874, he was the son of a farmer. Census records indicate that by 1910 he had moved to Pawhuska, apparently one of the many dreaming, desperate settlers. He opened a trading store and later became president of a bank. A 1926 photograph shows him dressed in the same style as Hale, with a sharp suit and a hat—a poor farmer's son transformed into a respectable businessman.

Much of his wealth, though, flowed from the deeply corrupt "Indian business"—the swindling of millionaire Osage. A court record noted that Burt had run a loan business targeting the Osage. During a 1915 hearing before a joint commission of Congress that was investigating American Indian affairs, a tribal attorney said that Burt would borrow money from other whites and then relend it to the Osage at astronomical interest rates.

One attorney accused Burt of using bizarre accounting methods to hide his corrupt practices. At the archive in Fort Worth, I pulled records from the U.S. Attorney's Office for the Western District of Oklahoma that dealt with the Osage murders. They contained something that I'd never seen anywhere before: the secret testimony of the grand jury that investigated the murders in 1926. Among the witnesses who testified were many of the main figures in the case, such as Ernest Burkhart and Dick Gregg. There was no mention of H. G. Burt's testifying. But a life-insurance agent stated that Burt had recommended an American Indian to target with an insurance-policy scheme.

I later found two other references to Burt amid the thousands of pages of records on the murders archived by the Bureau of Investigation. The first was an agent's report from a conversation with a trusted informant, who had revealed that Burt and Hale were "very intimate" associates. What's more, the informant said that Burt and Hale had "split on the boodle"—the sum of money—obtained from Bigheart. It wasn't clear from the report what, exactly, the amount was, but the bureau had noted that after Bigheart's death, Hale had presented a fake loan document in order to claim that Bigheart had owed Hale $6,000. Perhaps "the boodle" also included the $10,000 that Burt had tried to make off with instead of paying the Vaughan family.

Still, unlike the extremely valuable headrights that led to the slaying of Mollie Burkhart's family members—or even the $25,000 life-insurance policy in Henry Roan's death—none of these sums, especially if divided, seemed a big enough reward for murder. This may explain why the Justice Department never prosecuted William Hale for George Bigheart's killing or charged H. G. Burt. Yet it was clear that Tom White and his men were deeply suspicious of Burt. In a second report that I found in the bureau files, agents described Burt as a "murderer."

For days, I returned to the archive, trying to find a financial motive for the killing of Bigheart. As Martha had written to me in an email, "Ol' Pappy always said, 'Follow the money.'" I looked through records to see who would have profited from his death. But there was no evidence that Hale or Burt or any other white man had inherited Bigheart's fortune. Records showed it was passed down to Bigheart's wife and his young daughter. Bigheart's daughter, however, had a guardian, and this man would have had control of the money. I flipped through the records until I found the name of her guardian: H. G. Burt.

I felt my heart speed up as I reviewed the facts. I knew that Burt had been close to Hale. I knew that Burt had gained access to Bigheart's fortune by becoming the guardian of his daughter. I knew, from government records, that Burt had also been the guardian of several other Osage, including one who had died. I knew, from a local lawman's notes, that Burt and Hale had both been with Bigheart around the time he died from apparent poisoning. And I knew that the bureau considered Burt a killer.

Other pieces of evidence also tied Burt to a crime. There were the court records that had shown that Burt had stolen money Bigheart had meant for Vaughan. When Vaughan had gone to see Bigheart on his deathbed, perhaps Bigheart had tied not only Hale but also Burt to the murder plots.

The theory of Burt's involvement in the murder of Bigheart and Vaughan, though, was still based on circumstantial evidence. I didn't even know who was with Vaughan when he was thrown from the train. Then, while searching through old newspapers, I found an article in the *Pawhuska Daily Capital* about Vaughan's funeral. Partway through the story, it mentioned that Burt had boarded the train with Vaughan in Oklahoma City and was on the train when Vaughan disappeared from his cabin. According to another story in the newspaper, it was Burt who had reported Vaughan's disappearance.

Before I left the National Archives in Fort Worth, I came across a folder that had an interview with a bureau informant who had been close to Hale and who had provided critical evidence against him in the other murder cases. The informant was asked if he had any information regarding the murder of Vaughan.

"Yes," he replied. "I think Herb Burt pulled that."

I was aware of the unfairness of accusing a man of hideous crimes when he could not answer questions or defend himself. And when I called Martha Vaughan to tell her about my findings, I emphasized what we could and couldn't know for sure. I then went through the research I had gathered. I also mentioned that at a library in New Mexico I had come across notes from an unpublished interview with the Fairfax town marshal, who had investigated the Osage murders. He stated that Burt had been involved in Vaughan's killing and that a mayor of one of the boomtowns—a local tough guy—had helped Burt throw Vaughan off the train. The town marshal also said that during the bureau's investigation into the Osage murders in 1925, Burt was so scared that he considered fleeing. Indeed, Burt abruptly moved to Kansas that same year. When I finished going through all the details, Martha fell silent, then sobbed softly.

"I'm sorry," I said.

"No, it's a relief. This has been with my family for so long."

Not long after we spoke, I learned that Martha had died from heart failure. She was only sixty-five. Her heartbroken cousin Melville told me, "We lost another link to the past." While researching the murders, I often felt that I was chasing history even as it was slipping away.

24

Standing in Two Worlds

ONE NIGHT IN MAY 2013, THE CONSTANTINE THEATER, IN Pawhuska, was scheduled to show a video recording of a performance of the Osage ballet *Wahzhazhe*. The Osage have long been linked to the world of classical dance, having produced two of the greatest ballerinas, the sisters Maria and Marjorie Tallchief. Maria, considered America's first major prima ballerina, was born in Fairfax in 1925. In her autobiography, she recalled the oil riches and how her Osage father seemed to own the town: "He had property everywhere. The local movie theater on Main Street, and the pool hall opposite, belonged to him. Our ten-room, terra-cotta-brick house stood high on a hill overlooking the reservation." She also recalled that a house nearby had been "firebombed and everyone inside killed, murdered for their headrights."

Wahzhazhe chronicled the sweeping history of the Osage through dance, including the period of the Reign of Terror. *Wahzhazhe* means "Osage." I was eager to see the ballet, and after buying a ticket, I headed into the same theater where Mollie and Ernest Burkhart had once sat in the velvety chairs and where the oil barons had gathered for auctions during bad weather. In the early 1980s, the theater had been on the verge of being knocked down. But a group of local citizens volunteered to restore it, clearing away spiderwebs and vermin, polishing the brass plates on the front door, and removing layers of gunk on the lobby floor, revealing a mosaic in the shape of a star.

The auditorium was crowded, and I found my seat as the lights dimmed and the film began. An opening statement read, "In early missionary journals Osages were often described as being 'the happiest people in the world.' . . . They had a sense of freedom because they didn't own anything and nothing owned them. But the Osage Nation was in the way of the economic drive of the European world . . . and life as they once knew it would never be the same." The statement continued, "Today our hearts are divided between two worlds. We are strong and courageous, learning to walk in these two worlds, hanging on to the threads of our culture and traditions as we live in a predominantly non-Indian society. Our history, our culture, our heart, and our home will always be stretching our legs across the plains, singing songs in the morning light, and placing our feet down with the ever-beating heart of the drum. We walk in two worlds."

The ballet powerfully evoked these two colliding worlds. It showed the Osage from the time they roamed the plains to their first encounter with European explorers and missionaries, and to the black-gold rush. At one point, the dancers appeared dressed as flappers, twirling wildly to jazzy music. Suddenly, they were interrupted by the sounds of an explosion. The music and the dancing became mournful as several funereal dances conveyed the murderous Reign of Terror. One of the mourners, representing William Hale, wore a mask to hide his face of evil.

At the end of the show, many people in the audience lingered.

The courthouse where Ernest Burkhart was tried still looms over Pawhuska.

I didn't see Margie Burkhart in attendance, but she later told me that when she first saw the ballet's depiction of the Reign of Terror, "it hit me in the stomach." She added, "I didn't think it would affect me like that, but it did. There was so much emotion."

In the audience, I saw the museum director Kathryn Red Corn. She asked me how my research was going. When I mentioned the likely involvement of H. G. Burt—someone who had never been publicly linked to the killings—she showed little surprise and told me to come see her at the museum the following morning.

When I arrived, I found her sitting at her desk in her office, sur-rounded by artifacts. "Look at this," she said, handing me a copy of a brittle old letter. It was written in neat script and was dated No-

vember 27, 1931. "Look at the signature on the bottom," Red Corn said. The name was W. K. Hale.

She explained that Hale had sent the letter from prison to a member of the tribe and that not long ago a descendant had donated it to the museum. As I read through the letter, I was struck by the buoyant tone. Hale wrote, "I am in perfect health. I weigh 185 lbs. I haven't got a grey hair." When he got out of jail, he said, he hoped to return to the reservation: "I had rather live at Gray Horse than any place on earth." And he insisted, "I will always be the Osages true Friend."

Red Corn shook her head. "Can you believe it?" she said.

I assumed that she had invited me to the museum in order to

show me the letter, but I soon discovered that she had another reason. "I thought this might be a good time to tell you that story I mentioned before, about my grandfather," she said. She explained that after her grandfather divorced her grandmother, he wed a white woman, and in 1931 he began to suspect that he was being poisoned—by his new wife.

When relatives visited her grandfather's home, Red Corn recalled, he was scared. He would tell them, "Don't eat or drink anything in this house." Not long after, Red Corn's grandfather dropped dead; he was only forty-six years old. "Up until then he'd been in good health," Red Corn said. "There was nothing wrong with him. His wife made off with a lot of the money." The family was convinced that he had been poisoned, but there was never an investigation: "Back then, everyone covered these things up. The undertakers. The doctors. The police."

Red Corn did not know more than these details that had been relayed to her by relatives, and she hoped that I could investigate her grandfather's death. After a long pause, she said, "There were a lot more murders during the Reign of Terror than people know about. A *lot* more."

During my years researching the Osage murders, my small New York office became a grim archive. The floors and shelves were stacked with thousands of pages of FBI documents, autopsy reports, wills and last testaments, crime scene photographs, trial transcripts, analyses of forged documents, fingerprints, bank records, eyewitness statements, confessions, intercepted jailhouse notes, grand jury testimony, logs from private investigators, and mug shots. Whenever I found a new document, such as a copy of the Hale letter that Red Corn had shown me, I would label it and place it amid the stacks. Despite the darkness of the material, each new discovery gave me some hope that I might be able to fill in gaps in the historical chronicles—those spaces where there were no recorded witnesses or voices, only the silence of the grave.

The case of Red Corn's grandfather was one of those voids. Because there had been no investigation, and because all the people involved were dead, I couldn't find any trail of evidence to follow. Virtually all traces of her grandfather's life and death had seemingly been washed away.

The conversation with Red Corn, though, pushed me to search more deeply into perhaps the most puzzling of the Osage murder cases—that of Charles Whitehorn. The murder, which bore all the markings of a Hale-orchestrated hit, took place in May 1921— the same time period as the slaying of Anna Brown, in what was considered the beginning of the four-year Reign of Terror. Yet no evidence had ever surfaced tying Hale or his henchmen to Whitehorn's murder.

Though the case had never been solved, it had originally been a prime focus of investigators, and I had gathered evidence related to the crime. In one of the tottering piles in my office, I found the logs from the private detectives hired by Whitehorn's estate after his death.

As I read through the reports, I jotted down key details:

Whitehorn last seen alive in Pawhuska on May 14, 1921.
Witness spotted him around 8:00 p.m. outside Constantine Theater.

> Body discovered two weeks later—on a hill about a mile from downtown Pawhuska.

> According to undertaker, "The position of the body indicated that he had fallen in that position and had not been carried there."

> Weapon: a .32 revolver. Shot—twice . . .
> A professional hit?

The reports noted that the attorney W. W. Vaughan had been eager to help the private eyes. "Vaughan who is well acquainted with the Indians stated that his real interest in the case was to . . . have the guilty party prosecuted," a private detective wrote. Neither the investigators nor Vaughan had any inkling that within two years Vaughan, too, would be murdered. And I found myself pleading with them to see what they could not see.

A. W. Comstock—the attorney and guardian—had also tried to help with the investigation. A private detective noted that Comstock had reported that on May 14 an unidentified man had been seen lurking on the hill where Whitehorn's body was later found.

Because the Whitehorn case was officially unsolved, I expected the trails of evidence to disappear. But the reports were very clear. Based on tips from informants and other evidence, the private detectives began to develop a strong theory of the crime. After Whitehorn's death, his part-white, part-Cheyenne widow, Hattie, had married a dishonest white man named LeRoy Smitherman. The private eyes learned that the marriage had been set up by a "shrewd, immoral, capable woman," as one investigator put it. Her name was Minnie Savage, and she ran a boardinghouse in Pawhuska.

The private eyes suspected that Savage and Smitherman, as well as other conspirators, had arranged Whitehorn's killing in order to steal his headright and fortune. Over time, many of the investigators came to believe that Hattie Whitehorn, who had quickly spent some of her husband's fortune after his death, was also in on the scheme. An informant told a private eye that there was no doubt Hattie was a "prime mover in killing Charley Whitehorn."

An undercover private eye was placed in Hattie's boarding-house. "He could hear what was said over the telephone," another detective wrote in his report. Meanwhile, Minnie Savage's sister became a great source of information for investigators. She shared that she had seen what was likely the murder weapon. "Minnie was making up the bed and the gun was under the pillow. . . . It was a rather large gun, dark color." Despite all this, the private detectives somehow failed to get enough evidence to prosecute any of the suspects—or perhaps the private eyes were bought off.

When the first federal agents from the Bureau of Investigation began to work the case, in 1923, they also concluded that Savage, Smitherman, and Hattie Whitehorn were responsible for the murder. "From the evidence thus far gathered," an agent wrote, it appeared that "Hattie Whitehorn caused him to be murdered in order that she might get hold of his estate." Hattie had denied any involvement in the crime but told one agent, "I am as smart as you are. I have been warned about you." She added, "You are just getting into my confidence, and if I tell you, you will send me to the electric chair."

By that point, there had been several disturbing twists in the case. Hattie's new husband, Smitherman, had fled the country for Mexico, taking her car and a chunk of her money. Then a man named J. J. Faulkner—whom an agent called an "unprincipled, hypocritical crook"—began blackmailing Hattie with information that she'd shared with him about her role in the murder. (One of Hattie's sisters was heard insulting Faulkner and yelling at him that he should stop threatening Hattie in order to get money. Faulkner snapped back that he knew all about Hattie and the murder, and she'd better be careful about how she spoke to him.) In a report, Agent John Burger and a colleague stated, "We are strongly of the belief that Faulkner has succeeded in obtaining some sort of confession from Hattie, and is using it to make her do as he sees fit, by threatening her with prosecution and exposing her, and that his object is to gain control of her . . . property at her death, and get money from her while she lives."

Before long, Hattie became incurably sick. Agents noted that she seemed "liable to die at any time." Remarkably, none of the agents expressed suspicion over the nature of her illness, even though so many victims during the Reign of Terror had been poisoned. Faulkner had a wife, and she told agents that he was "refusing to allow Hattie to be sent to a hospital . . . in order to keep her under his influence." According to Hattie's sisters, Faulkner had begun to steal money from her while she was "under the influence of a narcotic."

Her sisters eventually managed to get Hattie admitted to a hospital. Agents, believing that she was about to die, tried to persuade her to give a confession. But Hattie never revealed anything further. Not surprisingly, she recovered from her mysterious illness after being removed from Faulkner's grip.

By the time Tom White showed up to begin his investigation, in 1925, the bureau had all but dropped the Whitehorn case.

Agent Burger wrote that it was an "isolated murder," unconnected to the Reign of Terror killings. The case did not fit into the bureau's dramatic theory of the murders: that a lone mastermind was responsible for all the killings, and that when William Hale and his henchmen were captured, the case of the Osage murders was solved. Yet, in hindsight, the fact that Hale appeared to have played no role in the Whitehorn plot was the very reason the killing was so important. Like the suspicious death of Kathryn Red Corn's grandfather, the plot against Charles Whitehorn—and the failed plot against his widow—exposed a secret history of the Reign of Terror. Hale was not the only evil killer targeting the Osage.

25

The Lost Manuscript

YOU MUST GO OUT THERE AND SEE WHAT IS HAPPENING,"
Kathryn Red Corn told me when I visited the Osage Nation again,
in June 2015. And so, following her directions, I drove through
Pawhuska and headed west across the prairie, through the tall
grasses, until I saw what she'd vividly described to me: a field of
metallic towers invading the sky. Each one stood 420 feet tall, the
equivalent of a thirty-story skyscraper, and had three whirring
blades. A single blade was as long as the wings of an airliner. The
towers were part of a windmill farm, which spanned more than
eight thousand acres and was expected to eventually supply electricity to some forty-five thousand homes in Oklahoma.

More than a hundred years after oil was discovered in Osage
territory, a new revolutionary source of energy was transforming
the region. But this time the Osage viewed it as a threat to their
underground reservation.

"Did you see them?" Red Corn said of the wind turbines when
I returned. "This company came in here and put them up without
our permission." The federal government, representing the Osage

The new windmill farm built above the Osage's underground reservation

Nation, had filed a lawsuit against Enel, the Italian energy company that owned the wind farm. Citing the terms of the 1906 Allotment Act, the lawsuit alleged that because the company had excavated limestone and other minerals while building the foundations for the turbines, it needed the Osage's approval to continue operations. Otherwise, Enel was violating the Osage's sovereignty over their underground reservation. The company insisted that it wasn't in the mining business, and thus did not need a lease from the Osage.

On July 10, 2015, at dawn, a chief and two dozen members of the Osage Nation gathered beneath the windmills for a prayer to Wah'Kon-Tah. As the first sunlight burned through the thin blue mist and radiated off the blades, a prayer leader said that the Osage were a "humble people, asking for your help."

Not long after, a court sided with Enel, saying that the "defendants have not marketed or sold minerals or otherwise engaged in mineral development. As a result, they are not required to obtain a lease." Plans were already under way for a second wind farm in the county.

New government environmental regulations for oil drilling were having an even more profound effect on the Osage's underground reservation. The regulations, issued in 2014, made it too expensive for many people to drill. An oil producer told a reporter, "For the first time in a hundred years, there's no drilling in Osage County."

I continued researching the murders, but there were fewer archives to examine, fewer documents to find. Then one day at the public library in Pawhuska, I noticed, tucked amid volumes of Osage history, a spiral-bound manuscript titled "The Murder of Mary DeNoya-Bellieu-Lewis." It appeared handmade, its pages printed on a computer. According to an introductory note, dated January 1998, the manuscript was compiled by Anna Marie Jefferson, the great-great-grandniece of Mary Lewis. "My great-grandmother . . . first told me the story about Mary," Jefferson wrote. She must have left a copy of the manuscript with the library, determined that the story not fall into the chasm of lost history.

I sat down and began to read. Mary Lewis, who was born in 1861, was an allotted member of the tribe. "With this money she was able to enjoy a prosperous life," Jefferson wrote. Lewis had two marriages that ended in divorce, and in 1918, in her midfifties, she was raising a ten-year-old adopted child. That summer, Lewis took her daughter on a trip to Liberty, Texas, a small city about forty miles from Houston, on the banks of the Trinity River. Lewis was accompanied by two white men: Thomas Middleton, who was a friend, and a companion of his. With Lewis's money, they bought a houseboat and stayed on the river. Then, on August 18, Lewis vanished. When authorities failed to investigate, her family hired a private detective. He discovered that after Lewis's disappearance, Middleton had pretended to be her adopted son in order to cash several of her checks. In January 1919, after the police detained Middleton and his companion, the private detective interrogated them. He told Middleton that he would "one hundred times rather find the old lady alive than dead," adding, "If you can give any information to locate her, that will help you."

Middleton insisted that he didn't know where she had gone. "I am not a bit afraid," he said.

He and his friend kept quiet. But two witnesses revealed that on the day Lewis disappeared, they had seen, a few miles from her houseboat, a car heading toward a snake-infested swamp. On January 18, investigators, with their pant legs rolled up, began to search the thick vegetation of the swamp. A reporter said that one of the lawmen had "scarcely stepped in the water of the bayou" before discovering Mary's body.

Middleton's companion confessed to killing Lewis, but he said it was Middleton's idea. After Lewis was dead, the plan was to use a female associate to pretend to be Lewis so that the friends could collect the headright payments. (This strategy was not unique— bogus heirs were a common problem.) Later that year, Middleton was convicted of murder and received a death sentence.

"There was a point in Mary's family that they were relieved the ordeal was over," Jefferson wrote. "However, the feeling of satisfaction would be followed by disbelief and anger." Middleton's sentence was changed to life in prison. Then, after he had served only six and a half years, he was pardoned by the governor of Texas. Middleton had a girlfriend, and Lewis's family believed that she had bribed authorities. "The murderer had gotten only a slap on the hand," Jefferson wrote.

After I finished reading the manuscript, I kept returning to one detail: she had been killed for her headright in 1918. According to most historical accounts, the Osage Reign of Terror spanned from the spring of 1921, when William Hale had Anna Brown murdered, to January 1926, when Hale was arrested. So Mary Lewis's murder meant that the killings over headrights had begun at least three years earlier than was widely assumed. And if Kathryn Red Corn's grandfather was poisoned in 1931, then the killings had also continued long after Hale's arrest.

These two cases showed that the Osage murders for their headrights were not the result of a single conspiracy orchestrated by Hale. He might have led the bloodiest and longest killing spree. But there were countless other killings—killings that were not included in the official victim count. And unlike the cases of Mary Lewis or Mollie Burkhart's family members, they were never investigated or even classified as homicides.

26

Blood Cries Out

I RETURNED TO THE ARCHIVES IN FORT WORTH AND RE-
sumed searching through the endless musty boxes and files that
had been wheeled on a cart into the small reading room where I
worked. I had stopped believing I would discover some hidden answer key that would unlock the secrets of the past.

Then, in one of the boxes, I found a tattered, fabric-covered logbook from the Office of Indian Affairs listing the names of guardians during the Reign of Terror. Written out by hand, the logbook
included the name of each guardian and, underneath, a list of his
Osage wards. If a ward passed away while under guardianship, a
single word was usually scrawled by his or her name: "Dead."

I searched for the name of H. G. Burt, the suspect in W. W.
Vaughan's killing. The log showed that he was the guardian of
George Bigheart's daughter and four other Osage. Beside the name
of one of these wards was the word "Dead." I then looked up Scott
Mathis, the owner of the Big Hill Trading Company. According to
the log, he had been the guardian of nine Osage, including Anna
Brown and her mother, Lizzie. As I went down the list, I noticed

that in addition to Anna and Lizzie, a third Osage Indian had died under Mathis's guardianship. And so had a fourth, and a fifth, and a sixth. Altogether, of his nine listed wards, seven had died. And at least two of these deaths were known to be murders.

I began to scour the log for other Osage guardians around this time. One had eleven Osage wards, eight of whom had died. Another guardian had thirteen wards, more than half of whom had been listed as dead. And one guardian had five wards, all of whom died. And so it went, on and on. The shocking number of dead wards could not have all happened naturally. Because most of these cases had never been investigated, however, it was impossible to determine precisely how many of the deaths were suspicious, let alone who might be responsible for any foul play.

But there were strong hints of widespread murder. In the FBI records, I found a mention of Anna Sanford, one of the names I had seen in the logbook with the word "Dead" written next to it. Though her case was never listed as a homicide, agents had clearly suspected poisoning.

Another Osage ward, Hlu-ah-to-me, had officially died of tuberculosis. But in the files was a telegram from an informant to the U.S. attorney claiming that Hlu-ah-to-me's guardian had deliberately denied her treatment and refused to send her to a hospital for care. Her guardian knew the hospital "was the lone place she could live, and if she stayed in Gray Horse she must die." The informant added that after her death, the guardian put himself in charge of her valuable estate.

In yet another case, the 1926 death of an Osage man named Eves Tall Chief was linked to alcohol. But witnesses testified at the time that he never drank and had been poisoned. "Members of the family of the dead man were frightened," an article from 1926 said.

Even when an Osage ward was mentioned as being alive in the log, it did not mean that he or she had not been targeted. The Osage ward Mary Elkins was considered the wealthiest member of the tribe because she had inherited more than seven headrights. On May 3, 1923, when Elkins was twenty-one, she married a second-rate white boxer. According to a report from an official at the Office of Indian Affairs, her new husband then locked her in their house, whipped her, and gave her "drugs, opiates, and liquor in an attempt to hasten her death so that he could claim her huge inheritance." In her case, the government official stepped in, and she survived. An investigation uncovered evidence that the boxer had not acted alone but had been part of a conspiracy of local citizens. Though the government official pushed for their prosecution, no one was ever charged, and the identities of the citizens were never revealed.

Then there was the case of Sybil Bolton, an Osage woman from Pawhuska who was under the guardianship of her white stepfather. On November 7, 1925, Bolton—whom a local reporter described as "one of the most beautiful girls ever reared in the city"—was found with a fatal bullet in her chest. Her death, at twenty-one, was reported by her stepfather to be a suicide, and the case was quickly closed. In 1992, Bolton's grandson Dennis McAuliffe Jr., an editor at the *Washington Post*, had investigated her death after discovering many contradictions and lies in the official account. As he shared in a memoir, *The Deaths of Sybil Bolton*, much of her headright money was stolen. And the evidence suggested that she had been assassinated outdoors, on her lawn, with her sixteen-month-old baby—McAuliffe's mother—beside her. According to the log, her guardian had four other Osage wards. They had also died.

The real number of Osage murders was undoubtedly higher

than the bureau's estimate of twenty-four. And while the bureau had closed its investigation after catching Hale and his henchmen, it was clear that at least some agents knew many more homicides had been systematically covered up. An agent described, in a report, just one of the ways the killers did this: "In connection with the mysterious deaths of a large number of Indians, the perpetrators of the crime would get an Indian intoxicated, have a doctor examine him and pronounce him intoxicated . . . and after the doctor's departure the [killers] would inject an enormous amount of morphine under the armpit of the drunken Indian, which would result in his death. The doctor's certificate would subsequently read 'death from alcoholic poison.'"

Others in Osage County noted that suspicious deaths were routinely blamed on "consumption," "wasting illness," or "causes unknown." Investigators who have since looked into the murders believe that the Osage death toll was in the several dozens, if not the hundreds. To get a better sense of just how many Osage were victims, McAuliffe looked at the *Authentic Osage Indian Roll Book,* which lists the deaths of many of the original allotted members of the tribe. He found that from 1907 to 1923 the Osage death rate was significantly higher than the national death rate for whites. "By all rights, their higher standard of living should have brought the Osages a *lower* death rate than America's whites," McAuliffe wrote. "Yet Osages were dying at more than one-and-a-half times the national rate."

The historian Louis F. Burns observed, "I don't know of a single Osage family which didn't lose at least one family member because of the head rights." And at least one bureau agent who left the case before White's arrival had realized that there was a culture of killing. In an interview with an informant, the agent was recorded as saying, "There are so many of these murder cases. There are hundreds and hundreds."

Even cases known to the bureau had hidden dimensions. During one of my last visits to the reservation, in June 2015, I went to the Osage Nation Court, where, in many criminal cases, the Osage now mete out their own justice. An Osage lawyer had told me that the Reign of Terror was "not the end of our history," adding, "Our families were victims of this conspiracy, but we're not victims."

In one of the courtrooms, I met Marvin Stepson. An Osage man in his seventies, he was serving as the chief trial court judge. He was the grandson of William Stepson, the steer-roping champion who had died of suspected poisoning in 1922.

Marvin Stepson is the grandson of William Stepson, who was a victim of the Reign of Terror.

Authorities never prosecuted anyone for Stepson's murder, but they came to believe that Kelsie Morrison—the man who had killed Anna Brown—was responsible. By 1922, Morrison had divorced his Osage wife. After Stepson's death, he married Stepson's widow, Tillie, making himself the guardian of her two children. One of his associates told the bureau that Morrison had admitted that he had killed Stepson so that he could marry Tillie and get control of her estate.

Stepson's death was usually included in the official tally of murders during the Reign of Terror. But as I sat with Marvin on one of the wooden courtroom benches, he revealed that his grandfather was not the family's only victim. After marrying Morrison, Tillie grew suspicious of him, especially after her new husband was overheard talking about the effects of the poison strychnine. Tillie confided to her lawyer that she wanted to keep Morrison from inheriting her estate and to cancel his guardianship of her children. But in July 1923, before she could make these changes, she, too, died of suspected poisoning.

Morrison stole much of her fortune. According to letters that he wrote, he planned to sell a portion of the estate he had swindled to none other than H. G. Burt, the banker who appeared to have been involved in the killing of W. W. Vaughan. Tillie's death was never investigated, though an associate said Morrison had admitted to him that he had killed her and asked him why he didn't get an "Indian squaw" and do the same. Marvin Stepson, who had spent years researching what had happened to his grandparents, told me, "Kelsie murdered them both, and left my father an orphan."

And that was not the end of the plot. After William Stepson and Tillie died, Marvin's father, who was three years old at the time, and his nine-year-old half sister became the next targets. In 1926, Morrison sent a note to William Hale while serving time in prison for killing Anna Brown. The error-filled note, which was intercepted by guards, read, "Bill, you know Tillies kids are going to have 2 or 3 hundred thousand dollars in a few years, and I have those kids adopted. How can I get possession or control of that money when I get out. You know I belive I can take these kids out of the State and they cant do a dam thing . . . they Could not get me for Kidnapping." It was feared that Morrison planned to kill both children. An Osage scholar once observed, "Walking through an Osage cemetery and seeing the gravestones . . . of young people who died in the period is chilling."

Marvin Stepson had the judicious air of someone who had spent his whole career serving the law. But he told me that when he first learned what Kelsie Morrison had done to his family, he feared what he might be capable of doing. "If Morrison walked in this room right now, *I'd . . . ,*" he said, his voice trailing off.

In cases where criminals escape justice, history can often at least expose them. Yet many of the Osage murders were so well hidden that is no longer possible, leaving families who lost loved ones still longing for answers. They sometimes carry out their own private investigations, which have no end. They live with doubts, suspecting dead relatives or old family friends or guardians—some of whom might be guilty and some of whom might be innocent.

When Dennis McAuliffe tried to find the killer of his grandmother, he first suspected his grandfather Harry, who was white. By then, Harry had died, but his second wife was still alive. She told McAuliffe, "You should be ashamed of yourself, Denny, digging up things about the Boltons. I can't understand why you'd want to do such a thing." And she kept repeating, "Harry didn't do it. He had nothing to do with it."

Later, McAuliffe realized that she was probably right. He came to believe, instead, that Sybil's stepfather was responsible. But there is no way to know with certainty. "I did not prove who killed my grandmother," McAuliffe wrote. "My failure was not just because of me, though. It was because they ripped out too many pages of our history. . . . There were just too many lies, too many documents destroyed, too little done at the time to document how my grandmother died." He added, "A murdered Indian's survivors don't have the right to the satisfaction of justice for past crimes, or of even knowing who killed their children, their mothers or fathers, brothers or sisters, their grandparents. They can only guess—like I was forced to."

Before I left Osage County to return home, I stopped to see Mary Jo Webb, a retired teacher who had spent decades investigating the suspicious death of her grandfather during the Reign of Terror.

Webb, who was in her eighties, lived in a single-story wooden house in Fairfax, not far from where the Smiths' home had exploded. A frail woman with a quavering voice, she invited me in and we sat in her living room. I had called earlier to arrange the visit, and she had brought out several boxes of documents that she'd gathered about the case of her grandfather Paul Peace. "He was one of those

Mary Jo Webb

victims who didn't show up in the FBI files and whose killers didn't go to prison," Webb said.

In December 1926, Peace suspected that his wife, who was white, was poisoning him. As the documents confirmed, he went to see the attorney A. W. Comstock, whom Webb described as one of the few decent white attorneys at the time. Peace wanted to get a divorce and change his will so his wife couldn't get his money. A witness later testified that Peace had claimed his wife was feeding him "some kind of poison, that she was killing him."

When I asked Webb how her grandfather might have been poisoned, she said, "There were these doctors. They were brothers. My mother said that everyone knew that's where people would get the dope to poison the Osage."

"What was their name?" I asked.

"The Shouns."

I remembered the Shouns. They were the doctors who had claimed that the bullet that had killed Anna Brown had disappeared. They were the doctors who had initially hidden that Bill Smith had given a last statement blaming William Hale, and who had arranged it so that one of them became the administrator of Rita Smith's valuable estate. They were the doctors whom investigators suspected of giving Mollie Burkhart poison instead of insulin.

Many of the cases seemed bound by a web of silent conspirators. Scott Mathis, the Big Hill Trading Company owner and the guardian of Anna Brown and her mother, was a member of the inquest into Anna's murder that failed to find the bullet. He also managed, on behalf of Mollie's family, the team of private eyes that conspicuously never cracked any of the cases.

A witness had told the bureau that after Henry Roan's murder, Hale was eager to get the body away from one undertaker and delivered to the funeral home at the Big Hill Trading Company. The murder plots depended upon doctors who falsified death certificates and upon undertakers who quickly and quietly buried bodies.

The guardian whom McAuliffe suspected of killing his grandmother was a prominent attorney working for the tribe who never interfered with the criminal networks operating under his nose. Nor did bankers, including the apparent murderer H. G. Burt, who were profiting from the criminal "Indian business." Nor did the crooked mayor of Fairfax—an ally of Hale's who also served as a guardian. Nor did countless lawmen and prosecutors and judges who had a hand in the blood money. In 1926, the Osage leader Bacon Rind remarked, "There are men amongst the whites, honest men, but they are mighty scarce."

Virtually every element of society was part of the murderous system. That is why just about any member of this society might have been responsible for the murder of Barney McBride in Washington, D.C. He threatened to bring down not only Hale but a vast criminal operation that was reaping millions and millions of dollars.

On February 23, 1927, weeks after Paul Peace vowed to disinherit and divorce the wife he suspected of poisoning him, he was killed in a hit-and-run car accident. Mary Jo Webb told me that the familiar forces had conspired to cover up her grandfather's death. "Maybe you could look into it," she said. I nodded, though I knew that in my own way I was as lost in the mist as Tom White or Mollie Burkhart had been.

Webb walked me outside, onto the front porch. It was dusk, and the fringes of the sky had darkened. The town and the street were empty, and beyond them the prairie, too.

"This land is saturated with blood," Webb said. For a moment, she fell silent, and we could hear the leaves of the blackjack trees rattling restlessly in the wind. Then she repeated, from the Bible, what God told Cain after he killed Abel: "The blood cries out from the ground."

The open prairie north of Pawhuska

Acknowledgments

I am grateful to all the people who contributed to this project, and none more so than the Osage who entrusted me with their stories and encouraged me to dig deeper. Over the years, many Osage shared with me not only their insights but also their friendship. I want to especially thank Chief Geoffrey Standing Bear, Margie Burkhart, Kathryn Red Corn, Raymond Red Corn, Joe Conner, Dolores Goodeagle, Dennis McAuliffe Jr., Elise Paschen, and Marvin Stepson as well as three people who sadly have since passed away, Jozi Tall Chief, Charles Red Corn, and Mary Jo Webb.

My research odyssey led me to many other generous individuals. The late Martha Vaughan and her cousin Melville shed light on their grandfather W. W. Vaughan. Tom White's relatives—including James M. White, Jean White, John Sheehan White, and Tom White III—were invaluable sources. So was Tom White III's spouse, Styrous, who dug up and developed archival photographs. Alexandra Sands relayed details about her grandfather James Alexander Street, who was one of the undercover operatives. Frank Parker Sr. sent me photographs and papers concerning his father, Eugene Parker—another undercover agent. Homer Fincannon and his brother, Bill, shared a wealth of information about their great-grandfather A. W. Comstock.

A number of scholars and experts patiently answered my never-ending questions. Garrick Bailey, an anthropologist who specializes in Osage culture, went beyond any reasonable bounds of duty and read the entire manuscript before publication. He is not accountable for anything I wrote, but the book is infinitely better because of him.

The FBI historian John F. Fox was a tremendous and invaluable resource. So was Dee Cordry, a former special agent with the Oklahoma State Bureau of Investigation who has spent years researching and writing about western lawmen. Garrett Hartness, Roger Hall Lloyd, and Arthur Shoemaker all shared some of their immense knowledge about the history of Osage County. David A. Ward, a professor emeritus of sociology at the University of Minnesota, provided me with a transcript of his interview with one of the prisoners who took Tom White hostage.

Louise Red Corn, the publisher of the *Bigheart Times* and an indefatigable reporter, found photographs for me and along with her husband, Raymond, was a kind host whenever I visited Osage County. Joe Conner and his wife, Carol, opened their house to me and turned it into a central place to conduct interviews. Guy Nixon spoke to me about his Osage ancestors. And Archie L. Mason, a member of the Osage Nation Congress, sent me a copy of the astonishing panoramic photograph of William Hale and the Osage.

There is no greater gift to an author than the Dorothy and Lewis B. Cullman Center for Scholars and Writers at the New York Public Library. The Cullman fellowship allowed me essential time for research and the opportunity to plumb the library's miraculous archives. Everyone at the center—Jean Strouse, Marie d'Origny, and Paul Delaverdac as well as the fellows—made for a year that was productive and fun.

The fellowship also guided me to an unexpected source. One day, Kevin Winkler, then the director of library sites and services, informed me that he knew about the Osage murders. It turned out that he was a grandson of Horace Burkhart, who was a brother of Ernest and Bryan Burkhart. Horace was considered the good brother, because he was not involved in any of the crimes. Winkler helped me to get in touch with his mother, Jean Crouch, and two of his aunts, Martha Key and Rubyane Surritte. They knew Ernest, and Key, who has sadly since died, had known Mollie as well. The three women spoke candidly about the family's history and shared with me a video recording of Ernest that was taken shortly before he died, in which he talked about Mollie and his past.

Several research institutions were critical to this project, and I am indebted to them and their staffs. Particularly, I want to thank David S. Ferriero, the archivist of the United States, as well as Greg Bognich, Jake Ersland, Christina Jones, Amy Reytar, Rodney Ross, Barbara Rust, and others at the National Archives; everyone at the Osage Nation Museum, including Lou Brock, Paula Farid, and the former director Kathryn Red Corn; Debbie Neece at the Bartlesville Area History Museum; Mallory Covington, Jennifer Day, Rachel Mosman, and Debra Osborne Spindle at the Oklahoma Historical Society; Sara Keckeisen at the Kansas Historical Society; Rebecca Kohl at the Montana Historical Society; Jennifer Chavez at New Mexico State University Library; Joyce Lyons, Shirley Roberts, and Mary K. Warren at the Osage County Historical Society Museum; Carol Taylor at the Hunt County Historical Commission; Carol Guilliams at the Oklahoma State Archives; Amanda Crowley at the Texas Ranger Hall of Fame and Museum; Kera Newby at the National Cowboy and Western Heritage Museum; and Kristina Southwell and Jacquelyn D. Reese at the University of Oklahoma's Western History Collections.

Several talented researchers assisted me in locating documents in distant corners of the country: Rachel Craig, Ralph Elder, Jessica Loudis, and Amanda Waldroupe. I can never thank enough Susan Lee, an extraordinarily gifted journalist who was indispensable to this project, helping me to ferret out records and devoting hours to fact-checking.

Aaron Tomlinson took exquisite photographs of Osage County and was a wonderful traveling companion. Warren Cohen, Elon Green, and David Greenberg are great journalists and even greater friends who provided wisdom and support throughout the process. And my friend Stephen Metcalf, who is one of the smartest writers, never tired of helping me to think through elements of the book.

At the *New Yorker,* I'm blessed to be able to draw on the advice of so many people brighter than I am, including Henry Finder, Dorothy Wickenden, Leo Carey, Virginia Cannon, Ann Goldstein, and Mary Norris. Eric Lach was a relentless fact-checker and provided keen editorial suggestions. I asked far too much of Burkhard Bilger, Tad Friend, Raffi Khatchadourian, Larissa MacFarquhar, Nick Paumgarten, and Elizabeth Pearson-Griffiths. They pored over portions of the manuscript, and in some cases all of it, and helped me to see it more clearly. Daniel Zalewski has taught me more about writing than anyone, and he spread his magical dust over the manuscript. And David Remnick has been a champion since the day I arrived at the *New Yorker,* enabling me to pursue my passions and develop as a writer.

To call Kathy Robbins and David Halpern, at the Robbins Office, and Matthew Snyder, at CAA, the best agents would not do them justice. They are so much more than that: they are allies, confidants, and friends.

As an author, I have found the perfect home at Doubleday. This book would not have been possible without my brilliant editor and publisher, Bill Thomas. He is the one who first encouraged me to pursue this subject, who guided me through the highs and lows, and who has edited and published this book with grace and wisdom. Nor would this book have been possible without the unfailing support of the late chairman of the Knopf Doubleday Publishing Group, Sonny Mehta. Nor would it have been possible without the remarkable team at Doubleday, including Todd Doughty, Suzanne Herz, John Fontana, Maria Carella, Lorraine Hyland, Maria Massey, Rose Courteau, and Margo Shickmanter.

It was Emily Easton, the co-publisher and vice president of Crown Books for Young Readers, who came up with the idea of adapting the original book to reach a new generation. Not only was she the guiding force behind this young readers' edition, but she herself spent countless hours adapting it with wisdom and sensitivity. Elizabeth Johnson contributed with essential copy edits. And because of Easton and her entire terrific team—including Cathy Bobak, Bob Bianchini, Melinda Ackell, Tim Terhune, and Claire Nist—you are now holding this book.

My family has been the greatest blessing of all. John and Nina Darnton, my in-laws, read the early manuscript not once but twice, and gave me the courage to keep going. My sister, Alison, and my brother, Edward, have been an unbreakable ballast. So have my mother, Phyllis, who offered the kinds of perfect touches to the manuscript that only she can, and my father, Victor, who recently passed away and who was, and continues to be, an inspiration.

Finally, there are those for whom my gratitude goes deeper than words can express: my children, Zachary and Ella, who have filled my house with the madness of pets and the beauty of music and the joyfulness of life, and my wife, Kyra, who has been my best reader, my greatest friend, and my eternal love.

Who's Who

A. W. Comstock: An attorney and guardian of several Osage. He assisted the authorities with investigations of the murders.

Al Spencer: A notorious Oklahoman bank robber and gang leader.

Alphonse Bertillon: A French criminologist who devised new scientific techniques for identifying criminals.

Andrew Lowe: The husband of Margie Burkhart, the granddaughter of Mollie and Ernest Burkhart.

Anna Brown: Mollie Burkhart's older sister, whose murder triggered many investigations.

Anna Burkhart: Mollie and Ernest Burkhart's younger daughter.

Asa Kirby: A thief and explosives expert who worked for Henry Grammer and was a suspect in the Reign of Terror.

Bacon Rind: A chief of the Osage people who fought to protect their rights.

Barney McBride: An oilman and friend of the Osage who traveled to Washington, D.C., to try to get federal authorities to investigate the murders.

Bessie White: Tom White's wife.

Bill Skelly: An oil baron who attended the auctions of Osage leases, which were held under the Million Dollar Elm.

Bill Smith: The husband of Rita Smith, Mollie Burkhart's sister, and a victim during the Reign of Terror.

Boxcar: An inmate at Leavenworth prison when Tom White was warden. He took White hostage during an attempted escape.

Bryan Burkhart: Ernest Burkhart's brother and a suspect in the Osage Reign of Terror.

Burt Lawson: A jailhouse informant who claimed he had information about the Osage murders.

Charles Whitehorn: An Osage man who was killed around the same time as Anna Brown.

Coley White: Tom White's brother who was sheriff of Travis County in Texas.

Colonel Ellsworth E. Walters: The auctioneer of Osage oil leases who was known for his showmanship under the Million Dollar Elm.

Curley Johnson: A partner of the outlaw Blackie Thompson and a suspect in the Osage murders.

Dennis McAuliffe Jr.: The grandson of Sybil Bolton who wrote a memoir about investigating her suspicious death.

Dick Gregg: A member of the Al Spencer Gang who refused to take part in the Reign of Terror.

Dudley White: Tom White's older brother who served as a Texas Ranger.

E. W. Marland: A wealthy oilman who attended the auctions of Osage leases and discovered Burbank—one of the highest-producing oil fields in the United States.

Elizabeth Burkhart: Mollie and Ernest Burkhart's older daughter.

Ernest Burkhart: Mollie Burkhart's second husband and William Hale's nephew.

Eves Tall Chief: A suspected victim during the Reign of Terror.

Frank Phillips: An oil baron who participated in the auction of Osage leases under the Million Dollar Elm.

Frank Smith: A member of Tom White's team investigating the Osage murders.

George Bigheart: The Osage chief James Bigheart's nephew and a victim during the Reign of Terror.

H. G. Burt: A corrupt banker and guardian in Osage County.

Harry Sinclair: An oil baron who attended the auctions of Osage leases and committed bribery in the Teapot Dome scandal.

Harve M. Freas: The sheriff of Osage County during the Reign of Terror.

Hattie Whitehorn: Charles Whitehorn's widow, who was suspected of plotting against him.

Henry Grammer: A rodeo star and infamous outlaw who controlled the illegal distribution of whiskey in Osage County and was a suspect in the Reign of Terror.

Henry Roan: An Osage man killed during the Reign of Terror.

Hlu-ah-to-me: A suspected victim of the Reign of Terror.

Irvin "Blackie" Thompson: A dangerous robber who gave information to authorities during their investigation into the Osage murders.

J. C. "Doc" White: Tom White's brother who was a former Texas Ranger and one of the Bureau of Investigation's frontier-style agents known as the Cowboys.

J. Edgar Hoover: The controversial new director of the Bureau of Investigation who was responsible for assigning Tom White to assemble and lead the team probing the Osage murder cases.

James Bigheart: One of the Osage's greatest chiefs, who helped to negotiate the deal that gave the tribe control of all the oil under their land.

James "Cowboy" Burkhart: Mollie and Ernest Burkhart's son.

James and David Shoun: Brothers who were doctors in Osage County and suspected of playing a part in the Reign of Terror.

Jean Paul Getty: An oil baron who operated in Osage County and went on to found Getty Oil Company.

Joe Allen: A man questioned by authorities in Anna Brown's murder.

Joe Bates: An Osage victim during the Reign of Terror.

John Burger: A bureau agent and a member of Tom White's team.

John Cobb: Mollie Burkhart's third husband.

John Florer: A Kansas frontiersman who established the first trading post in Gray Horse.

John Leahy: A lawyer who helped prosecute some of the key suspects in the Osage murders.

John Palmer: A celebrated lawyer and advocate for the Osage people.

John Ramsey: A cow rustler who worked for the outlaw Henry Grammer and was involved in the violence against the Osage.

John Wren: A bureau agent and an American Indian who was part of Tom White's investigative team.

Kathryn Red Corn: A director of the Osage Nation Museum.

Kelsie Morrison: A bootlegger and drug dealer who became an informant for the Bureau of Investigation.

LeRoy Smitherman: Hattie Whitehorn's unscrupulous second husband.

Lizzie: Mollie Burkhart's mother, who was a victim during the Reign of Terror.

Louis F. Burns: A respected Osage historian.

Margie Burkhart: Mollie Burkhart's granddaughter.

Martha Vaughan: W. W. Vaughan's granddaughter.

Marvin Stepson: William Stepson's grandson.

Mary Elkins: One of the wealthiest Osage, who was targeted during the Reign of Terror.

Mary Jo Webb: An Osage elder and teacher who investigated the suspicious death of her grandfather, Paul Peace, during the Reign of Terror.

Mary Lewis: An Osage victim during the Reign of Terror.

Melville Vaughan: The grandson of W. W. Vaughan and Martha Vaughan's cousin.

Minnie Savage: The owner of a Pawhuska boardinghouse who was believed to be involved in one of the plots against the Osage.

Minnie Smith: Mollie Burkhart's younger sister.

Mollie Burkhart: An Osage woman who, along with her family, became a prime target during the Reign of Terror.

Ne-kah-e-se-y: Mollie Burkhart's father, who was later known as Jimmy.

Nettie Brookshire: Rita and Bill Smith's servant, who became a victim during the Reign of Terror.

Oda Brown: Anna Brown's former husband.

Rita Smith: Mollie Burkhart's sister and a victim during the Reign of Terror.

Robert Emmett White: Tom White's father and the sheriff of Travis County in Texas.

Rose Osage: A suspect in Anna Brown's murder.

Scott Mathis: The owner of the Big Hill Trading Company and the guardian of several murdered Osage.

Sybil Bolton: A suspected victim during the Reign of Terror.

Tillie Stepson: The widow of William Stepson, who later married Kelsie Morrison.

Tom White: The agent who led an undercover investigation into the Osage murders.

W. W. Vaughan: A local attorney who tried to help track down the killers of the Osage.

Wah-Ti-An-Kah: An Osage chief who suggested his people purchase land in what is now part of Oklahoma.

Warren G. Harding: The U.S. president whose aides became entangled in the Teapot Dome scandal.

William K. Hale: Ernest Burkhart's uncle and a powerful cattle baron who became known as the King of the Osage Hills.

William Stepson: An Osage champion steer-roper who was a victim during the Reign of Terror.

Glossary

Accomplice: A person who assists in the commission of a crime.

Alibi: The statement given by a potential suspect about where they were at the time their alleged crime was committed, usually to establish their innocence.

Allegations: A claim or charge that has not yet been proven true.

Allotment: The share of surface land given to each Osage on the tribal roll, after the U.S. government had forced the breakup of their communal reservation.

Appeal: The process for a convicted criminal to formally request a higher judicial authority to overturn their guilty sentence after reviewing their case for potential factual or legal errors.

Attorney General: The head of the Department of Justice.

Autopsy: A thorough examination of a body to determine the cause of death.

Black Gold: Another name for oil.

Boomtown: A town enjoying very fast growth in business success and population.

Breechcloth: A type of traditional clothing once worn by Osage men that ties around the waist and extends down to cover the upper legs.

Bureau of Investigation: A division of the Department of Justice responsible for investigating federal crimes. It later became known as the Federal Bureau of Investigation (FBI).

Coroner: A public official in charge of investigating suspicious or unexplained deaths.

Deliberations: The secret discussions and debates between jurors at the end of a trial, as they attempt to agree upon the defendant's guilt or innocence based on the evidence.

Deserter: A soldier, sailor, or any member of the military who leaves his or her assigned post without permission.

Desperado: A bold or violent criminal, most often associated with the western United States in the nineteenth and early twentieth centuries.

Double Agent: A spy who pretends to be working for one side while secretly working on behalf of its enemy.

Felony: A serious crime that comes with severe penalties ranging from at least a year and up to a lifetime in federal prison.

First-Degree Murder: The most serious of all murder charges, reserved for murders that were intentionally planned in advance.

Forensics: The application of scientific knowledge to help solve crimes.

Grand Jury: A group of citizens who listen to evidence and ask questions to help determine whether criminal charges should be brought against a suspect. The proceedings of a grand jury investigation are kept secret both so that future trial juries may hear the case without bias and to protect the rights of a suspect who is not charged with a crime.

Headright: An individual's portion of the money from the Osage Nation's oil income, which could only be inherited, not sold.

Immunity (from prosecution): When a person is protected from criminal charges in return for giving important information that could help solve a more serious crime.

Informant: A person who shares inside knowledge of a group or organization with law enforcement.

Inquest: A formal investigation led by a coroner into how someone died.

Juror: A member of a jury, which is a group of people responsible for deciding guilt or innocence in a legal case.

Justice of the Peace: A local official with the power to judge minor civil and criminal cases.

Lynching: Deadly mob violence, most frequently in the form of hanging, without legal authority.

Missionary: A person who devotes his or her life to spreading religious beliefs to others.

Moccasins: A soft leather shoe traditionally worn by many Native Americans.

Mole: A person who poses as part of the group they are investigating to collect evidence against them.

Moonshine: Any kind of alcohol that is made secretly and illegally.

Obstruction of Justice: When someone interferes with a government's ability to investigate or prosecute a crime.

Oil Derrick: A machine used to draw oil out of the ground.

On the Take: Slang term for taking bribes.

Pardoned: When someone who is guilty of a crime is protected from the consequences of that crime.

Parole: The early release of a prisoner based on their agreeing to certain conditions. They can be returned to prison to serve the rest of their sentence if they don't fulfill all the agreed-upon terms.

Per Capita: A Latin phrase that means "by head" or "per person." It is often used as a way to measure the average wealth of members of a population.

Perjury: The intentional act of lying under oath, which is a crime.

Posse: A large group with a common interest or purpose, often called by law enforcement to search for an alleged criminal.

Preliminary Hearing: When the prosecution and defense attorney demonstrate to the judge that they have enough evidence to force a defendant to stand trial.

Prohibition: The period of time between 1920 and 1933, when transporting, possessing, or drinking intoxicating alcohol was made illegal by the passing of the Eighteenth Amendment to the U.S. Constitution. The Twenty-First Amendment reversed it after Prohibition ended up creating criminal empires and casual lawbreaking.

Prosecutor: A lawyer in a criminal case who tries to prove that the accused person is guilty.

Roustabout: An unskilled laborer in an oil field. It also came to mean somebody who stirs up trouble.

Scapegoat: Someone who is wrongly blamed for others' faults or wrongdoings.

Speakeasy: A secret bar serving illegal liquor during the Prohibition era.

Stickup Man: A thief who uses a gun to rob individuals or institutions like banks.

Testimony: Evidence from a witness who has sworn a legal oath to tell the truth.

Tomahawk: A type of ax once used by Native American warriors.

Verdict: The jury's decision of guilt or innocence at the end of a trial.

Wildcatter: A person who drills for oil wells where none have been found before.

A Note on the Sources

This book is based extensively on primary and unpublished materials. They include thousands of pages of FBI files, secret grand jury testimony, court transcripts, informants' statements, logs from private eyes, pardon and parole records, private correspondence, an unpublished manuscript co-authored by one of the detectives, diary entries, Osage Tribal Council records, oral histories, field reports from the Bureau of Indian Affairs, congressional records, Justice Department memos and telegrams, crime scene photographs, wills and last testaments, guardian reports, and the murderers' confessions. These materials were drawn from archives around the country. Some records were obtained through the Freedom of Information Act, while FBI documents that had been redacted by the government were provided to me, uncensored, by a former law-enforcement officer. Moreover, several private papers came directly from descendants, among them the relatives of the victims of the Reign of Terror; further information was often gleaned from my interviews with these family members.

I also benefited from a number of contemporaneous newspaper dispatches and other published accounts. In reconstructing the history of the Osage, I would have been lost without the seminal works of two Osage writers: the historian Louis F. Burns and the prose poet John Joseph Mathews. In addition, I was greatly aided by the research of Terry Wilson, a former professor of Native American studies at the University of California, Berkeley, and Garrick Bailey, a leading anthropologist of the Osage.

The writers Dennis McAuliffe Jr., Lawrence Hogan, Dee Cordry, and the late Fred Grove had conducted their own research into the Osage murders, and their work was enormously helpful. So was Verdon R. Adams's short biography *Tom White: The Life of a Lawman.* Finally, in detailing the history of J. Edgar Hoover and the formation of the FBI, I drew on several excellent books, particularly Curt Gentry's *J. Edgar Hoover,* Sanford J. Ungar's *FBI,* Richard Gid Powers's *Secrecy and Power,* and Bryan Burrough's *Public Enemies.*

In the bibliography, which can be found in the adult version of the book, I have delineated these and other important sources. If I was especially indebted to one, I tried to cite it in the notes as well. Anything that appears in the text between quotation marks comes from a court transcript, diary, letter, or some other account. These sources are cited in the notes, except in cases where it is clear that a person is speaking directly to me.

Archival and Unpublished Sources

Comstock Family Papers, private collection of Homer Fincannon

FBI	Federal Bureau of Investigation declassified files on the Osage Indian murders
FBI/FOIA	Federal Bureau of Investigation records obtained under the Freedom of Information Act
HSP	Historical Society of Pennsylvania
KHS	Kansas Historical Society
LOC	Library of Congress
NARA-CP	National Archives and Records Administration, College Park, Md.
	Record Group 48, Records of the Office of the Secretary of the Interior
	Record Group 60, Records of the Department of Justice
	Record Group 65, Records of the Federal Bureau of Investigation
	Record Group 129, Records of the Bureau of Prisons
	Record Group 204, Records of the Office of the Pardon Attorney
NARA-DC	National Archives and Records Administration, Washington, D.C.
	Records of the Center for Legislative Archives
NARA-FW	National Archives and Records Administration, Fort Worth, Tex.
	Record Group 21, Records of District Court of the United States, U.S. District Court for the Western District
	Record Group 75, Records of the Bureau of Indian Affairs, Osage Indian Agency
	Record Group 118, Records of U.S. Attorneys, Western Judicial District of Oklahoma
NMSUL	New Mexico State University Library
	Fred Grove Papers, Rio Grande Historical Collections
OHS	Oklahoma Historical Society
ONM	Osage Nation Museum
OSARM	Oklahoma State Archives and Records Management
PPL	Pawhuska Public Library
SDSUL	San Diego State University Library
TSLAC	Texas State Library and Archives Commission
UOWHC	University of Oklahoma Western History Collections

Vaughan Family Papers, private collection of Martha and Melville Vaughan

Notes and Selected Bibliography

Key to abbreviations

n.p.: not published

n.d.: no date

quoted in: words cited are from other speakers, not the author of the work

citations in "name" to "name" format are from a variety of correspondence, such as letters and telegrams.

A complete bibliography can be found in the adult edition of *Killers of the Flower Moon*.

1: THE VANISHING

3   "gods had left": Mathews, John Joseph. *Talking to the Moon*. Norman: University of Oklahoma Press, 1981: 61.

3   On May 24: My description of Anna Brown's disappearance and the last day she visited Mollie Burkhart's house is drawn primarily from the testimony of witnesses who were present. For more information, see records at NARA-CP and NARA-FW.

4   "peculiar wasting illness": Quoted in Franks, Kenny Arthur. *The Osage Oil Boom*. Oklahoma City: Western Heritage Books, 1989: 117.

4   "Lo and behold": Sherman Rogers, "Red Men in Gas Buggies," *Outlook*, Aug. 22, 1923.

5   "circle of expensive": Elmer T. Peterson, "Miracle of Oil," *Independent* (N.Y.), April 26, 1924.

6   "even whites": Estelle Aubrey Brown, "Our Plutocratic Osage Indians," *Travel*, Oct. 1922.

6   "He was not the kind": *Oklahoma City Times*, Oct. 26, 1959.

9   Ernest's brothers, Bryan: His birth name was Byron, but he went by Bryan. To avoid confusion, I have simply used Bryan throughout the text.

11   "She was drinking": Grand jury testimony of Martha Doughty, NARA-FW.

12   "Do you know": Grand jury testimony of Anna Sitterly, NARA-FW.

12   "I thought the rain": Ibid.

12   Fueling the unease: Information concerning Whitehorn's disappearance is drawn largely from local newspapers and from private detectives and FBI reports at the National Archives.

12   Friendly and funny: It should be noted that one newspaper account

says that Whitehorn's wife was part Cherokee. However, the FBI files refer to her as part Cheyenne.

12 "popular among": *Pawhuska Daily Capital*, May 30, 1921.

13 "Oh Papa": Quotations from the hunters come from their grand jury testimony, NARA-FW.

2: AN ACT OF GOD OR MAN?

15 A coroner's inquest: My descriptions of the inquest were drawn primarily from eyewitness testimony, including that of the Shoun brothers. See records at NARA-CP and NARA-FW.

16 "She's been shot": Grand jury testimony of Andy Smith, NARA-FW.

17 "An officer was": Quoted in Cordry, Dee. *Alive If Possible—Dead If Necessary*, Mustang, Okla.: Tate, 2005: 238.

17 "terror to evil": Thoburn, Joseph Bradfield. *A Standard History of Oklahoma*. Chicago: American Historical Society, 1916: 1833.

17 "I had the assurance": Grand jury testimony of Roy Sherrill, NARA-FW.

19 Mollie relied: My description of the funeral is drawn primarily from statements by witnesses, including the undertaker, and from my interviews with descendants.

19 "devotion to his": A. F. Moss to M. E. Trapp, Nov. 18, 1926, OSARM.

19 "It was getting": Statement by A. T. Woodward, U.S. House Committee on Indian Affairs, *Modifying Osage Fund Restrictions, Hearings Before the Committee on Indian Affairs on H.R. 10328*. 67th Cong., 2nd sess., March 27–29 and 31, 1922: 103.

3: KING OF THE OSAGE HILLS

21 "TWO SEPARATE MURDER": *Pawhuska Daily Capital*, May 28, 1921.

21 "set adrift": Burns, Louis F. *A History of the Osage People*. Tuscaloosa: University of Alabama Press, 2004: 442.

22 "Someday": *Modesto News-Herald*, Nov. 18, 1928.

22 So Mollie turned: My portrait of William Hale is drawn from a number of sources, including court records, Osage oral histories, FBI files, contemporaneous newspaper accounts, Hale's correspondence, and my interviews with descendants.

22 "fight for life": Sargent Prentiss Freeling in opening statement, *U.S. v. John Ramsey and William K. Hale*, Oct. 1926, NARA-FW.

22 "He is the most": Article by Merwin Eberle, "'King of Osage' Has Had Long Colorful Career," n.p., OHS.

23 "like a leashed animal": *Guthrie Leader*, Jan. 5, 1926.

23 "high-class gentleman": Pawnee Bill to James A. Finch, n.d., NARA-CP.

23 "Some did hate": C. K. Kothmann to James A. Finch, n.d., NARA-CP.

24 "I couldn't begin": M. B. Prentiss to James A. Finch, Sept. 3, 1935, NARA-CP.

24   "I never had better": William K. Hale to Wilson Kirk, Nov. 27, 1931, ONM.

24   "We were mighty": *Tulsa Tribune,* June 7, 1926.

24   "willing to do": J. George Wright to Charles Burke, June 24, 1926, NARA-CP.

26   "How did she go": Testimony of Mollie Burkhart before tribal attorney and other officials, NARA-FW.

27   "When you brought": Coroner's inquest testimony of Bryan Burkhart, in bureau report, Aug. 15, 1923, FBI.

27   "You understand": Grand jury testimony of Ernest Burkhart, NARA-FW.

28   "the greatest criminal": Boorstin, Daniel J. *The Americans: The Democratic Experience.* New York: Vintage, 1974: 81.

29   "perhaps any": James G. Findlay to William J. Burns, April 23, 1923, FBI.

29   "the meanest man": McConal, Patrick M. *Over the Wall: The Men Behind the 1934 Death House Escape.* Austin: Eakin Press, 2000: 19.

30   "absolutely no": Private detective logs included in report, July 12, 1923, FBI.

30   "ANNA BROWN": *Pawhuska Daily Capital,* July 23, 1921.

30   "There's a lot": Quoted in Crockett, Art. *Serial Murderers.* New York: Pinnacle Books, 1993: 352.

31   "the hands of parties": *Pawhuska Daily Capital,* May 30, 1921.

32   "*Have pity*": Frank F. Finney, "At Home with the Osages," Finney Papers, UOWHC.

4: UNDERGROUND RESERVATION

33   The money had: In describing the history of the Osage, I benefited from several excellent accounts. See Burns, *History of the Osage People;* Mathews, John Joseph. *Wah'kon-Tah: The Osage and the White Man's Road.* Norman: University of Oklahoma Press, 1981; Wilson, Terry P. *The Underground Reservation: Osage Oil.* Lincoln: University of Nebraska Press, 1985; Tixier, Victor. *Tixier's Travels on the Osage Prairies.* Norman: University of Oklahoma Press, 1940; Bailey, Garrick Alan. *Changes in Osage Social Organization, 1673–1906.* Eugene: University of Oregon, 1973. I also drew on field reports and Tribal Council documents held in the Records of the Osage Indian Agency, NARA-FW.

33   "we must stand": Burns, *History of the Osage People,* 140.

33   "finest men": Ibid.

33   "It is so long": Quoted in Ambrose, Stephen E. *Undaunted Courage: Meriwether Lewis, Thomas Jefferson, and the Opening of the American West.* New York: Simon & Schuster, 2002: 343.

34   "to make the enemy": Mathews, John Joseph. *The Osages: Children of the Middle Waters.* Norman: University of Oklahoma Press, 1973: 271.

35   Lizzie also grew up: Existing records do not indicate her Osage name.

35   "industrious": Probate records of Mollie's mother, Lizzie, "Application for Certificate of Competency," Feb. 1, 1911, NARA-FW.

35   "The race is": Tixier, *Tixier's Travels on the Osage Prairies*, 191.

36   "I am perfectly": Quoted in Brown, Meredith Mason. *Frontiersman: Daniel Boone and the Making of America*. Baton Rouge: Louisiana State University Press, 2009: 245.

36   "Why don't you": Wilder, Laura Ingalls. *Little House on the Prairie*. New York: Harper & Brothers, 1935: 46–47.

36   "The question will": Quoted in Wilson, Terry P, *Underground Reservation: Osage Oil*, 18.

37   "broken, rocky": Isaac T. Gibson to Enoch Hoag, in Office of the Commissioner of Indian Affairs. *Report of the Commissioner of Indian Affairs to the Secretary of the Interior for the Year 1871*, Washington, D.C.: Government Printing Office, 1872: 906.

37   "My people": Mathews, *Wah'kon-Tah*, 33–34.

37   "The air was filled": Quoted in Burns, *History of the Osage People*, 448.

38   The biggest one: The Office of Indian Affairs was renamed the Bureau of Indian Affairs in 1947.

38   "This little remnant": Gibson to Hoag, in *Report of the Commissioner of Indian Affairs to the Secretary of the Interior for the Year 1871*, 487.

38   "It was like": Finney, James Edwin, and Joseph B. Thoburn, "Reminiscences of a Trader in the Osage Country," *Chronicles of Oklahoma* 33 (Summer 1955), 149.

39   "every buffalo dead": Quoted in Merchant, Carolyn. *American Environmental History: An Introduction*. New York: Columbia University Press, 2013: 20.

39   "We are not dogs": Mathews, *Wah'kon-Tah*, 30.

39   "Tell these gentlemen": Information on the Osage delegation, including any quotations, comes from Mathews's account in ibid., 35–38.

41   "Likewise his daughters": Frank F. Finney, "At Home with the Osages."

43   "The Indian must conform": Burns, *History of the Osage People*, 91.

44   "big, black mouth": Mathews, John Joseph. *Sundown*. Norman: University of Oklahoma Press, 1988: 23.

44   "It is impossible": Quoted in McAuliffe, Dennis. *The Deaths of Sybil Bolton: An American History*. New York: Times Books, 1994: 215–16.

45   "His ears are closed": Mathews, *Wah'kon-Tah*, 311.

47   "A RACE FOR LAND": *Daily Oklahoma State Capital*, Sept. 18, 1893.

48   "Men knocked": *Daily Oklahoma State Capital*, Sept. 16, 1893.

48   "Let him, like these whites": Quoted in Trachtenberg, Alan. *The Incorporation of America: Culture and Society in the Gilded Age*. New York: Hill and Wang, 2007: 34.

48   "great storm": *Wah-shah-she News*, June 23, 1894.

49   "to keep his finger": Russell, Orpha B. "Chief James Bigheart of the Osages," *Chronicles of Oklahoma* 32 (Winter 1954–55): 892.

49   "the most eloquent": Thoburn, *Standard History of Oklahoma*, 2048.

49   "That the oil": Quoted in U.S. Congress. House Subcommittee of the Committee on Indian Affairs. *Leases for Oil and Gas Purposes, Osage National Council, on H.R. 27726: Hearings Before a Subcommittee of the Committee on Indian Affairs.* 62nd Cong., 3rd sess., Jan. 18–21, 1913: 154.

50   Like other Osage: Many white settlers managed to finagle their way onto the roll and eventually reaped a fortune in oil proceeds that belonged to the Osage. The anthropologist Garrick Bailey estimated that the amount of money taken from the Osage was at least $100 million.

50   "Bounce, you cats": Quoted in Franks, *Osage Oil Boom*, 75.

50   "ack like tomorrow": Mathews, John Joseph. *Life and Death of an Oilman: The Career of E. W. Marland.* Norman: University of Oklahoma Press, 1989: 116.

51   "It was pioneer days": Gregory, Robert. *Oil in Oklahoma.* Muskogee, Okla.: Leake Industries, 1976: 13–14.

5: THE DEVIL'S DISCIPLES

53   "the foulness": Probate records of Anna Brown, "Application for Authority to Offer Cash Reward," NARA-FW.

53   "We've got to stop": H. L. Macon, "Mass Murder of the Osages," *West,* Dec. 1965.

54   "turned brutal crimes": Summerscale, Kate. *The Suspicions of Mr. Whicher: A Shocking Murder and the Undoing of a Great Victorian Detective.* New York: Bloomsbury, 2009: xii.

54   "depart from": Pinkerton's National Detective Agency, *General Principles and Rules of Pinkerton's National Detective Agency,* LOC.

55   "I fought in France": William G. Shepherd, "Lo, the Rich Indian!", *Harper's Monthly,* Nov. 1920.

56   That summer: Descriptions of the activities of the private eyes derive from their daily logs, which were included in bureau reports by James Findlay, July 1923, FBI.

56   "Mathis and myself": Report by Findlay, July 10, 1923, FBI.

56   "Everything was": Grand jury testimony of Anna Sitterly, NARA-FW.

57   "This call seems": Report by Findlay, July 10, 1923, FBI.

57   "General suspicion": Ibid.

58   "weakens the whole": Pinkerton's National Detective Agency, *General Principles and Rules of Pinkerton's National Detective Agency,* LOC.

59   "clue that seems": Report by Findlay, July 13, 1923, FBI.

59   "We are going": Report by Findlay, July 10, 1923, FBI.

59   "she came out": *Mollie Burkhart et al. v. Ella Rogers,* Supreme Court of the State of Oklahoma, NARA-FW.

59   "a love that": Ibid.

60   "the sacred bond": Ibid.

61   "a little baby": Grand jury testimony of Bob Carter, NARA-FW.

61   "The fact he": In proceedings of *Ware v. Beach,* Supreme Court of the State of Oklahoma, Comstock Family Papers.

63   "kind-hearted": *Washington Post,* Nov. 17, 1935.

64   "Be careful": *Washington Post,* Sept. 6, 1922.

64   "the most brutal": *Washington Post,* July 14, 1923.

64   "CONSPIRACY BELIEVED": *Washington Post,* March 12, 1925.

6: THE MILLION DOLLAR ELM

65   "There is a touch": *Ada Evening News,* Dec. 24, 1924.

65   "Come on boys": *Daily Journal-Capital,* March 29, 1928.

66   "It was not unusual": Gunther, Max. *The Very, Very Rich and How They Got That Way.* Hampshire, UK: Harriman House, 2010: 124.

66   "the oil men": Quoted in Allen, Frederick Lewis. *Only Yesterday: An Informal History of the 1920s.* New York: John Wiley & Sons, 1997: 129.

67   "I understand": Quoted in McCartney, Laton. *The Teapot Dome Scandal: How Big Oil Bought the Harding White House and Tried to Steal the Country.* New York: Random House, 2009: 113.

67   On January 18: My description of the auction is drawn from local newspaper articles, particularly a detailed account in the *Daily Oklahoman,* Jan. 28, 1923.

70   "Where will it": Shepherd, "Lo, the Rich Indian!"

70   "The Osage Indians": Brown, "Our Plutocratic Osage Indians."

71   some of the spending: For more on this subject, see Harmon, Alexandra. *Rich Indians: Native People and the Problem of Wealth in American History.* Chapel Hill: University of North Carolina Press, 2010: 181.

71   "the greatest, gaudiest": Fitzgerald, F. Scott. *The Crack-Up.* New York: New Directions, 2009: 87.

72   "The last time": Gregory, *Oil in Oklahoma,* 40.

72   "like a child": U.S. Congress. House Committee on Indian Affairs. *Modifying Osage Fund Restrictions, Hearings Before the Committee on Indian Affairs on H.R. 10328.* 67th Cong., 2nd sess., March 27–29 and 31, 1922: 73.

72   "racial weakness": From the decision in the case of *Barnett v. Barnett,* Supreme Court of Oklahoma, July 13, 1926.

72   "Every white man": H. S. Traylor to Cato Sells, in *Indians of the United States: Investigation of the Field Service,* 204.

73   "There is a great": House Committee on Indian Affairs. *Modifying Osage Fund Restrictions*, 60.

73   "We have many little": *Pawhuska Daily Capital*, Nov. 19, 1921.

73   "a flock of buzzards": Transcript of proceedings of the Osage Tribal Council, Nov. 1, 1926, ONM.

74   "bunched us": U.S. Congress. House Subcommittee of the Committee on Indian Affairs. *Indians of the United States: Investigation of the Field Service: Hearing by the Subcommittee of the Committee on Indian Affairs*, 66th Cong., 2nd sess., 1920: 281.

7: THIS THING OF DARKNESS

75   One day, two men: My description of the discovery of Roan's body and the autopsy comes from the testimony of the witnesses present, including the lawmen. For more information, see records at NARA-FW and NARA-CP.

75   "He must be drunk": Grand jury testimony of J. R. Rhodes, NARA-FW.

76   "Roan considered": Pitts Beatty to James A. Finch, Aug. 21, 1935, NARA-CP.

76   "We were good": Lamb, Arthur H. *Tragedies of the Osage Hills*. Pawhuska, Okla.: Raymond Red Corn, 2001: 178.

77   "Henry, you better": Testimony of William K. Hale, *U.S. v. John Ramsey and William K. Hale*, Oct. 1926, NARA-FW.

77   "$20 in greenback": Grand jury testimony of J. R. Rhodes, NARA-FW.

77   "HENRY ROAN SHOT": *Osage Chief*, Feb. 9, 1923.

78   So she decided: Mollie's secrecy regarding her marriage to Roan was later revealed in *U.S. v. John Ramsey and William K. Hale*, Oct. 1926, NARA-FW.

78   "Travel in any direction": *Daily Oklahoman*, Jan. 6, 1929.

79   "do away with her": Report by Findlay, July 13, 1923, FBI.

79   "paralyzing fear": Manuscript by Fred Grove with Tom White, n.p., NMSUL.

79   "dark cloak": *Manitowoc Herald-Times*, Jan. 22, 1926.

79   Bill Smith confided: My description of Bill and Rita Smith during this period and of the explosion is drawn largely from witness statements made to investigators and during court proceedings; some details have also been gleaned from local newspaper accounts and the unpublished manuscript by Grove with White. For more information, see records at NARA-CP and NARA-FW.

79   "Rita's scared": Manuscript by Grove with White, n.p., NMSUL.

79   "Now that we've moved": Ibid.

80   "expect to live": Report by John Wren, Oct. 6, 1925, FBI.

82   "It seemed that the night": Manuscript by Grove with White, n.p., NMSUL.

82   "It shook everything": Statement by Ernest Burkhart, Jan. 6, 1926, FBI.

82   "It's Bill Smith's house": Quoted in Hogan, Lawrence J. *The Osage Indian Murders: The True Story of a Multiple Murder Plot to Acquire the Estates of Wealthy Osage Tribe Members.* Frederick, Md: Amlex, 1998: 66.

84   "Come on men": *Osage Chief,* March 16, 1923.

84   "He was halloing": Grand jury testimony of David Shoun, NARA-FW.

84   "Rita's gone": Manuscript by Grove with White, n.p., NMSUL.

85   "blown to pieces": Grand jury testimony of Horace E. Wilson, NARA-FW.

85   "The time of the deed": Report by John Burger and Tom F. Weiss, Aug. 12, 1924, FBI.

85   "They got Rita": Report by Frank Smith, James Alexander Street, Burger, and J. V. Murphy, Sept. 1, 1925, FBI.

86   "should be thrown": Report by Wren, Dec. 29, 1925, FBI.

86   Amid this terrible corruption: Details of Vaughan's investigation and murder were drawn from several sources, including FBI records, newspaper accounts, the Vaughan family's private papers, and interviews with descendants.

89   "Yes, sir, and had": Grand jury testimony of Horace E. Wilson, NARA-FW.

89   "I didn't want": Grand jury testimony of C. A. Cook, NARA-FW.

90   "Lie still": Testimony of Frank Smith, included in Ernest Burkhart's clemency records, NARA-CP.

90   "a horrible monument": Bureau report titled "The Osage Murders," Feb. 3, 1926, FBI.

91   "in failing health": Mollie Burkhart's guardian records, Jan. 1925, NARA-CP.

8: DEPARTMENT OF EASY VIRTUE

95   "important message": Tom White to J. Edgar Hoover, Nov. 10, 1955, FBI/ FOIA.

96   "as God-fearing": Tom H. Tracy, "Tom Tracy Tells About—Detroit and Oklahoma," *Grapevine,* Feb. 1960.

96   "In those days": Transcript of interview with Tom White, NMSUL.

97   "bullet-spattered": Karl G. Hastedt, "White Brothers of Texas Had Notable FBI Careers," *Grapevine,* Feb. 1960.

97   During President Harding's term: For more information on J. Edgar Hoover and the early history of the FBI, see Gentry, Curt. *J. Edgar Hoover: The Man and the Secrets.* New York: W.W. Norton, 2001; Ungar, Sanford J. *FBI.* Boston: Little Brown, 1976; and Burrough, Bryan. *Public Enemies: America's Greatest Crime Wave and the Birth of the FBI, 1933–34.* New York: Penguin, 2009. For more background on the Teapot Dome scandal, see McCartney's *Teapot Dome Scandal;* Dean, John W. *Warren G. Harding.* New York: Times Books, 2004; and Stratton, David H. *Tempest*

over Teapot Dome: The Story of Albert B. Fall. Norman: University of Oklahoma Press, 1998.

100 "any continued": C. S. Weakley to Findlay, Aug. 16, 1923, FBI.

101 "responsible for failure": Hoover to W. D. Bolling, March 16, 1925, FBI.

101 "I want you": Transcript of interview with White, NMSUL.

101 "I am human": White to Hoover, Aug. 5, 1925, FBI/FOIA.

9: THE UNDERCOVER COWBOYS

104 "unbroken chain": Transcript of interview with White, NMSUL.

104 "almost universal": Report by Weiss and Burger, Aug. 12, 1924, FBI.

104 Hoover had kept in the bureau: Information on the members of Tom White's team comes largely from the agents' personnel files, which were obtained through the Freedom of Information Act; White's FBI reports, letters, and writings; newspaper accounts; and the author's interviews with descendants of the agents.

104 White first recruited: The former New Mexico sheriff was named James Alexander Street.

104 White then hired: Eugene Hall Parker was the former Texas Ranger who was part of White's undercover team.

104 "where there is": Personnel file of Parker, April 9, 1934, FBI/FOIA.

105 In addition, White: The deep undercover operative was an agent named Charles Davis.

105 "Pistol and rifle": Personnel file of Frank Smith, Aug. 13, 1932, FBI/FOIA.

105 "The Indians, in general": Report by Weiss and Burger, Dec. 31, 1923, FBI. Prior to Tom White's taking over the investigation, Burger had worked on the case with Agent Tom F. Weiss; all of Burger's reports were filed jointly with him.

106 "PROCEED UNDER COVER": Harold Nathan to Gus T. Jones, Aug. 10, 1925, FBI.

10: ELIMINATING THE IMPOSSIBLE

107 One after the other: My descriptions of the bureau's investigations into the murders come from several sources, including FBI reports; agents' personnel files; grand jury testimony; court transcripts; and White's private correspondence and writings.

107 Finally, Agent John Wren arrived: Wren also pretended at times to be representing certain cattle interests.

108 "My desk was": Grand jury testimony of Horace E. Wilson, NARA-FW.

108 "I don't know": Ibid.

108 "made a diligent": Grand jury testimony of David Shoun, NARA-FW.

108 "When you have eliminated": Doyle, Arthur Conan. *The Sign of Four.* London: Spencer Blackett, 1890: 93.

109 "I never had a quarrel": Report by Burger and Weiss, April 22, 1924, FBI.

109 "very self-contained": Ibid.

109 "Were you thick": Report by Weakley, Aug. 7, 1923, FBI.

110 "We interviewed": Report by Weiss and Burger, Feb. 2, 1924, FBI.

111 When Hoover became: The bureau's Identification Division initially collected fingerprints from files maintained by the U.S. Penitentiary in Leavenworth penitentiary and by the International Association for Chiefs of Police.

111 "the guardians of civilization": Quoted in Powers, Richard Gid. *Secrecy and Power: The Life of J. Edgar Hoover.* New York: Free Press, 1988: 150.

111 "We have his picture": Report by Weiss and Burger, Feb. 2, 1924, FBI.

112 Morrison soon reported back: Morrison initially claimed, falsely, that Rose implicated her boyfriend.

112 "Why'd you do it": Report by Weiss and Burger, Feb. 2, 1924, FBI.

112 "If he is not": Report by Weiss and Burger, Aug. 16, 1924, FBI.

11: THE THIRD MAN

114 "paid by suspects": Weiss and Burger to Burns, March 24, 1924, FBI.

115 "We old fellows": Grand jury testimony of Ed Hainey, NARA-FW.

116 "They went straight": Report by Weakley, Aug. 15, 1923, FBI.

116 "perjured himself": Report by Weiss and Burger, Jan. 8, 1924, FBI.

117 "Third man is": Report by Weiss and Burger, Jan. 10, 1924, FBI.

117 "Stop your foolishness": Ibid.

12: A WILDERNESS OF MIRRORS

118 "seen part": Report by Frank Smith, Sept. 28, 1925, FBI.

118 "handed to": Eustace Smith to Attorney General, March 15, 1925, FBI.

119 "frightened out": Report by Weiss and Burger, July 12, 1924, FBI.

119 "Look out": Report by Weiss and Burger, Aug. 16, 1924, FBI.

119 "Keep your balance": Transcript of interview with White, NMSUL.

119 "has known": Report by Weiss and Burger, Feb. 11, 1924, FBI.

120 "It is quite": Report by Weiss and Burger, April 11, 1924, FBI.

120 "shape an alibi": Grand jury testimony of Elbert M. Pike, NARA-FW.

121 "discuss this case": Report by Weiss, Nov. 19, 1923, FBI.

13: A HANGMAN'S SON

122 "I was raised": Adams, Verdon R. *Tom White: The Life of a Lawman.* El Paso: Texas Western Press, 1972: 6.

123 "If a mob attempts": *Bastrop Advertiser,* Aug. 5, 1899.

126 "Get all the evidence": Leonard Mohrman, "A Ranger Reminisces," *Texas Parade,* Feb. 1951.

126 "We had nothing": Hastedt, "White Brothers of Texas Had Notable FBI Careers."

128 "avoid killing": Adams, *Tom White,* 16.

128 "An officer who": Quoted in Parsons, Chuck. *Captain John R. Hughes: Lone Star Ranger.* Denton: University of North Texas Press, 2011: xvii.

14: DYING WORDS

131 "If Bill Smith": Grand jury testimony of David Shoun, NARA-FW.
131 "often leave": Ibid.
131 "If she says": Ibid.
131 "He never did say": Grand jury testimony of James Shoun, NARA-FW.
131 "Gentlemen, it is a mystery": Grand jury testimony of David E. Johnson, NARA-FW.
131 "You know, I only": Ibid.
131 "I would hate": Grand jury testimony of James Shoun, NARA-FW.
132 "If he did": Report of Smith, Street, Burger, and Murphy, Sept. 1, 1925, FBI.
133 "Did he know what": Grand jury testimony of David Shoun, NARA-FW.
134 "The blackest chapter": U.S. Congress. Senate Committee on Indian Affairs. *Survey of Conditions of the Indians in the U.S. Hearings Before the United States Senate Committee on Indian Affairs, Subcommittee on S. Res. 79.* 78th Cong., 1st sess., Aug. 2 and 3, 1943: 23018.
134 "shamelessly and openly": Gertrude Bonnin, "Oklahoma's Poor Rich Indians: An Orgy of Graft and Exploitation of the Five Civilized Tribes and Others," 1924, HSP.
134 "A group of traders": *St. Louis Post-Dispatch,* May 10, 1925.
135 "For her and her": Memorandum by Gertrude Bonnin, "Case of Martha Axe Roberts," Dec. 3, 1923, HSP.
135 "There is no hope": Ibid.
135 "Your money": Shepherd, "Lo, the Rich Indian!"

15: THE HIDDEN FACE

136 "controlled everything": Report by Wren, Davis, and Parker, Sept. 10, 1925, FBI.
138 "I knew the questions": *Tulsa Tribune,* Aug. 6, 1926.
138 "Absolutely": Grand jury testimony of John McLean, NARA-FW.
138 "Bill, what are you": Grand jury testimony of W. H. Aaron, NARA-FW.
138 "Hell, yes": *U.S. v. John Ramsey and William K. Hale,* Oct. 1926, NARA-FW.
139 "If I were you": Manuscript by Grove with White, n.p., NMSUL.
140 "is absolutely controlled": Report by Wright, April 5, 1923, FBI.
140 "capable of anything": Report by Weiss and Burger, Jan. 10, 1924, FBI.

16: THE QUICK-DRAW ARTIST, THE YEGG, AND THE SOUP MAN

143 "many new angles": Edwin Brown to Hoover, March 22, 1926, FBI/FOIA.
143 "a crook and": Report by Wren, Oct. 6, 1925, FBI.
144 Hoover, meanwhile, was growing impatient: For more information regarding Hoover's transformation of the bureau, see Gentry, *J. Edgar*

Hoover; Powers, *Secrecy and Power;* Burrough, *Public Enemies;* and Ungar, *FBI.* For more on the dark side of Progressivism, also see Thomas C. Leonard's journal articles "American Economic Reform in the Progressive Era" and "Retrospectives."

145 "I made peace": *Osage Chief,* July 28, 1922.

146 "Gregg is 100 percent": Report by Weiss and Burger, Aug. 12, 1924, FBI.

146 "A very small man": White to Fred Grove, June 23, 1959, NMSUL.

147 "a cold cruel": Criminal record of Dick Gregg, Jan. 9, 1925, KHS.

147 "gone places": White to Grove, June 23, 1959, NMSUL.

148 "Bill Smith and": Statement by Dick Gregg, June 8, 1925, FBI.

148 "That's not my style": Quoted in article by Fred Grove in *The War Chief of the Indian Territory Posse of Oklahoma Westerners* 2, no. 1 (June 1968).

148 "on the level": White to Grove, June 23, 1959, NMSUL.

148 "an outlaw": Ibid.

148 "Johnson knows": Report by Weiss and Burger, Aug. 14, 1924, FBI.

149 "CHEROKEES NO MATCH": *Muskogee Times-Democrat,* Aug. 5, 1909.

149 "that Indian deal": Report by Burger, Nov. 30, 1928, FBI.

151 "taking care": Grand jury testimony of John Mayo, NARA-FW.

152 "Hale knows": Report by Weiss and Burger, July 2, 1924, FBI.

152 "damned neck": Report by Weiss and Burger, Aug. 16, 1924, FBI.

152 "I'm too slick": Document titled "Osage Indian Murder Cases," July 10, 1953, FBI.

152 "like he owned": Transcript of interview with White, NMSUL.

17: THE STATE OF THE GAME

153 "We've been getting": Manuscript by Grove with White, n.p., NMSUL. In bureau records, Lawson's first name is spelled Burt; in other records, it is sometimes spelled Bert. To avoid confusion, I have used Burt throughout the text.

154 "We understand from": Manuscript by Grove with White, n.p., NMSUL.

154 "Some time around": Report by Smith and Murphy, Oct. 27, 1925, FBI.

156 "Have confession": White to Hoover, Oct. 24, 1925, FBI.

156 "Congratulations": Hoover to White, Oct. 26, 1925, FBI.

156 "Once, when he": Homer Fincannon, interview with author.

157 "not to drink": Report by Wren, Oct. 6, 1925, FBI.

157 "illness is very suspicious": Brown to Wright, July 18, 1925, NARA-CP.

158 "Understand I'm wanted": Manuscript by Grove with White, n.p., NMSUL.

158 "like a leashed": *Guthrie Leader,* Jan. 6, 1926.

160 "We all picked Ernest": Statement by Oscar R. Luhring in grand jury proceedings, NARA-FW.

160 "small-town dandy": Transcript of interview with White, NMSUL.

160 "We want to talk": Manuscript by Grove with White, n.p., NMSUL.

161 "If he didn't": Gentry, *J. Edgar Hoover,* 386.

161 "perfect": *Tulsa Tribune,* Jan. 5, 1926.

163 "Blackie, have": Grand jury testimony of Smith, Jan. 5, 1926, NARA-CP.

164 "After being so warned": Statement by Ernest Burkhart, Jan. 6, 1926, FBI.

165 "I relied on": Manuscript by Grove with White, n.p., NMSUL.

165 "Hale had told": Statement by Ernest Burkhart, Feb. 5, 1927, NARA-CP.

165 "Just a few days": Statement by Ernest Burkhart, Jan. 6, 1926, FBI.

165 "You have got": Grand jury testimony of Frank Smith, NARA-FW.

165 "All that story": Transcript of interview with White, NMSUL.

166 "When it happened": Statement by Ernest Burkhart, Jan. 6, 1926, FBI.

166 "I know who killed": Grand jury testimony of Frank Smith, NARA-FW.

166 "There's a suspect": Manuscript by Grove with White, n.p., NMSUL.

166 "like a nervy": *Tulsa Tribune,* March 13, 1926.

166 "I guess": Grand jury testimony of Frank Smith, NARA-FW.

166 "a little job": Statement by John Ramsey, Jan. 6, 1926, FBI.

167 "white people": Manuscript by Grove with White, n.p., NMSUL.

168 "Weren't you giving": Grand jury testimony of James Shoun, NARA-FW.

169 "We are all your friends": Testimony of Mollie Burkhart before tribal attorney and other officials, NARA-FW.

169 "My husband": Macon, "Mass Murder of the Osages."

170 "ever saw until": Quoted in Gregory, *Oil in Oklahoma,* 57.

170 "We have unquestioned": Manuscript by Grove with White, n.p., NMSUL.

170 "money will buy": Report by Weiss and Burger, Feb. 2, 1924, FBI.

171 "We don't think": Manuscript by Grove with White, n.p., NMSUL.

171 "I'll fight it": Ibid.

18: A TRAITOR TO HIS BLOOD

172 "an evidently": *Literary Digest,* Jan. 23, 1926.

172 "more blood-curdling": *Evening Independent,* Jan. 5, 1926.

172 "King of the Killers": Holding, "King of the Killers."

173 "Hale kept my husband": Lizzie June Bates to George Wright, Nov. 21, 1922, NARA-FW.

173 "OLD WILD WEST": *Evening Independent,* March 5, 1926.

173 "The Tragedy": White to Hoover, Sept. 18, 1926, FBI.

173 "We Indians": Bates to Wright, Nov. 21, 1922, NARA-FW.

174 "Members of the Osage": Copy of resolution by the Society of Oklahoma Indians, NARA-FW.

174 "Townspeople": *Lima News,* Jan. 29, 1926.

174 "not only useless": Brown to A. G. Ridgley, July 21, 1925, FBI.

175   "ablest legal talent": *Sequoyah County Democrat*, April 9, 1926.

176   "I never killed": Lamb, *Tragedies of the Osage Hills*, 174.

176   "not to worry, that he": Statement by Burkhart in deposition, Feb. 5, 1927, NARA-CP.

176   The bureau put: One night in December 1926, Luther Bishop, a state lawman who had assisted on the Osage murder cases, was shot and killed in his house. His wife was charged with the murder but was later acquitted by a jury. Dee Cordry, a former police investigator and an author, examined the case in his 2005 book, *Alive If Possible—Dead If Necessary*. He suspected that Hale, in a final act of revenge, ordered the killing.

176   "Kelsie said": Report by Smith, Feb. 8, 1926, FBI.

176   "get her out": Grand jury testimony of Dewey Selph, NARA-FW.

177   "We'd better": Manuscript by Grove with White, n.p., NMSUL.

177   "Before this man": White to Hoover, March 31, 1926, FBI.

177   "Whatever you do": Report by Burger, Nov. 2, 1928, FBI.

177   "bumped off": Grand jury testimony of Ernest Burkhart, NARA-FW.

177   "I'll give you": Transcript of interview with White, NMSUL.

177   "We think": White to Hoover, June 26, 1926, FBI.

177   "intentionally guilty": Wright to Burke, June 24, 1926, NARA-CP.

178   "That is all": Testimony of Mollie Burkhart before tribal attorney and other officials, NARA-FW.

178   "Dear husband": Mollie to Ernest Burkhart, Jan. 21, 1926, NARA-FW.

178   "It appeared": Manuscript by Grove with White, n.p., NMSUL.

179   "Bill, I have": Ibid.

179   "Very few, if any": White to Hoover, July 3, 1926, FBI.

179   "Seldom if ever": *Tulsa Tribune*, March 13, 1926.

180   "new and exclusive": *Bismarck Tribune*, June 17, 1926.

180   "Hale is a man": *Tulsa Tribune*, March 13, 1926.

180   "*Judge Not*": Quoted in Hogan, *Osage Indian Murders*, 195.

180   "Your honor, I demand": Manuscript by Grove with White, n.p., NMSUL.

181   "traitor to his": *Tulsa Daily World*, Aug. 20, 1926.

181   "This man is my client": *Tulsa Daily World*, March 13, 1926.

181   "He's not my attorney": Manuscript by Grove with White, n.p., NMSUL.

181   "nerve went": White to Hoover, June 5, 1926, FBI.

182   "I never did": Testimony from Ernest Burkhart's preliminary hearing, included in *U.S. v. John Ramsey and William K. Hale*, NARA-FW.

182   "Hale and Ramsey": Transcript of interview with White, NMSUL.

19: THE DOUBLE AGENT

183   "I looked back": *Tulsa Tribune*, May 30, 1926.

184   "PRISONER CHARGES": *Washington Post*, June 8, 1926.

184   "ridiculous": White to Grove, Aug. 10, 1959, NMSUL.

184 "fabrication from": White to Hoover, June 8, 1926, FBI.

184 "I'll meet the man": Manuscript by Grove with White, n.p., NMSUL.

185 "the whole damn": Kelsie Morrison testimony, in *State of Oklahoma v. Morrison*, OSARM.

185 "bump that squaw": Morrison's testimony at Ernest Burkhart's trial, later included in ibid.

186 "He raised her": Ibid.

186 "I stayed in the car alone": Statement by Katherine Cole, Jan. 31, 1926, NARA-FW.

187 "Don't look": My description of Burkhart changing his plea derives from trial coverage in local papers, Grove's nonfiction manuscript, and a 1927 letter written by John Leahy and held at the NARA-CP in Burkhart's clemency records.

187 "I'm through lying": *Tulsa Daily World*, June 10, 1926, and manuscript by Grove with White, n.p., NMSUL.

188 "I wish to discharge": *Tulsa Daily World*, June 10, 1926.

188 "I'm sick and tired": Manuscript by Grove with White, n.p., NMSUL.

189 "I feel in my heart": *Daily Journal-Capital*, June 9, 1926.

189 "Then your plea": *Tulsa Daily World*, June 10, 1926.

189 "BURKHART ADMITS": *New York Times*, June 10, 1926.

190 "That put us": Transcript of interview with White, NMSUL.

20: SO HELP YOU GOD!

191 "The stage is set": *Tulsa Tribune*, July 29, 1926.

191 "not testify against him": Report by Burger, Nov. 2, 1928, FBI.

192 "It is a question": *Tulsa Tribune*, Aug. 21, 1926.

193 "Gentlemen of the jury": *Tulsa Daily World*, July 30, 1926.

193 "the veteran of legal battles": *Tulsa Tribune*, July 29, 1926.

194 "Hale said to me": *Tulsa Daily World*, July 31, 1926.

194 "I never devised": Lamb, *Tragedies of the Osage Hills*, 179.

194 "the ruthless freebooter": *Tulsa Daily World*, Aug. 19, 1926.

194 "The richest tribe": *Daily Journal-Capital*, Aug. 20, 1926.

194 "Is there any": For this quotation and other details from the scene, see *Oklahoma City Times*, Aug. 25, 1926.

196 "I will kill": Report by H. E. James, May 11, 1928, FBI.

196 "Such practices": *Daily Oklahoman*, Oct. 8, 1926.

196 "Will you state your name": *U.S. v. John Ramsey and William K. Hale*, Oct. 1926, NARA-FW.

197 "Your wife is": Ibid.

197 "I don't work": Statement by Ernest Burkhart at his 1926 trial, NMSUL.

197 "The time now": Closing statement of Luhring, *U.S. v. John Ramsey and William K. Hale*, Oct. 1926, NARA-FW.

198 "There never has been": Ibid.

198 "Hale's face": *Daily Oklahoman*, Oct. 30, 1926.

198 "A jury has found": *Tulsa Daily World*, Oct. 30, 1926.

199 "KING OF OSAGE": *New York Times*, Oct. 30, 1926.

199 "one of the greatest": Leahy to U.S. Attorney General, Feb. 1, 1929, FBI/FOIA.

199 "if I ever get the Chance": Morrison to Hale, included in *State of Oklahoma v. Kelsie Morrison*, OSARM.

199 "Did you go out": Testimony of Bryan Burkhart, ibid.

200 "Sheriffs investigated": *St. Louis Post-Dispatch*, Nov. 4, 1926.

201 "NEVER TOLD": Newspaper article, n.p., n.d., FBI.

201 "So another": *The Lucky Strike Hour*, Nov. 15, 1932, accessed from otrr. org/.

202 "We express": Quoted in Adams, *Tom White*, 76.

202 "I hate to give up": Mabel Walker Willebrandt to Hoover, Feb. 15, 1927, FBI/FOIA.

202 "I feel that": Hoover to Willebrandt, Dec. 9, 1926, FBI/FOIA.

203 "Why, hello": *Daily Oklahoman*, n.d., and transcript of interview with White, NMSUL.

21: THE HOT HOUSE

204 "How do you raise": Adams, *Tom White*, 84.

204 "ugly, dangerous": Rudensky, Red. *The Gonif*. Blue Earth, Minn.: Piper, 1970: 32.

205 "Warden White showed": Ibid., 33.

205 White tried to improve: Believing it was imperative for prisoners to keep busy, White allowed Robert Stroud, a convicted murderer, to maintain an aviary in his cell with some three hundred canaries, and he became known as the Birdman. In a letter, Stroud's mother told White how grateful she was that someone who understood "human nature and its many weaknesses" was in a position of authority over her son.

205 "The Warden was strict": Adams, *Tom White*, 133.

205 "treated as": White to Morris F. Moore, Nov. 23, 1926, NARA-CP.

205 "It was a business": Deposition of Hale, Jan. 31, 1927, NARA-CP.

205 He allegedly arranged: Hale appealed his conviction, and in 1928 an appeals court shockingly overturned his verdict. A man who had assisted the defense team subsequently confessed that Hale had someone who had "done the fixing." But Hale was promptly tried again and convicted, as was Ramsey.

206 "IT IS FURTHER": Probate records of Mollie Burkhart, File No. 2173, NARA-FW.

206 On December: My descriptions of the escape attempt are drawn primarily from FBI records obtained through the Freedom of

Information Act; a transcript of an interview with one of the convicts that was conducted by the author David A. Ward; Tom White's letters; newspaper accounts; and Adams, *Tom White.*

208 "I know you're going": *Dunkirk Evening Observer,* Dec. 12, 1931.

208 "Shoot him": Adams, *Tom White,* 114.

208 "White asked me": *Pittsburgh Press,* Dec. 14, 1939.

209 "I am sure": *Dunkirk Evening Observer,* Dec. 12, 1931.

209 "come back": Ward, David A. *Alcatraz: The Gangster Years.* Berkeley: University of California Press, 2009: 6.

209 "The funny part": Ibid.

210 "I looked up": Quoted in Gentry, *J. Edgar Hoover,* 58.

211 "appreciate a personal": Special Agent in Charge in El Paso to Hoover, Feb. 12, 1951, FBI/FOIA.

212 "I would be glad": White to Hoover, Sept. 3, 1954, FBI/FOIA.

212 "certainly bear": Hoover to White, Sept. 9, 1954, FBI/FOIA.

213 "unjust, unfair": Wren to Hoover, Aug. 2, 1932, FBI/FOIA.

213 "I would like to keep": White to Grove, Aug. 10, 1959, NMSUL.

213 "I hope this": White to Hoover, March 20, 1958, FBI/FOIA.

213 "I am hoping": White to Grove, Jan. 4, 1960, FBI/FOIA.

214 "I am sincerely sorry": J. E. Weems to Grove, June 28, 1963, NMSUL.

214 "born on this land": White to Hoover, Feb. 15, 1969, FBI/FOIA.

214 "He died as he had lived": Adams, *Tom White,* in postscript.

22: GHOSTLANDS

217 "Stores gone": Morris, John W. *Ghost Towns of Oklahoma.* Norman: University of Oklahoma Press, 1978: 83.

218 "only shreds and tatters": Burns, *History of the Osage People,* xiv.

221 Over several weekends: For more detailed information on Osage dances, see Callahan, Alice Anne. *The Osage Ceremonial Dance I'n-Lon-Schka.* Norman: University of Oklahoma Press, 1993.

221 "To believe": Burns, *History of the Osage People,* 496.

224 "Mrs. Mollie Cobb": *Fairfax Chief,* June 17, 1937.

224 "anyone convicted": Copy of Osage Tribal Council Resolution, No. 78, Nov. 15, 1937, NARA-FW.

224 "should have been hanged": *Daily Journal-Capital,* Aug. 3, 1947.

227 "OSAGE OIL WEALTH FADING": *Literary Digest,* May 14, 1932.

228 "In five years": *Hamilton Evening Journal,* Sept. 28, 1929.

230 "*Because she died*": Paschen, Elise. *Bestiary.* Pasadena, Calif: Red Hen Press, 2009.

231 "I think somewhere": Webb-Storey, Anna. "Culture Clash: A Case Study of Three Osage Native American Families." Ed.D. thesis, Oklahoma State University, 1998: 115.

23: A CASE NOT CLOSED
235 "sufficient evidence": Report by Smith, Sept. 28, 1925, FBI.
239 "very intimate": Report by Weiss and Burger, April 11, 1924, FBI.
239 "split on the boodle": Ibid.
239 "murderer": Report by Wren, Nov. 5, 1925, FBI.
241 "I think Herb Burt": Report by Smith, April 3, 1926, FBI.

24: STANDING IN TWO WORLDS
242 "He had property": Tallchief, Maria. *Maria Tallchief: America's Prima Ballerina*. With Larry Kaplan. New York: Henry Holt, 1997: 4.
242 "firebombed and everyone": Ibid., 9.
245 "I am in perfect health": Hale to Wilson Kirk, Nov. 27, 1931, ONM.
248 "Vaughan who is": Report by Findlay, July 13, 1923, FBI.
248 "shrewd, immoral": Report by Burger, Aug. 12, 1924, FBI.
249 "prime mover": Report by Findlay, July 13, 1923, FBI.
249 "He could hear": Ibid.
249 "Minnie was making": Ibid.
249 "From the evidence": Report by Burger, Aug. 12, 1924, FBI.
249 "I am as smart": Report by Burger, Aug. 13, 1924, FBI.
250 "unprincipled, hypocritical": Report by Weiss and Burger, Jan. 10, 1924, FBI.
250 "We are strongly": Ibid.
250 "liable to die": Report by Weiss and Burger, Dec. 26, 1923, FBI.
250 "refusing to allow": Report by Weiss and Burger, Jan. 2, 1924, FBI.
250 "under the influence": Report by Weiss and Burger, Jan. 10, 1924, FBI.
251 "isolated murder": Report by Burger, Aug. 13, 1924, FBI.

25: THE LOST MANUSCRIPT
254 "defendants have not": U.S. District Court for the Northern District of Oklahoma, *U.S. v. Osage Wind, Enel Kansas, and Enel Green Power North America*, Sept. 30, 2015.
254 "For the first time": *Tulsa World*, Feb. 25, 2015.
255 "scarcely stepped": *Pawhuska Daily Capital*, Jan. 30, 1919.

26: BLOOD CRIES OUT
258 "Members of the family": *Daily Oklahoman*, Oct. 25, 1926.
259 "drugs, opiates": Quoted in Wilson, *Underground Reservation*, 144.
259 "one of the most beautiful": Quoted in McAuliffe, *Deaths of Sybil Bolton*, 109.
260 "In connection with": Bureau report titled "Murder on Indian Reservation," Nov. 6, 1932, FBI.
260 "I don't know": *Osage Tribal Murders*. Directed by Sherwood Ball. Los Angeles: Ball Entertainment, 2010, DVD.

261 "There are so many": Interview by F. G. Grimes Jr. and Edwin Brown, June 17, 1925, FBI.

263 "Bill, you know": Report by Smith, Oct. 30, 1926, FBI.

263 "Walking through": Robert Allen Warrior, "Review Essay: The Deaths of Sybil Bolton: An American History," *Wicazo Sa Review* 11 (1995): 52.

264 "You should be ashamed": McAuliffe, *Deaths of Sybil Bolton*, 137.

264 "Harry didn't do it": Ibid., 139.

264 "I did not prove": From McAuliffe's revised and updated edition of *The Deaths of Sybil Bolton*, which was renamed *Bloodland: A Family Story of Oil, Greed, and Murder on the Osage Reservation*. San Francisco: Council Oak Books, 1999: 287.

266 "There are men": Quoted in Wallis, Michael. *Oil Man: The Story of Frank Phillips and the Birth of Phillips Petroleum*. New York: St. Martin's Press, 1999, 152.

Illustration Credits

ii–iii	Courtesy of Archie Mason
7	Corbis
8	Courtesy of Raymond Red Corn
10	Courtesy of Raymond Red Corn
16	Courtesy of the Federal Bureau of Investigation
19	Courtesy of the Osage Nation Museum
25	(top) Courtesy of the Bartlesville Area History Museum
	(bottom) Courtesy of the Oklahoma Historical Society
28	Courtesy of the Bartlesville Area History Museum
29	Courtesy of the Bartlesville Area History Museum
37	Courtesy of the Osage Nation Museum
38	Courtesy of the Western History Collections, University of Oklahoma Libraries, Finney No. 231
42	(top) Courtesy of the Western History Collections, University of Oklahoma Libraries, Finney No. 215
	(bottom) Courtesy of the Western History Collections, University of Oklahoma Libraries, Finney No. 224
45	Courtesy of Raymond Red Corn
46	Courtesy of the Western History Collections, University of Oklahoma Libraries, Cunningham No. 184
49	Courtesy of the Library of Congress
52	Courtesy of the Bartlesville Area History Museum
55	Courtesy of the Osage Nation Museum
60	Corbis
63	Courtesy of the Osage Nation Museum
66	Courtesy of the Bartlesville Area History Museum
68	(top) Courtesy of Guy Nixon
	(bottom) Courtesy of the Osage County Historical Society Museum
70	Courtesy of the Bartlesville Area History Museum
71	Courtesy of Raymond Red Corn
76	Corbis
80	Courtesy of the Montana Historical Society
81	Courtesy of the Federal Bureau of Investigation
83	(top) Corbis
	(bottom) Corbis

88	Courtesy of Melville Vaughan
90	Courtesy of the Osage Nation Museum
97	Courtesy of the Western History Collections, University of Oklahoma Libraries, Rose No. 1525
99	Courtesy of the Library of Congress
106	Courtesy of Frank Parker Sr.
109	Courtesy of the Federal Bureau of Investigation
111	Courtesy of Wikimedia Commons
115	Courtesy of Alexandra Sands
117	Courtesy of the National Archives at Kansas City
123	Courtesy of James M. White
125	Courtesy of Austin History Center, Austin Public Library
127	(top) Courtesy of James M. White (bottom) Courtesy of the Western History Collections, University of Oklahoma Libraries, Rose No. 1525
128	Courtesy of the Western History Collections, University of Oklahoma Libraries, Rose No. 1806
133	Courtesy of Raymond Red Corn
141	Courtesy of the Oklahoma Historical Society, Oklahoman Collection
146	Courtesy of the Kansas Historical Society
147	Courtesy of Homer Fincannon
149	Courtesy of the National Cowboy and Western Heritage Museum
151	Courtesy of the Federal Bureau of Investigation
159	Courtesy of the Oklahoma Historical Society, Oklahoman Collection
162	Corbis
175	Courtesy of the Oklahoma Historical Society, Oklahoman Collection
185	Courtesy of the Osage Nation Museum
189	Courtesy of Raymond Red Corn
192	Courtesy of the Oklahoma Historical Society, Oklahoman Collection
195	Courtesy of the Oklahoma Historical Society, Oklahoman Collection
203	Courtesy of the Library of Congress
207	Courtesy of Margie Burkhart
211	Courtesy of the Library of Congress Courtesy of Tom White III
212	Unknown

218	Aaron Tomlinson
220	Courtesy of Archie Mason
223	Aaron Tomlinson
226	(top) Courtesy of the Oklahoma Historical Society, Oklahoman Collection
	(bottom) Courtesy of Margie Burkhart
229	Aaron Tomlinson
244	Aaron Tomlinson
253	Aaron Tomlinson
261	Aaron Tomlinson
265	Aaron Tomlinson
268	Aaron Tomlinson

Index

Allen, Joe, 58, 109, 112
Al Spencer Gang
  final train robbery by, 217
  Gregg and, 29, 145–148, *146*
  Kansas City Massacre and, 210
  Leavenworth prisoners from, 204,
    206–210
  Spencer and, 29, 145–148, 165,
    217
  threats against FBI by, 177
Associated Press, 65
Austin (Travis County, Texas) jail,
  122–125, *125*
Authentic Osage Indian Roll Book,
  260

Barker, Ma and Fred, 210
Bates, Joe, 63, 173
Bertillon, Alphonse, 110
Bigheart, George, 172, 219
Bigheart, James (Osage chief), 48–
  49, *49*, 52
Big Hill Trading Company, 14, 54–
  55, *55*, 82, 231–232, 257, 266
Bolton, Sybil, 259
Boxcar (prison inmate), 206–210
Brookshire, Nettie, 79–85, *81*, *83*,
  102, 157
Brown, Anna (Wah-hrah-lum-pah;
    Mollie's sister)
  Bryan Burkhart's trial and, 195
  coroner's inquest and, 15–20, 31,
    108, 131

disappearance of, 3–14, *16*, 114,
  230
early investigation into death of,
  21–32, 53–64, 79
FBI investigation into death
  of, 102, 167–169, 174, 176
  (*see also* Osage murders-FBI
  investigation)
Grammer and, 80
guardianship system and, 257
legacy of, 230–231
Morrison's testimony and trial,
  184–186, 199–200
Osage name of, 40
photos of, *10*, *19*, *90*, *185*
pregnancy of, 61, 170–171
skull of, *16*, 108, 220
Brown, Oda, *10*, *20*, 57–58
Bunch, Roy, 139
Bureau of Indian Affairs. *See* Office of
  Indian Affairs (U.S. Department
  of the Interior)
Bureau of Investigation. *See* Federal
  Bureau of Investigation
Burger, John, 104–105, *109*, 109–
  112, 113–117, 250, 251
Burkhart, Anna (Mollie's and Ernest's
    daughter), 78, 91, 186–187
Burkhart, Bryan (Ernest's brother)
  Anna Brown's death investigation
    and, 26–27, 56–57
  Anna Brown's disappearance and,
    9–12, 14

Burkhart, Bryan (Ernest's brother)
(cont'd)
Ernest Burkhart's trial and, 185–
186, 189
as FBI suspect, 113–117, 117, 119–
121, 154, 167
headright inheritance scheme of,
140–142
late life of, 225
Morrison's trial and, 199–200
trial of, 195
Burkhart, Elizabeth (Mollie's and
Ernest's daughter), 8, 178,
225–227, 227, 232
Burkhart, Ernest
Anna Brown's disappearance and
death, 6, 19, 20, 200
arrest of, 182
divorce of, 224
as FBI suspect, 113–114, 121, 130–
135
grand jury testimony of, 238
Hale's trial and, 177–182, 191,
193–194, 197
headright inheritance scheme of,
140–142
investigation of Anna Brown's
death and, 24–27
late life and legacy of, 223–227
marriage to Mollie, 8, 19
oil lease auctions attended by,
65
photos of, 8, 141, 189, 227
Smith family's house explosion
and, 82, 232
stolen car of, 90
trial of, 182, 183–190, 192, 217,
225, 244
as wife's financial guardian, 73
Burkhart, Horace (Ernest's
brother), 9

Burkhart, James "Cowboy" (Mollie's
and Ernest's son), 8, 225–226,
227, 232
Burkhart, Margie (Mollie's and
Ernest's granddaughter), 223,
223–232, 244
Burkhart, Mollie
(Wah-kon-tah-he-um-pah)
Anna Brown's disappearance and
early investigation, 3–14, 21–
27, 29–31, 53–56, 59–61, 64,
79 (see also Brown, Anna)
Catholic education of, 8, 20, 43–
45, 45
daughter's death, 186–187
divorce of, 224
Ernest's trial and, 183–190
father of (Ne-kah-e-se-y/Jimmy),
20, 34, 35, 38, 39, 41, 42
financial guardians and family of,
72–74
at Hale's trial, 172, 177–180
legacy of, 219, 229, 229, 230–
231 (see also Osage County
(modern-day))
marriage to Cobb, 206, 224
marriage to Ernest, 8, 19 (see also
Burkhart, Ernest)
marriage to Roan, 77–78, 196–
197
Mollie and Osage name of, 40, 41
mother of (Lizzie), 8–9, 18, 19, 21,
22, 31–32, 35, 38, 53–55, 72,
140–142, 219, 229, 229, 257
oil lease auctions attended by, 65
photos of, 7, 10, 19, 90, 141, 207
poisoning of, 90–91, 157, 167–
169, 266
Smith family's house explosion
and, 82, 232 (see also Smith,
Bill; Smith, Rita)

stolen car of, 90
wealth and lifestyle of, 5–6
see also headrights and
    guardianship system; Osage
    murders-FBI investigation
Burns, Louis F., 218, 221
Burt, H. G., 236–241, 244, 257, 262,
    266

Cherokee Nation, 36–37, *46*, 46–48,
    47
Cobb, John, 206, 224
Cole, Katherine, 176, 185–186
Comstock, A. W., 61–63, 146, *147*,
    156, 248, 265, 271
Constantine Theater, 67, 242–244
Coolidge, Calvin, 98
corruption
    gambling/bootlegging in
        Oklahoma and, 17, 53, 62–63,
        63, 80–81, 157
    jury tampering, 192–196, 237
    of oil leases, 86
    in Osage County law enforcement,
        103–104, 143–144
    Teapot Dome and, 67, 97–98, 101
    White on, 174
    witness tampering, 176, 192–196
    see also Freas, Harve M.; Hale,
        William K.
courts
    federal vs. state court for Roan
        murder trial, 174–175, 178, 190
    grand jury investigation (1926),
        238
    jury tampering, 192–196, 237
    Oklahoma Supreme Court, 237
    Osage Nation Court, 34, 261–263
    Pawhuska courthouse, 217, *244*
    witness tampering, 176, 192–196
    see also trials

Dalton Gang, 17
Davis, Herman Fox, 86
deaths, investigations of. *See* Osage
    murders-FBI investigation;
    poisoning/suspected poisoning
The Deaths of Sybil Bolton (McAuliffe),
    259
DeNoya-Bellieu-Lewis, Mary, 254–
    256
Dictograph, 60
Dillinger, John, 210

Elkins, Mary, 259
Enel, *253*, 253–254

Fairfax Chief, 224
Faulkner, J. J., 250
FBI. *See* Federal Bureau of
    Investigation
The FBI Story (movie), 211–212, 231
Federal Bureau of Investigation
    (FBI)
    Bureau of Investigation creation,
        96
    calls for national investigation of
        Osage deaths, 89, 91
    "Cowboys" of, 96
    Department of Justice role of, 97
    fingerprinting by Identification
        Division, 111–112, 201
    Lindbergh kidnapping and Kansas
        City Massacre, 210
    name of, 210
    publicity about trial outcome,
        200–202
    on Whitehorn murder, 249–251
    see also Hoover, J. Edgar; Osage
        murders-FBI investigation;
        trials; White, Tom
Fitzgerald, F. Scott, 71
Florer, John, 41, 42, 49

flower-killing moon belief, 3, 230–231

Freas, Harve M.
coroner's inquest of Brown and, 17
Hale's arrest and, 179
investigation of Anna Brown's death by, 30, 53–54, 59, 62–63
reelection of and resumed involvement in Osage murders case, 157–158

Freeling, Sargent Prentiss, 176, 181, 196–197

Getty, George, 51
Getty, Jean Paul, 51, 66
Getty Oil Company, 51
Grammer, Henry, 17, 80, *80*, 148–150, *149*, 165–166, 194
Grann, David, research by, 218–219, 233–241. *See also* Osage County (modern-day); unsolved crimes
Gray Horse, Oklahoma. *See* Osage County (modern-day); Osage territory
Gregg, Dick, 29, 145–148, *146*, 238
Grove, Fred, 213–214
Gulf Oil, 69
Gypsy Oil Company, 69

Hale, William K.
Anna Brown's disappearance and, 11, 30–31
Anna Brown's pregnancy and, 170–171
business of, 6–9, 22–24, *25*, 27
depicted in *Wahzhazhe* (ballet), 243
early investigation and, 53–54, 60, 62

Ernest Burkhart's interrogation about, 156–167
as FBI suspect, 107, 113, 130–135, 143–152, 153–156, 170–171, 172–173
George Bigheart's death and, 240
on guardianship system, 73
imprisonment of, 203, 205–206, 224–225
inheritance scheme of, 140–142
insurance scheme of, 136–140
as "King of the Osage Hills," 23–24
letter written from prison by, 245
photos of, *25, 151, 159, 192, 195, 220*
Roan's death and, 76–77
on Smith house bombing, 90
trial of, 173–182, 190, 191–195, 196–199, 203
unsolved cases and, 233

Harding, Warren G., 66, 97, 98
Harper's Monthly Magazine, 70
"Have pity on me, O Great Spirit!" (Osage mourning prayer), 32
headrights and guardianship system
bogus heir schemes, 255–256
financial guardians imposed on Osage people, 50, 55, 61, 70–74, *71*, 133–135, 139–142, 240, 257
guardianship system ended, 206
logbook of guardians, 257–259
Pine on, 184
Hlu-ah-to-me, 258
Hoover, J. Edgar
Ernest Burkhart's trial and, 184
fingerprinting by FBI and, 111–112, 201
photos of, *211, 212*

White hired by, 95–101, 99, 104, 106

White's investigation and, 143–145, 156, 161, 162, 177, 200–202

White's post-FBI contact with, 210–214

Indian Rights Association, 134–135

I'n-Lon-Schka (Osage ceremonial dance), 221–223

insurance agent (FBI investigator), 105, 107, 136–140

jails. *See* prisons and jails

Jefferson, Anna Marie, 254–256

Jefferson, Thomas, 33–34

Jimmy (Ne-kah-e-se-y; Mollie's father). *See* Ne-kah-e-se-y (Jimmy; Mollie's father)

Johnson, Curley, 148, 150, 162–165

juries, tampering with, 192–196, 237

justice of the peace (Fairfax, Oklahoma), 15–16, 26, 31, 76, 84–85, 89, 108

Kansas, Osage territory in, 33–36

Kansas City Massacre, 210

Kaw Indian woman (alleged witness), 58, 109, 112

Kirby, Asa, 150, 155, 165–166, 188–189

La Tuna prison, 208–210

law enforcement

Bertillonage process, 110–111, *111*

coroner's inquest of Brown and, 15–20, 31, 108, 131

corruption in Osage case found by FBI, 143–144

Dictograph used in, 60

Emmett White's career in, 122–125, *125*

fingerprinting used by FBI, 111–112, 201

gambling/bootlegging in Oklahoma and, 17, 53, 62–63, *63*, 80–81, 157

handwriting and document analysis, 138

Osage County corruption, 103–104

private investigators and, 32, 53–64, 100, 145

Sherlock Holmes stories about, 54, 58, 108

state-level investigation of Osage deaths, 86

see also courts; Osage murders-FBI investigation

Lawson, Burt, 153–157, 160, 161, 165, 233

Leahy, John, 187–188

Leavenworth Penitentiary

Hale's imprisonment at, 203, 205–206, 224–225

hostage crisis of, 206–210

as "Hot House," 204–205

Smith's assignment to warden of, 202–203, *203*

Lewis, Mary, 254–256

Lindbergh, Charles, 210

Literary Digest, 227–228

Little House on the Prairie (Wilder), 36

Lizzie (Mollie's mother)

Anna Brown's death and, 18

death of, 31–32

early life of, 35

financial guardians and family of, 72, 257

headright inheritance scheme and, 140–142

Lizzie (Mollie's mother) *(cont'd)*
  investigation of Anna Brown's
    death, 21, 22
  investigation of death of, 53–55
  legacy of, 219, 229, *229 (see also*
    Osage County (modern-day))
  marriage of, 38
  photos of, *19*
  residence of, 8–9
Louisiana, Territory of, 33–34
Lowe, Andrew, 225–226, 232
The Lucky Strike Hour (radio program),
  201
lynchings, 123

Marland, E. W., 51, 66, 71–72, 86
Mathews, John Joseph, 3, 44
Mathis, Scott, 14, 19–20, 54–55, *55*,
  84, 143–144, 257–258, 266
McAuliffe, Dennis, Jr., 259, 260, 263–
  264
McAuliffe, Harry, 263–264, 266
McBride, Barney, 63–64, 67, 76, 87,
  172, 233–234, 267
Middleton, Thomas, 255–256
Miller, Lloyd (alias of Kelsie
  Morrison), 110
Million Dollar Elm, auctions at, 65,
  67, *70*, 217
Million Dollar Elm Casinos, 228
moonshine still (Osage County),
  28
Morrison, Kelsie
  Ernest Burkhart's trial and, 184–
    186
  as FBI informant, 110–112, 140,
    145
  Freas and, 17
  as suspect, 152, 167, 170
  threats to wife of, 176
  trial of, 199–200

Moss, Flint, 188
"The Murder of Mary DeNoya-
  Bellieu-Lewis" (Jefferson), 254–
  256
Muskogee Times-Democrat, 149

Nash, Frank "Jelly," 29, 210
Ne-kah-e-se-y (Jimmy; Mollie's
  father), 20, 34, 35, 38, 39, 41,
  42
  see also Jimmy (Ne-kah-e-se-y;
    Mollie's father)
New Mexico sheriff (FBI agent), 104–
  105, 107, *115*
New York Times, 199

Office of Indian Affairs (U.S.
  Department of the Interior)
  archives of, 237–238, 240
  Bates's death and, 173
  Bureau of Indian Affairs name of,
    24
  Catholic education of Osage
    children by, 43–45, *45*
  hearing about Anna Brown's death
    by, 24–27
  on Indian Territory land, 37
  on Mollie Burkhart's illness/
    poisoning, 91, 157
  on Osage culture, 35, 36
  Pawhuska office of, 38
  ration system of, 39–40
  see also headrights and
    guardianship system
oil
  bribery by oil barons, 97–98
  Burbank oil field discovery, 51, 71
  headrights of Osage, 50, 139–142,
    202, 227–228
  lease auctions in Pawhuska, 65–
    74, *66, 68, 70,* 228

mineral rights and Allotment
Act (1906), 46–52, 252–254,
253
oil strike in Osage territory, 52
Osage fortunes and Great
Depression, 227
wealth of Osage from, 4–6, 55, 61,
70–74, 71, 133–135 (*see also*
headrights and guardianship
system)
wildcatters, 50–52
see also headrights and
guardianship system
Oklahoma
federal vs. state cases, 174–175,
178, 190
Oklahoma Supreme Court, 237
Osage forced migration to, 36–
40, 38
statehood of, 48, 50
Osage, Rose, 58, 109, 224
Osage County (modern-day), 217–
232
Burkhart descendants and Reign
of Terror legacy, 223, 223–232,
226, 229
former oil boomtowns of, 217–
219, 218, 231–232
I'n-Lon-Schka (ceremonial dance)
held in, 221–223
Osage Nation Museum in, 219–
221, 220
during Reign of Terror (*see* Osage
murders-FBI investigation;
Osage Reign of Terror; Osage
territory)
Osage murders-FBI investigation
Bryan Burkhart as suspect of,
113–117, 117, 119–121
depiction in popular culture, 214,
221–223, 242–244

Ernest Burkhart as suspect of, 107,
113–114, 121, 130–135, 156–
167
grand jury investigation (1926),
238
hired assassins suspected by FBI,
103, 148, 176, 182, 189
mole suspected within
investigation, 118–121
news about (*see individual names of
newspapers*)
White hired by Hoover for, 95–
101
White's hiring of investigation
team, 102–106, 107–112
White's search for witnesses in,
143–152, 153–156
see also courts; trials; unsolved
crimes
Osage Nation (people and culture)
bison and hunting by, 35–36, 38–
39, 230
death and burial traditions, 18,
20, 32, 37
flower-killing moon belief, 3, 230–
231
"Have pity on me, O Great Spirit!"
(Osage mourning prayer), 32
massacre of Osage (1870), 36
modern-day population and
governance, 218–219, 228
naming traditions, 40
oil income and lifestyle change,
4–6, 55, 61, 70–74, 71, 133–
135 (*see also* headrights and
guardianship system)
Osage Nation Court, 34, 261–
263
Osage Nation Museum, 219–221,
220
Osage Roll, 4

Osage Nation (people and culture)
(cont'd)
Osage Tribal Council, 100, 175,
201–202
prejudice toward, 105–106, 167,
193
smallpox and diseases of, 38
traditional clothing and
appearance of, 5–7, 9, 14, 34–
35, 39–41, 44, 45, 222
Travelers in the Mist, 21
Wah'Kon-Tah (life force), 18, 20,
222, 253
Wahzhazhe (ballet), 242–244
Osage Reign of Terror, 75–91
Burkhart descendants and legacy
of, 223, 223–232, 226, 229
death toll (1923), 89
dog poisoning and, 80
fear of, 78–79, 89–91, 145
naming of, 85
personal funds of Osage spent on
investigation, 32, 53–64, 100,
145
timeline of, 247, 256
victims of (see Bigheart, George;
Brown, Anna; McBride, Barney;
Roan, Henry; Smith, Bill; Smith,
Rita; unsolved crimes; Vaughan,
W. W.; Whitehorn, Charles;
individual Burkhart family
members' names)
see also unsolved crimes
Osage territory, 33–52
cultural changes to, 40–46 (see
also Osage Nation (people and
culture))
forced migration to Kansas, 34–
36
forced migration to Oklahoma,
36–40, 38
law enforcement in Osage County,
overview, 28, 29–30

Pawhuska and Gray Horse
established in Osage County,
38
physical description of, 3
ration system in, 39–40
white settlers' move to, 40–45
see also oil
Outlook magazine, 4

Palmer, John, 49, 101
Paschen, Elise, 230–231
Pawhuska, Oklahoma. See oil; Osage
County (modern-day); Osage
territory
Pawhuska Daily Capital, 21, 30, 240
Pawnee Bill (Wild West showman),
23
Peace, Paul, 264–265, 267
Phillips, Frank, 51, 66, 67
Pike (private detective), 54, 62, 119–
121
Pine, William B., 184
Pinkerton, Allan, 54, 58
poisoning/suspected poisoning
of Bates, 173
of dogs, 80
of George Bigheart, 172, 237–
241
of Johnson, 148
of Lizzie, 32, 130
of Mollie Burkhart, 90–91, 157,
167–168, 266
trial testimony about, 193–194
uninvestigated/unsolved crimes,
246, 250–251, 256, 258, 260–
263, 265–267
prisons and jails
Austin (Travis County, Texas),
122–125, 125
La Tuna prison, 208–210
Leavenworth Penitentiary, 203,
203, 205–210, 224–225
private investigators, 53–64

hired in Osage death
investigations, 32, 54–64, 100,
145
Pinkerton and, 54, 58
role of, 53–54

racism
lynchings of African Americans,
123
prejudice toward Native
Americans, 105–106, 167,
193
see also headrights and
guardianship system
Ramsey, John
Ernest Burkhart's trial and, 183,
188–189
imprisonment of, 203, 204
Smith family's house explosion
events, 165–167
trials of, 174–180, 182, 191–195,
192, 196–199, 203
Red Corn, Kathryn, 219–221, 244–
247, 251, 252, 256
Rind, Bacon (Osage chief), 74, *133*,
266
Roan, Henry
death of, 75–81, *76*
descendants of, 231
Hale's trial for murder of, 174–
175, 178, 190, 193–197 (*see also*
Hale, William K.)
insurance scheme and, 136–140
legacy of, 219, 229, *229* (*see also*
Osage County (modern-day))
Mollie Burkhart's marriage to, 77–
78, 196–197
undertaker used for, 266
White's investigation of death of,
102, 143, 150–151, 161, 166–
167, 170
see also Osage murders-FBI
investigation

Roosevelt, Theodore, 48, 96
Rudensky, Red, 204–205

Sanford, Anna, 258
Savage, Minnie, 248–249
Shoun, David
Bill Smith's death and, 130–132
coroner's inquest of Brown by,
15–16, 31, 108
FBI suspicion about, 108
Mollie Burkhart's poisoning and,
91, 157, 168, 266
Roan's death and, 77
Smith house bombing and, 84, 85
Shoun, James
Bill Smith's death and, 130–132
coroner's inquest of Brown by,
15–16, 31, 108
FBI suspicion about, 108
insurance scheme and, 137
Mollie Burkhart's poisoning and,
91, 157, 168, 266
Roan's death and, 77
Smith house bombing and, 79,
84
Sinclair, Harry, 66–67, 97
Skelly, Bill, 67
Skirvin, W. B., 234
Smith, Bill
Anna Brown's body discovery and,
14
Anna Brown's death investigation
by, 32, 53, 59
death of, 79–85, *81*, *83*, 102, 232
Ernest Burkhart's trial and, 188–
189
FBI investigation of death of, 102
Hale's trial and, 197 (*see also* Hale,
William K.)
headright inheritance scheme
and, 140–142
legacy of, 229, *229*
on Lizzie's death, 32

Smith, Bill (cont'd)
  marriages of, 59
  suspects in murder of, 148–151,
    153–157, 161–171
  see also Osage murders-FBI
    investigation
Smith, Frank (FBI agent), 105, 153,
  156–167, 170–171, 177, 183
Smith, Minnie (Wah-sha-she; Mollie's
  sister), 4, 10, 20, 31, 40, 59, 90
Smith, Rita (Me-se-moie; Mollie's
  sister)
  Anna Brown's body discovery and,
    14
  Anna Brown's death investigation
    and, 56, 59–60, 60
  death of, 79–85, 81, 83, 102
  Ernest Burkhart's trial and, 188–
    189
  FBI investigation of death of, 102
  Hale's trial and, 197 (see also Hale,
    William K.)
  headright inheritance scheme
    and, 140–142
  husband of (see Smith, Bill)
  Osage name of, 40
  photo of, 90
  suspects in murder of, 148–151,
    153–157, 161–171
  see also Osage murders-FBI
    investigation
Smitherman, LeRoy, 248–249
Society of Oklahoma Indians, 174
"soup man." See Kirby, Asa
Spencer, Al, 29, 147, 165, 217. See also
  Al Spencer Gang
Springer, Jim, 176, 196
St. Lewis, Roy, 175, 175, 194–196
St. Louis Post-Dispatch, 200
St. Louis School (Pawhuska), 43–45,
  45

Standard Oil, 67
Stepson, Marvin, 261, 261–263
Stepson, William, 62–63, 63, 261–
  263
Stone, Harlan Fiske, 98

Tall Chief, Eves, 258
Tallchief, Maria and Marjorie, 242
Tarbell, Ida, 111
Teapot Dome scandal, 67, 97–98,
  101
Texas
  Austin (Travis County) jail, 122–
    125, 125
  La Tuna prison, 208–210
  Texas Rangers and White family,
    126, 129
Texas Ranger (FBI agent hired by
  White), 104–105, 106, 107
Thompson, Irvin "Blackie," 29, 100–
  101, 148, 162, 162–165, 191,
  200
The Tragedy of the Osage Hills
  (newsreel), 173
Trail of Tears, 37
Travelers in the Mist, 21
trials, 172–182, 183–190, 191–203
  of Bryan Burkhart, 195
  of Ernest Burkhart, 182, 183–190,
    192, 217, 225, 244
  FBI publicity about outcome of,
    200–202
  federal vs. state cases, 174–175,
    178, 190
  of Hale, 173–182, 190, 191–195,
    196–199, 203
  of Morrison, 199–200
  of Ramsey, 174–180, 182, 191–
    195, 192, 196–199, 203
  White's Leavenworth job
    following, 202–203, 203

Tulsa Daily World, 17, 87
Tulsa Tribune, 179, 180, 191
Turner, Ted, 230

undertaker. *See* Mathis, Scott
unsolved crimes, 242–251, 252–256,
    257–267
  of Bolton's death, 259, 263–264,
    266
  logbook of guardians and, 257–
    259
  Osage death statistics and, 259–
    261
  of Peace's death, 264–265, 267
  of Red Corn family member's
    death, 244–247, 251, 252, 256
  as society-wide, 265–267
  of Stepson's death, 261–263
U.S. Congress
  on inheritance of headrights,
    202
  on Osage wealth, 72–74
  Pine on guardianship system, 184
  Teapot Dome corruption and, 67,
    97–98, 101
U.S. Department of Justice
  FBI's role in, 97 (*see also* Federal
    Bureau of Investigation)
  on federal vs. state cases, 174–175,
    178, 190
  on jury tampering, 196
  on Mollie Burkhart's poisoning,
    157
  on Osage Hills fugitives, 29
  Osage Tribal Council and, 100
  personal funds of Osage spent on
    investigation, 32, 53–64, 100,
    145
  see also FBI
U.S. National Archives, 236–238, 240
U.S. Supreme Court, 178, 190

Vaughan, Martha, 86–89, *88*, 234–
    241
Vaughan, Melville, 234–241
Vaughan, Rosa, *88*, 235–237
Vaughan, W. W., 86–89, *88*, 172,
    233–241, 248, 257, 271

Wah'Kon-Tah (Osage life force), 18,
    20, 32, 34, 222, 253
Wah-Ti-An-Kah (Osage chief), 37, *37*,
    39–40
Wahzhazhe (Osage ballet), 242–244
Walters, Ellsworth E. "Colonel," 65–
    70, *70*
Walton, Jack C., 86
Washington Post, 64, 184
Webb, Mary Jo, 264–265, *265*, 267
White, Bessie Patterson, 128–129
White, Coley, 126, *127*
White, Dudley, 122, *123*, 126–129,
    127, *128*, 204
White, J. C. "Doc," 96, 97, 104, *123*,
    126–128, *127*, 210, 214
White, Robert Emmett, 122–124,
    127
White, Tom
  Bryan Burkhart's trial and, 195
  death of, 214
  early life of, 122–129
  Ernest Burkhart's interrogation
    and trial, 156–167, 182,
    183–190, 192, 225 (*see also*
    Burkhart, Ernest)
  FBI investigation team of, 102–
    106, 107–112 (*see also* Osage
    murders-FBI investigation)
  FBI publicity about investigation
    of, 200–202
  Hale's interrogation and trials,
    170–171, 172, 174–182 (*see
    also* Hale, William K.)

White, Tom *(cont'd)*
  Hoover's contact with, following
    Osage case, 210–214
  Hoover's hiring of, for Oklahoma
    City office, 95–101, 104, 106
  as La Tuna warden, 208–210
  as Leavenworth warden, 202–203,
    203, 203–210
  Morrison's trial and, 199–200
  photos of, *211, 212*
  Ramsey's trial and, 174–180, 182,
    191–195, 203
  search for witnesses by, 143–152,
    153–156
  suspects identified in
    investigation of, 113–117, *117,*
    118–121, 130–135
  on Vaughan's murder, 239
  Whitehorn case and, 250–251
Whitehorn, Charles
  coroner's inquest of, 31
  disappearance and death of, 12,
    13, 17, 21, 53, 62–63
  early investigation into death of,
    21
  FBI investigation of death of, 102
  legacy of, 219 (*see also* Osage
    County (modern-day))
  unsolved murder of, 247–251
  see also Osage murders-FBI
    investigation
Whitehorn, Hattie, 62, 79, 248–251
"Wi'-gi-e" (Paschen), 230–231
Wilder, Laura Ingalls, 36
Wren, John
  FBI firing of, 105, 213
  Osage murder investigated by,
    105–106, 107, 152, 157–158,
    166, 177

The Years of Fear (Grove), 214
yegg (safecracker), 150–151

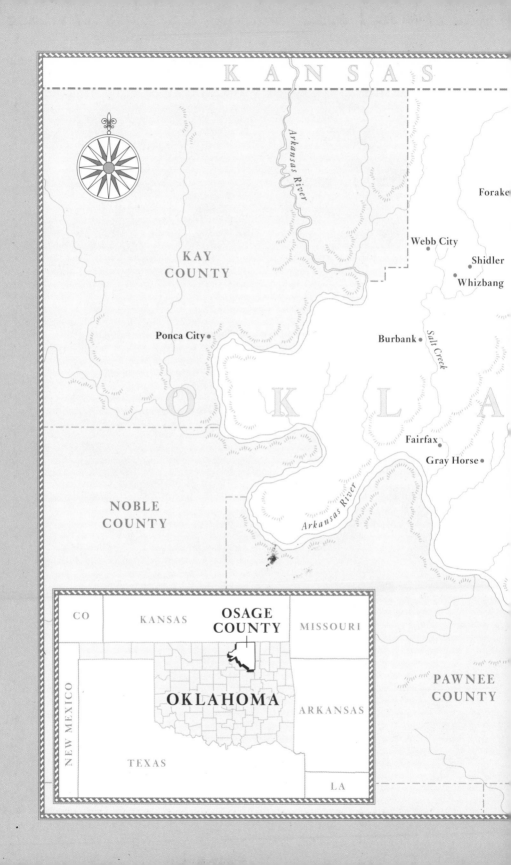